MANAGING
HUMAN SERVICE
ORGANIZATIONS

Recent Titles from Quorum Books

The Tort of Discovery Abuse
Warren Freedman

Classic Failures in Product Marketing: Marketing Principle Violations and How to Avoid
Them
Donald W. Hendon

The Management of International Advertising: A Handbook and Guide for Professionals
Erdener Kaynak

Public Sector Privatization: Alternative Approaches to Service Delivery
Lawrence K. Finley, editor

The Work/Life Dichotomy: Prospects for Reintegrating People and Jobs
Martin Morf

Financial Management for Health Care Administrators
Ronald John Hy

Computer Simulation in Business Decision Making: A Guide for Managers, Planners,
and MIS Professionals
Roy L. Nersesian

A Stakeholder Approach to Corporate Governance: Managing in a Dynamic Environment
Abbass F. Alkhafaji

The Impact of Intergovernmental Grants on the Aggregate Public Sector
Daniel P. Schwallie

Managing Employee Rights and Responsibilities
Chimezie A. B. Osigweh, Yg., editor

The Coming Crisis in Accounting
Ahmed Belkaoui

MANAGING HUMAN SERVICE ORGANIZATIONS

Edited by
LYNN E. MILLER

Q

QUORUM BOOKS
NEW YORK • WESTPORT, CONNECTICUT • LONDON

Library of Congress Cataloging-in-Publication Data

Managing human service organizations.

  Bibliography: p.
  Includes index.
  1. Social work administration—United States.
2. Human services—United States—Management.
3. Corporations, Nonprofit—United States—Management.
I. Miller, Lynn E.
HV95.M267   1989   361'.0068   88-35682
ISBN 0-89930-305-6 (lib. bdg. : alk. paper)

British Library Cataloguing in Publication Data is available.

Library of Congress Catalog Card Number: 88-35682
ISBN: 0-89930-305-6

First published in 1989 by Quorum Books

Greenwood Press, Inc.
88 Post Road West, Westport, Connecticut 06881

Printed in the United States of America

The paper used in this book complies with the
Permanent Paper Standard issued by the National
Information Standards Organization (Z39.48–1984).

10 9 8 7 6 5 4 3 2 1

Contents

Figures and Exhibits

EXHIBITS

Preface

In contrast to the tremendous expansion of the not-for-profit sector in the 1960s and early 1970s, the past decade has witnessed funding cutbacks accompanied by greater scrutiny of the quality and efficiency of human service organizations. At the present time, an emphasis on quality management has become well entrenched, and the management record of an agency is often an important factor in funding decisions.

This greater concern with management skills has not been entirely externally motivated, however. As agencies have matured, their administrators have encountered new sets of problems. Changing environments have challenged many agencies to reevaluate their fundamental missions. The growth experienced by some organizations has been accompanied by problems in communication, coordination, and decision making. In many agencies, funding cutbacks and competition from other agencies have motivated administrators to seek new sources of funding and more cost-effective programs. In general, these new issues and concerns have provided the impetus for many human service agency managers to reevaluate their roles and technical management skills.

Since 1981, La Salle University has been awarded grants from foundations and corporations in the Philadelphia area to conduct programs of workshops, management training, and technical assistance for the executives of local small to medium-sized nonprofit agencies. Although often formally trained in clinical rather than managerial areas, many of the human service agency administrators who enrolled in these programs were found to be running their organizations quite successfully. They frequently reported that they were attending the programs in order to have an opportunity to think about their management philosophies and refine the skills they had acquired through their experiences as managers.

Our purpose in writing this book was to provide conceptual frameworks to help managers think broadly about different aspects of managing their organizations, as well as to provide specific suggestions and tools that would complement these frameworks. We did not intend to compile a handbook that would present the basic ABCs of managing human service organizations. Indeed, we hoped to write a book that would transcend the view that all organizations should be run basically the same way. Although most of the contributing authors are affiliated with academic institutions, all have extensive practical consulting experience and have attempted to combine theory and practice in the hope of helping human service managers better carry out the purposes of their organizations.

The funding for this project was provided by a grant from the William Penn Foundation to the Nonprofit Management Development Center at La Salle University. This support is gratefully acknowledged. The editor and contributors are also grateful to the administrators and other personnel at La Salle who provided abundant support and assistance.

PART I
GENERAL MANAGEMENT

1
Strategic Planning in Human Service Agencies

RADHA CHAGANTI
AND EVERETT FRANK

DEFINITION OF STRATEGIC PLANNING

Strategic planning refers to planning for the future of the agency as a whole, not just for particular programs or units in the agency. This plan does not merely say what the agency should be doing in the next year, but it lays the groundwork for the long run, covering at least the next three to five years and often covering the next seven or even ten years. For this plan management asks and answers questions about the future of their agency, such as: Where is our agency headed for the future? Where should it be headed for the future? How do we get our agency to where we want it to be?

How is strategic planning different from other kinds of planning? After all, agencies are planning when they prepare annual budgets, or when they prepare proposals requesting funding for individual programs. The difference lies mainly in the perspective the management takes and the scope of the planning process. Policymakers in the agency take a long-range view so that they know how to make the best use of future trends in order to achieve the agency objectives. In addition, they seek to identify the direction for the entire organization rather than for individual programs or activities.

When the agency formulates such a comprehensive long-range plan, this does not imply that things change drastically in one sweep. Commitment to the new direction builds slowly, and the principal managers nudge the policies, programs, and personnel slowly but consciously in the desired direction. Matters are not put together for a final and complete solution as in a puzzle, but managers deal with different parts one at a time, selecting people, assigning tasks, and building consensus. They identify the broad overall goals and the thrust of the agency for the future, invite proposals to achieve these goals, and make resource commitments slowly, making sure to reassess them often. They do not commit the agency to one course of action irrevocably, but always have other alternatives open to respond to as new facts emerge.

Strategic planning is long-range for the entire agency. In this sense it is not synonymous with long-range planning, since some long-range plans cover only particular programs or activities.

Simply put, strategic planning provides a framework for consistent and effective decisions. It provides a means for everyone in the agency to understand the overall direction for the agency's future and thus provides unity of purpose.

Who does this planning? It is mainly the top management of the agency, because these individuals and groups have the final responsibility for what the agency does or does not do. Therefore, an important question is, Who is the top management of the agency? The answer is not going to be the same across agencies. For example, it may be the executive director alone, or the executive director with the second-level managers and the board of directors. In short, top management comprises all of those individuals and groups who have a significant influence on key decisions in the agency, for example, decisions on the major programs of the agency, or decisions regarding the agency's objectives.

While the top management has the primary role in preparing and implementing the strategic plan, we advise that key professional personnel also be included in the planning process, since they would be both knowledgeable about the agency matters and concerned about the future of the agency. The planning process should always be a joint effort with the professional staff, especially at the stage of defining the mission of the agency and evaluating its strengths and weaknesses. Members of the client community are another group that should be closely involved in the planning process. Involvement of these groups is critical for building commitment to the plan and for facilitating problem-free implementation.

How is this planning for the future of the agency done? There are five broad steps to the process of carrying out strategic planning. In the next section we describe the main steps involved in formulating strategic plans, and in the last section we will discuss some examples of strategic planning that took place in different kinds of human service agencies.

STEPS IN STRATEGIC PLANNING

Step 1. Define the Mission of the Agency and Related Objectives

The top management takes the initiative in this stage, but the best results are likely to be obtained by involving all the key constituencies, such as the board, senior executives, staff, clients, and funding sources. Distinctions can be drawn between the mission statement and the statement of objectives. The mission statement is an enduring statement of the broad and basic purposes of the agency, whereas the statement of objectives is more limited both in scope and in the time frame over which it will apply.

In identifying the mission, the agency defines its most important values and organizational philosophies. The overall mission is then translated into a set of specific objectives the agency wishes to achieve over a specific time frame in the future. These objectives take into consideration the conditions prevalent in the agency's external and internal environments. Hence it is quite likely the objectives may be revised when conditions change significantly. But the mission statement should hold for the entire life of the organization. Policymakers should recognize this difference while conducting the planning process.

Some questions that can be used to help in this step are:

a. What does the agency stand for? What should its overall mission be? Whom does it want to serve? Are there some groups whom it would not want to serve? What are its organizational philosophies about the kind of internal environment it wants to provide for its staff?

b. What specific goals and objectives should the agency set for itself over the next two, three, five, and seven years? What are its objectives relating to the groups it would serve (e.g., the kinds of new groups the agency would like to serve) and the types of programs and services it would provide (e.g., would it expand, maintain, or reduce current services?)? What are its objectives for its personnel?

Step 2. Analysis of the External Environment

Here the agency looks at what is happening outside the agency in order to identify the potential opportunities and problems. The intent here is not to passively accept and adjust to the anticipated trends, but wherever possible to influence the trends so that they are more favorable to the agency's mission and objectives. Some questions that help management in this step are:

a. What are the major forces in the external environment that have affected our agency in the past?

b. What are the trends in the needs of the principal communities it serves? What are the new programs and services being demanded? What are the key changes expected in the demographic and other characteristics of these communities?

c. What are likely to be the trends in its key funding sources and in its sources of volunteer and paid service professionals? How would these trends affect our agency?

d. What other organizations are providing, or will provide, programs and services similar to our agency's? How have their activities influenced our agency in the past? What were the strategies used by the more effective organizations? What can our agency learn from their strategies? What will the strategies of these ''competing'' organizations be like in the future? How will they affect our agency's programs and results in the future?

e. What will be the trends in other important aspects, such as governmental policies affecting human service agencies, lifestyles, economy and technology, and other societal aspects which may influence our agency's future?

Two substeps are useful in looking at these trends in the external environment: first, list all trends in the outside environment and then separate the more important from the less important trends; second, separate the unfavorable and the favorable trends. When we advise managers to probe into the future trends in the external environment, we recognize that it is not easy to forecast exactly what will happen. Therefore, we suggest that managers develop simple alternative scenarios. For example, it would be useful to develop scenarios that would project what the environment would look like (a) if the key trends are highly favorable, (b) if the key trends are moderately favorable, and (c) if the key trends are highly unfavorable. Such forecasting will help the managers prepare contingency plans to cope with an uncertain future.

Several techniques and models can be used to analyze the environment. We briefly outline the model developed by Porter (1980) as an example. This is a simple model that can be easily adapted to analyze the different kinds of pressures human service agencies face from the various organizations and groups with which they deal. This model points out that an agency is affected primarily by five types of environmental or "competitive" pressures, as follows:

a. "Buyers" or client communities

b. "Suppliers" or sources of funds, manpower, and other important resources

c. "Rivals" or other organizations and agencies that offer similar types of programs and services to roughly the same client communities

d. "New entrants" or new organizations that might begin offering similar types of services in the future

e. "Producers of substitute services" or agencies that may develop in the future new types of programs that may make our agency's programs less attractive to the client communities and hence make it more difficult for the agency to obtain funding

Thus, in dealing with environmental pressures, it is necessary for the agency to identify its "competition" very carefully and understand well what drives these organizations. For example, a private day care center may find it faces competition for clients as well as funds and other resources from publicly supported day care centers, the child care arrangements that employer organizations provide, churches, and at-home baby-sitters. Agencies can gather information about the different facets of their environment from a variety of sources, such as news media, professional associations of human service agencies, public documents on the costs and budgets of other agencies, client community members, and consultants. Trends in broad demographic and societal forces can be analyzed with data from numerous public sources.

Step 3. Assessment of the Organization's Internal Environment

In this step, the agency identifies the values of the organization, tabulates the resources and talents available within the agency now, and analyzes its strengths and weaknesses. Some questions management should ask are:

a. Programs. What is the main thrust behind the programs and activities of the agency? How well are the current programs achieving the agency's goals? How well are they utilizing the agency's resources (including personnel, finances, physical facilities, and other resources)? How well are the agency's programs growing relative to those of other similar ("competing") agencies?

b. Resources. What are the major resources that the agency uses, and where are they coming from? What are the likely trends in their future supply? What are the gaps between the types and amounts of resources needed and what is likely to be available? What are the actions needed to meet these gaps? How satisfactory is the utilization of the various resources? Because human resources are crucial, the agency should analyze specifically how satisfactory is the utilization of its personnel, for example, in terms of recruitment, skills and performance of the staff, job satisfaction and turnover, and career development.

c. Strengths and weaknesses. What is it that the agency does better than other comparable (or competing) agencies? What is it that this agency does less well than they? What are the key factors that determine the agency's success, that is, what must the agency do well in order to succeed? Are there some things that the agency does particularly well, that is, what are the distinctive competencies of the agency that give it an edge over similar human service agencies?

d. Consistencies. How well do the agency's programs and activities build on its strengths and avoid its weaknesses? How well do the programs take advantage of the potential opportunities? How consistent are the current and future programs and activities with the organization's basic mission and philosophy?

The best way to analyze the strengths and weaknesses and make sure there are no premature judgments is to give each person time to present views as each of the items (a) through (d) are being analyzed. Ask each committee member to speak for a brief, predetermined amount of time (say, for ten minutes) about the item if they wish to present their own points. At this time the speakers should be asked to present strictly their own ideas and not be allowed to comment or respond to points made by others. By restricting the time and again limiting them to presenting their own ideas, the members will have greater opportunity to bring a variety of ideas out into the open. In fact, if there is concern that the more powerful and aggressive members may inhibit expression by the others, then the members can be asked to write down their ideas on each of the four items anonymously on four different cards, and then these ideas can be listed on a blackboard for all to consider. After all the categories of items are covered, then the issues identified and the pros and cons of the arguments on each point should be discussed. This exercise can lead to a consensus if carried out without an attempt to channel conclusions in a predetermined direction—even if it appears to be time-consuming and uses up a lot of paper.

Step 4. Formulation of Future Strategy

By the time the agency completes the first three steps, the management has evaluated its mission, assessed its resources and strengths and weaknesses, and examined the type of external environment with which it has to cope. We do not suggest that all agencies should follow—nor do we imply that agencies in fact do follow—the first three steps in the strict order described above. As a matter of fact, agencies often may have to retrace to step 1 after completing step 3, because the objectives may have to be redefined and refined based on the assessment of the environmental trends and of the agency's strengths and weaknesses. However, we do believe that information on the first three aspects is a prerequisite for a sound choice of future strategy—which constitutes the next step.

In this fourth step, management identifies the various directions in which the agency can move in the future to accomplish its objectives. Then it evaluates and chooses the direction that would be best for the agency, given its values, resources, and environment. Some questions that will help management in this step are as follows:

What are the different types of programs that the agency can adopt in the future? (For example, a child care service agency can consider such alternatives as adding a number of new types of educational programs to its current menu of services or opening operations in new locations.) Which of these best meet the agency's objectives and match the agency's strengths? What are some nonprogram activities—such as changes in funding sources, types of client communities served, physical facilities, and personnel and administrative practices—that the agency should consider for the future? Are there some ways in which the agency can secure a more favorable environment? What changes would be required in the agency's present activities in order to have the right programs in place for the future? How feasible are these changes given the agency's resources, weaknesses, and organizational values and the preferences of key constituencies? How well would each alternative help the agency achieve its long-run and short-run objectives?

In identifying alternatives, it is essential that the agency explore several alternatives before selecting a final plan of action. Too often, managers allow themselves to prematurely settle upon a favored solution. When they take it upon themselves to examine a wide range of alternatives, the agency's decision makers become cognizant of the preferences of its various constituencies and, hopefully, the final selection is made through a process of consensus.

The plan of action that the agency chooses after deliberating all these issues

Exhibit 1.1
Framework for Selecting Strategies

Future Conditions in the External Environment

Favorable   Unfavorable

	Favorable	Unfavorable
High Strength of Agency Programs	Cell A Current programs are strong and will do well in future. Continue as is/ do nothing different.	Cell B Current programs are strong, but unattractive for the future. So new programs should replace these in the future.
Low	Cell C Current programs are weak now but are attractive for the future. Take action to strengthen them.	Cell D Current programs are weak now and will be unattractive for the future. So replace them now. If not, agency may soon cease to exist.

makes up the organizationwide long-range plan for the agency or, in other words, the agency's strategy.

Several models are available in the business literature for help in the formulation of strategy, and we reinterpret one model to illustrate that agency managements may find these models useful in the context of making strategy for human services.

The Strategy Portfolio Matrix developed by the Boston Consulting Group (BCG, 1968) is useful for evaluating the current activities of an organization and for laying out the broad strategy prescriptions for the future. This model is not comprehensive, yet its simplicity and clarity help in identifying and selecting between the alternatives. The matrix can be applied to the human service agencies in a modified form, as suggested by McConkey (1981) and as shown in Exhibit 1.1.

This matrix presents a summary assessment of future conditions in the agency's external environment on the one hand, and the strengths of the agency's current programs and services on the other. Each cell of the matrix points to some broad prescriptions for future strategies that follow from this analysis. This matrix does not specify which types of program alternatives the agency should pursue if the present programs are unattractive for the future, and in this respect its prescriptions are incomplete. Hence the agency should proceed to elaborate the specific strategic alternatives available under each set of conditions, evaluate their feasibility given the strengths and weaknesses of the agency, and select the appropriate action. For example, if the agency finds itself in Cells B or D, some specific alternatives to be considered would be: merging some or all of its programs with programs of other agencies, improving the quality and distinctiveness of its programs through innovation, improving the cost efficiencies to make the programs more viable, sharing some resources and services with other agencies to improve the levels of resource utilization, introducing new programs, and providing the same services to a different client community.

Step 5. Implementation of the Strategic Plan

The agencywide strategic plan is translated into action by preparing appropriate detailed operational plans such as plans for individual programs, annual budgets that break down the long-range strategy's financial allocations, longer-term financial plans in capital budgets, staffing plans, and utilization plans for other resources.

This detailed operational planning will be the primary task of the operating staff, but it should be an interactive process involving the staff and the top management. The staff is responsible for results in particular areas and they prepare and implement areawide plans that match the agency strategy for their area. For instance, if a human service agency's strategy in educational programs is to focus on employment-oriented training, then the educational programs staff in the agency will have the primary responsibility to develop and implement a detailed program plan that is consistent with this strategy. They may decide, for example, to offer a mix of programs such as computer literacy training, equipment repair, auto mechanics, and secretarial training.

Successful implementation also requires setting up the appropriate procedures and guidelines for managing operations. Some of the tasks involved are: assigning specific responsibilities for results, developing yardsticks for evaluating the achievement of the planned results, and instituting a rewards and incentive system that motivates individuals to achieve the desired results.

Monitoring is an important part of implementation. First, it is a prerequisite for rewarding the right performance. Second, close monitoring allows management to know when results are off-track. Early knowledge buys management the time to take steps to bring things back on track. Monitoring involves not only tracking results or actual performance, but also sensing any changes that may be occurring in the environment.

In sum, specific action-steps, a time frame, and resource and responsibility assignment are prerequisites for implementation of the formulated strategy. As the strategy is in execution, there is need for accurate monitoring and review of results and for an effective reward system. One format that helps this happen is:

a. State the general objective. For example, the general objective might be to improve fund-raising from private sources by 10 percent in three years.

b. Develop and define the subobjectives in all necessary areas. To follow with the example above, one subobjective that flows from the general objective might be: hire a part-time consultant to establish a fund-raising program.

c. Define the needed resources. In the above case, one resource may be the financial resources for fund-raising activities, for example, allocate $10,000 between 1990 and 1992.

d. Set up the control systems. For example, progress in the fund-raising may be reviewed every six months, and if certain milestone amounts are not procured, the agency may have to reassign the personnel or revise the objective itself.

A successful planning process is one that never stops. The end result is a continuous cycle with constant involvement from the top managers as well as from the lower levels. Redirection and refinement go on all the time.

Finally, our discussion so far may have given the impression that strategic planning is a highly formalized and systematic process that depends exclusively on reason and logic and leaves no room for intuition, creativity, and imagination. We do not mean to imply this. The "do's" that we have outlined are merely pointers regarding the kinds of factors that managers should keep in mind while formulating a strategy for their agency. As Mintzberg (1987) points out in the following quotes, the phrase "crafting strategy" probably describes more accurately how strategies are actually made than the phrase "formulating strategy."

Like a potter manages her craft, so too managers have to craft their strategy. [The potter's] mind is on the clay, but she is also aware of sitting between her past experiences and her future prospects. . . . She has an intimate knowledge of her work, her capabilities, and her market. As a craftsman she senses rather than analyzes them, her knowledge is "tacit." The product that emerges on the wheel is likely to be in the tradition of her past work, but she may break away and embark in a new direction. . . . Like the potter, . . . managers bring to their work an intimate knowledge . . . of past capabilities and future opportunities [for the agency]. . . . Strategies can emerge in the process of responding to an evolving situation, as well as be deliberately formulated (pp. 66, 68).

EXAMPLES OF STRATEGIC PLANNING IN HUMAN SERVICE AGENCIES

In this section we will present some examples of strategic planning carried out in selected human service agencies (the names and dates are disguised) to illustrate the problems and prospects in the practice of strategic planning. The examples will be grouped as well as possible into the five steps in strategic planning outlined in the previous section. However, real-life issues do not neatly partition themselves into categories, and hence overlap is inevitable.

The basic principle for effective strategic planning is that it must be adapted to the needs of each specific organization. In particular, the planning process in human service agencies should take into consideration the following two factors:

a. Long-term capital requirements—especially physical plant requirements that make it imperative to develop a plan that extends far enough in time to ensure a payback of capital funds. If capital is not a factor, strategic planning can generally be done on a shorter-term basis, with more emphasis on operations. If capital is a factor, more detailed long-term planning is necessary.

b. The size of the organization. This often determines the nature and extent of the problems, the resources available, and the degree to which the board of directors needs to be involved. An agency with a staff of ten and a budget of $100,000 can shift gears in strategy more quickly and has a staff that is more aware of the agency's strategy than an agency with a staff of 200 and a budget of $3 million. Some reasons are that the planning process in the larger agency is likely to be slower and cooperation more difficult. Hence a large agency has to strive harder to deliberately involve the key groups from the start. Also, the implementation of the resulting plan needs the help of systematic motivation and control systems to a much greater extent, because the top managers cannot personally provide the oversight.

The Planning Committee

We mentioned in the earlier section that the key groups should be involved. One agency we know of, which was primarily seeking to serve the black community in the Greater Philadelphia area of Pennsylvania, failed to include representatives of its clientele on the planning committee. It finally had to abandon its strategic plan in the face of strong criticism from the client groups.

An effective working size for the committee is 6 to 12 people, and an outside consultant or advisor is particularly helpful when there are strong intergroup differences in objectives and preferences. We have observed that the best results are produced when the committee as a whole meets to develop and clarify the mission of the agency. But the detailed operating plans are best designed by subgroups that include people who have the implementing responsibility— whether or not these individuals are on the agencywide planning committee. To illustrate, one agency in the Philadelphia area created a very effective eight-member planning committee consisting of the executive director, four other members from the board of directors, and three other staff members. This committee held five meetings, each lasting four hours, to draft the mission. In addition, these members reconstituted themselves into three-person subcommittees to draft individual sections of the detailed plan—membership, physical plant, new programs, review of current programs, personnel, and fund-raising.

Step 1. Defining the Mission of the Agency

The mission statement should be one that board and staff members can endorse and work from. It is not a statement merely for marketing or fund-raising purposes, though a clear statement of direction can help in attracting prospective donors. It is a statement of the management's values relating to the groups to be served, financing, quality of service, board-staff relations, and its self-concept.

Defining the mission is not always a straightforward task, as seen in the case of the Southern Neighborhood Agency. This agency was founded in 1910 as the Southern Neighborhood Athletic Center to provide athletic facilities for teenaged boys in a relatively low-income area. The primary purpose was to give the boys constructive outlets for their development.

After World War II, vocational training was added to the agency's programs, and during the sixties, a day care facility was also added to meet the changing needs of the neighborhood. The youth and the day care programs operated independently of each other. The board consisted of 14 members, 9 of whom were also involved with recreational activity in the agency.

The communities around the agency demanded that it should broaden its services to cater to the needs of the total population, the women, elderly, and minorities. The board was split on this issue. The agency management and the board saw this as the right occasion to formulate a coherent long-range strategic plan. Hence they formed a planning committee and gave themselves the charge of finding acceptable answers to the following questions: Who are we? Are we a neighborhood full-service agency, or a specialized recreational and vocational agency? The committee debated these questions for three days in a row and came to the conclusion that their agency should move in the following directions:

- The agency will serve the total population in the area.
- Recreational activities will remain the centerpiece in the services.
- One new recreational service for the general public will be added in the next six months to fulfill the larger mission.
- The board will be reconstituted to better represent the community.

It is evident from this statement that, in reality, human service agencies—or for that matter any organization—cannot conduct one step of the strategic planning process in isolation from the others. In arriving at this statement, the planning group implicitly examined its environment and the agency's internal resources. However, while it is indeed essential that the mission be relevant for the particular agency, it should be reiterated that in developing the mission statement, the concern should be with identifying the lifelong purpose of the agency. Hence the agency's policymakers should resist the temptation to be influenced by the short-term "here and now" concerns.

Another example is the following mission statement developed by a women's service group:

We are a private nonprofit membership organization of women in Aberdeen County established to enhance the well-being of all women in the county by working to protect and advance the rights of females, by providing quality services for employment and counseling and by providing support and assistance to families of single female parents.

A day care center declared its mission as follows:

The Arden Day Care Center is a nonprofit corporation licensed by the city of Allentown. It serves the immediate community surrounding Arden by providing a warm nurturing atmosphere in which each child feels accepted and cared for as an individual. The center also seeks to provide developmental learning designed to stimulate each child's curiosity and creativity. Dedicated to combating racism, it encourages each child to reach his or her potential and foster mutual understanding within the rich diversity of the Arden community.

Staffed by caring teachers with appropriate training and expertise, the center's program is based on a developmental model which includes a planned sequence of learning skills. Financed primarily by tuition fees, the center seeks to maintain enrollment that provides financial stability, meets our educational goals and allows for racial, sexual and economic diversity.

The important contribution of each of these mission statements was that they provided a purpose upon which all board and staff members could agree. In both cases there were serious disagreements about the main purpose of the agency before the process started, and hence the statement served as a tool for forging consensus among all the members of the organization.

Step 2. Evaluating the External Environment

As we pointed out earlier, this step consists of examining the economic, technological, demographic, political, and social factors that might affect the agency in the next several years. One youth service agency carried out this analysis by developing a list of crucial questions for its future and updating the answers periodically. Some of these questions were as follows:

- What is the economic outlook going to be like in the next several years? What effect will that have on our funding and our clients? Will we have to offer different kinds of services?
- What is happening to the neighborhood we serve? Is it changing? Which characteristics of this neighborhood are changing? Should we move out, or even close?
- Who is our competition? What are they doing? How do our cost and quality compare? What can we do to be comparable or, preferably, superior to them?

Step 3. Assessment of Internal Resources

One agency developed the following list to provide focus for its internal assessment:

Service level and quality

Facilities

Equipment

Public relations

Information base

Cost performance

Funding

For evaluating each area this agency developed a variety of documentary support including a client demographics analysis, an operating financial statement for the agency as a whole and for the major programs, client-participation rates for the important programs, and organization charts for the key units in the agency.

Steps 4 and 5. Selection of Strategies and Implementation

When the previous steps are completed, it is time to develop a strategy. By now, the managers might have gained a good understanding of the risks, opportunities, and threats posed by the external environment as well as the internal strengths and weaknesses of the agency. Then they pose the question What are the critical issues we have to deal with if we are to achieve our mission? The list of critical issues should preferably not exceed six to eight points.

We present below an example from one small center providing counseling programs for people of all ages with drug, alcohol, and related problems. The problems of this agency had mainly to do with personnel, programming, and fund-raising. The physical plant was not involved. Because it was a small agency, strategy selection was intermingled with mission definition and operational planning. This agency's management identified the following areas of weakness:

• Personnel: Low salaries make it difficult to attract and retain competent staff; lack of professionalism is evident among the staff.

• Quality of programs: Quality of programs is weaker than that of similar (competing) agencies.

• Relations with board: Agency lacks support from the board and hence fund-raising is difficult.

• Community support: Community lacks awareness about the agency.

• Finances: Agency is urgently in need of additional funding

The planning committee then developed the following set of actions for addressing the problems:

• Within one year, the agency will raise the number and levels of its staff positions and salaries to equal average levels in other local agencies.

• The board has been requested to provide by the end of the next quarter a set of recommendations that will make the agency's programs competitive in quality and improve its image in the community. The board members will then also take up part of the responsibility for raising funds.

- The agency will include representatives of the community in its planning committee by the end of the current planning year.
- The agency has generated a list of income and financial goals to guide the fund-raising efforts.

The planning committee assigned the tasks of formulating the detailed plans for each area and monitoring the progress to separate subcommittees. Each of these subgroups had three members, one each from the planning committee, the board, and the appropriate functional unit within the agency. Examples of the action plans, including budgets of different types, developed by these subcommittees were:

- A personnel/staff budget was developed showing the dollar needs for the agency to bring up the number and salaries of professional staff on par with competing agencies. The subcommittee surveyed other local agencies for the required data.
- An operating budget was prepared after comparing the current income and expenditure levels with the income and expenditure levels required for bringing the staffing as well as program quality up to the average levels for comparable agencies.
- A policy manual for personnel procedures was formulated. A recommendation was made to use outside experts to improve professionalism among the agency staff.
- Action plans were prepared for recruiting new board members, especially from the surrounding community. Also, a memorandum was distributed to clarify the agency's expectations regarding the roles and responsibilities of the board members, the types of subcommittees required, and the subcommittees' tasks.
- An action plan to improve the agency's image was developed, with ideas for developing a logo to present a recognizable image to the community, for surveying the client groups for ideas on programs, and for fund-raising.
- Another plan specified how to diversify the sources of outside funding and how to allocate the dollar goals and timetables for fund-raising to the different board members and the senior staff.

Once these plans were finalized and adopted, implementation commenced immediately.

Another example is the Elktown Youth Services Association, a much larger community organization, which developed a capital budgeting plan to build a $500,000 physical fitness center as part of its future growth strategy. This plan extended over five years and included the following specific implementation steps:

February 1985: Submit grant proposal for $200,000.

March 1985: Name development committee to raise the first $100,000.

March 1985: Arrange facilities to borrow $200,000 to be paid back over the next ten years from expanded memberships and from user fees at the new physical fitness center.

December 1985: Deadline for raising $500,000.

January 1986: Make final decision on selection of architect and construction firm for the fitness center.

October 1986: Hire director for the fitness center. Develop a promotion campaign for the center.

December 1986: Complete construction and recruit additional staff by mid-December. Launch the promotion campaign by last week of December.

January 1987: Open the center. Continue the promotion effort.

December 1987: Agency membership should increase by 50 percent. Net increase in agency membership and user fees from the physical fitness center should bring in an additional $20,000.

December 1989: Membership increases and user fees of physical fitness center should contribute $45,000 annually.

Concluding Remarks

We have presented here a few examples to expand the theoretical "do's" and "don'ts" discussed in the first section. These examples by no means exhaust the ways in which human service agencies develop and implement strategic plans. We have found that each agency finds ways and methods uniquely suited to its requirements, and as long as agencies focus on developing a comprehensive viable future strategy for the organization, the various methods tend to work equally well. Further, although we focused primarily on "successful" examples, this does not mean that these agencies or others did not face problems in crafting strategy or making it work. Strategic planning does not guarantee success, but assists in harnessing the intimate knowledge, intuition, and creativity of human service professionals in formulating a plan that helps the agency fulfill its mission more effectively.

REFERENCES

Boston Consulting Group (1968). Strategy and market segment research. In *Perspective*. Boston, MA: Boston Consulting Group.

McConkey, D. D. (Summer 1981). Strategic planning in nonprofit organizations. *Business Quarterly* 18 (2), 36–41.

Mintzberg, H. (1987). Crafting strategy. *Harvard Business Review* 65 (4), 66–77.

Porter, M. (1980). *Competitive strategy*. New York: Free Press.

Quinn, B. (1980). *Strategies for change: Logical incrementalism*. Homewood, IL: Irwin.

ANNOTATED BIBLIOGRAPHY

The strategic planning field is rich with academic and practitioner-oriented literature—in books and journals. Typically, much of it discusses the issues in the context of business corporations. In fact, the term "business policy" is often used synonymously with strategic planning. The *Harvard Business Review* and the *Journal of Business Strategy* are two major journals in strategy targeted mainly for the practitioner audience. The *Strategic Management Journal* is more academically oriented. We are listing below a handful of the books and articles that managers of human service agencies may want to refer to for further information on theory and techniques in strategic planning. As the reader may notice, many of these books and articles have been written with large business corporations, and occasionally large public-sector agencies, in mind. Hence, managers of the smaller human service organizations need to do a lot of translating, cutting down, and adapting of the concepts and techniques.

Books

Hirschhorn, J. A. (1981). *Cutting back*. New York: Jossey-Bass. Directly focuses on the service organizations. It deals with the subject of how to adapt the strategies and the management processes in these organizations to the cutbacks in external resources. Some of the techniques that this book suggests for analyzing the environment and current and new programs are useful not only for strategic planning under a cutback environment, but for any planning process.

Mason, R. O., and I. I. Mitroff (1981). *Challenging strategic planning assumptions*. New York: John Wiley. Provides a technique for analyzing the key groups within and outside who can influence the strategy of an organization. It makes the point that when strategic planning goes on and organizations choose certain strategies over others, planners are always making many assumptions about what these various groups would or would not do. These assumptions are very critical and hence the strategic planners should be explicitly aware of them. Within this framework, the book explains a group formation and group discussion technique called the Strategic Assumption Surfacing and Testing (SAST). This technique is helpful for (1) identifying the various key external and internal groups (called stakeholders) that can impact the strategies of the organization, (2) analyzing how they influence the strategies of the organization, and (3) examining the feasibility of the different strategies under consideration in terms of the behaviors they require from the key stakeholders. Then the planning group selects the actual strategies through consensus. The authors provide examples from large businesses and government agencies.

Peters, T. J. (1984). *A passion for excellence*. New York: Harper and Row. A companion volume to the 1982 book that carries forward the same theme, but cites numerous examples from the small business field and some governmental and nonprofit organizations.

Peters, T. J., and R. H. Waterman (1982). *In search of excellence*. New York: Harper and Row. The thesis of this book is that a well-managed organization does everything well, including strategic planning. Hence organizations should strive to follow the principles of "excellent management." This highly readable best-seller then goes on to describe these principles by describing the ways in which the best-managed companies in American are run. The principles would be useful to managers of human service organizations as well.

Porter, M. (1980). *Competitive strategy*. New York: Free Press. A lucid, excellent analysis of the types of environments faced by business corporations and the strategies appropriate under each set of conditions. The concepts need reinterpretation for the context of human service organizations.

Unterman, I. and R. H. Davis (1984). *Strategic management of not-for-profit organizations*. New York: Praeger. Very relevant for human service agencies. Does much of the translating of the strategic planning literature from the large business and government context to the field of the human service agencies.

Articles

Boston Consulting Group (1968). Strategy and market segment research. In *Perspective*. Boston, MA: Boston Consulting Group. Develops the broad rule-of-thumb technique called the "growth-share matrix." This technique tries to classify the growth in the market (or in the parlance of service organizations, the overall picture of the organization's environment) and the market share (or the present standing of its programs and activities), into high versus low categories. Then, by placing the programs and services into the categories, this matrix gives broad pointers on which types of strategies the organization should choose under various conditions. The technique is explained in the terminology of business, but it is quite helpful in analyzing the environments of human service organizations.

Lindblom, C. E. (1959). The science of muddling through. *Public Administration Review* 19 (1), 79–88. Argues that changes take place very slowly and gradually in any organization and that this is true of all areas, including strategy making.

2

Organizational Structure in Human Service Agencies

RICHARD M. WEISS

The notion of providing human services through a bureaucracy almost seems paradoxical. Undeniably, many human service agencies in the governmental sector may be characterized as having numerous impersonally administered rules and procedures carried out by individuals with strictly delimited areas of responsibility within a hierarchy of authority. However, this arrangement is unlikely to be admired by those providing human services in the voluntary sector. Rather, many of these voluntary-sector agencies pride themselves on the extent of their divergence from that image.

Nevertheless, although bureaucracy has no shortage of detractors, its drawbacks should not be permitted to overshadow completely its intended—and occasionally realized—positive functions. Situations such as the inflexible application of rules by bureaucrats who insist that there is nothing they, personally, can do about a particular situation most certainly can be infuriating. However, would we really prefer organizations in which a functionary's personal feelings toward various clients (perhaps based on the receipt of gifts) were translated into unequal outcomes among equally deserving individuals?

Limiting the range of authority of employees and requiring them to carry out their roles in a manner that is consistent with written rules that are applied uniformly to all clients can reduce that sort of injustice. Requiring employees to hold off on certain actions until receiving approval from a number of individuals above them in a hierarchical chain of command is likely to slow down the delivery of services; however, it also is likely to heighten accountability.

Figure 2.1
Jane and Original Volunteers

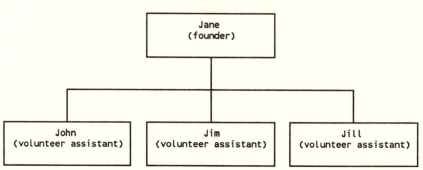

Although very few of us are in favor of red tape, probably even fewer support the notion that decisions concerning issues such as the disbursement of funds or the delivery of services should be based on favoritism or whim.

Instead of either embracing or rejecting bureaucratic structuring of human service agencies, this chapter will attempt to identify some of the circumstances under which various characteristics of bureaucratic organizational structures are more or less appropriate. We begin with a story of a fictional agency that began simply and very nonbureaucratically, but changed substantially as it became more successful. The organization described here evolved slowly, beginning from the voluntary efforts of a small group of people. Although not all agencies develop in this fashion, this illustration should suggest the various functions and limitations of different organizational structures.

THE EVOLUTION OF AN ORGANIZATIONAL STRUCTURE

Jane Doe is the executive director of the Northside Community Services Center, a human service agency that she founded some years ago. When she started out, her organization not only was far smaller than it is today, but it did not even have a name. Its simple origin was the Thanksgiving dinner that Jane served in her home for needy citizens of her community. Preparing the dinner was a big job, but she did it all herself, and a chart to represent this "organization" would be rather superfluous, requiring simply a box with Jane's name in it.

By the third Thanksgiving, however, Jane's culinary, organizational, and promotional skills (and a substantial downturn in the local economy) had led to such a large turnout that she could no longer put together the entire dinner without some help, and three neighbors volunteered to assist her. In Figure 2.1 we see the organizational chart for Jane's third dinner. The three neighbors, John, Jim, and Jill, were supervised by Jane and all functioned at approximately the same level of responsibility in helping her with a variety of tasks such as shopping, cooking, serving, and cleaning up.

Figure 2.2
Volunteer Force Expands

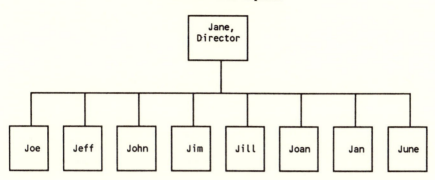

Because of Jane's skill and experience (and because this was still essentially her dinner), the assistants always checked with her before doing anything she had not already specifically asked them to do. Over the next two years the number of people who attended the dinner continued to grow, and five more volunteers were now helping Jane, much the same as did her original three volunteers; Figure 2.2 shows the organizational chart at this point.

By the sixth year, the fame of her cranberry sauce and turkey dressing had spread far and wide, and Jane had a team of twelve volunteers working on what she hoped would be the best dinner yet. But this time, things didn't go very well. Although Jane had succeeded in raising all the money needed for that year's bigger-than-ever dinner, too few cranberries and turkeys had been purchased, the birds came out too tough and the gravy too thin, and four days after Thanksgiving Jane found herself cleaning up the mess that remained in the church basement where the dinner had been held.

Of course, there are many possible explanations for what suddenly went wrong. Perhaps Jane had fallen victim to burnout or stress after these years of selfless and wearying altruism. Perhaps she lacked the skills to motivate her assistants properly or to facilitate cooperation among the group's members. However, rather than attributing Jane's problem to poor interpersonal skills, we will consider the possibility that they may have resulted from a failure of organization, and we will attempt to show how Jane's group might have been structured for greater effectiveness.

With the greatly increased demand for the service that Jane was providing, she found that an increasing amount of her time was being spent meeting with the religious, civic, and other charitable groups that could provide the resources she needed, such as money for food and a facility in which to cook and serve the dinner. In the past Jane had been able to conduct these interactions with outside groups as well as supervise a crew of volunteers. However, the extent of these external activities and the difficulty of directly overseeing the work of

Figure 2.3
Original Volunteers Given Supervisory Responsibilities

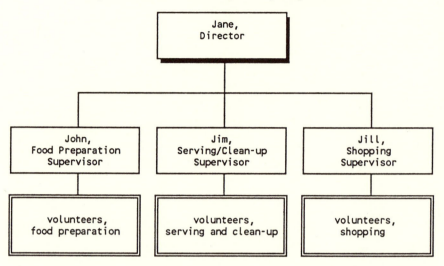

not just three or four, but a dozen people carrying out a variety of tasks, had overtaxed even Jane.

In the years that they all had been working with Jane, her first three volunteers, John, Jim, and Jill, had become knowledgeable about the functioning of the operation and repeatedly had demonstrated their trustworthiness. Although Jane felt somewhat ill at ease about the idea of instituting a hierarchical chain of command in her organization, she decided that in order to relieve herself of the time-consuming pressure of answering every assistant's questions about relatively minor details, she would ask her three most tenured helpers to serve as supervisors. The other assistants were now to ask questions of, take directions from, and bring their problems to John if they were involved in food preparation, to Jill if they were assigned to shopping for the food, and to Jim if their task was to serve the meal or to clean up afterward. These three, in turn, took direction from Jane. The organizational chart at this point, shown in Figure 2.3, now had three levels in its hierarchy, and was arranged according to functions (shopping, cooking, and serving and cleaning up).

As pleased as Jane and her associates were to see the happiness they had been bringing to their dinner guests at Thanksgiving, they regretted that so many of these individuals were alone and hungry at Christmastime, and the group decided to hold dinners at both of these times of the year. However, in discussing the implementation of this expansion of their services, they realized that many of their volunteers were not entirely willing to essentially double their commitment of time to the organization. Figure 2.4 illustrates the organization structure that emerged in response to that dilemma. John and Jill became the directors of,

Figure 2.4
Creation of Two "Divisions"

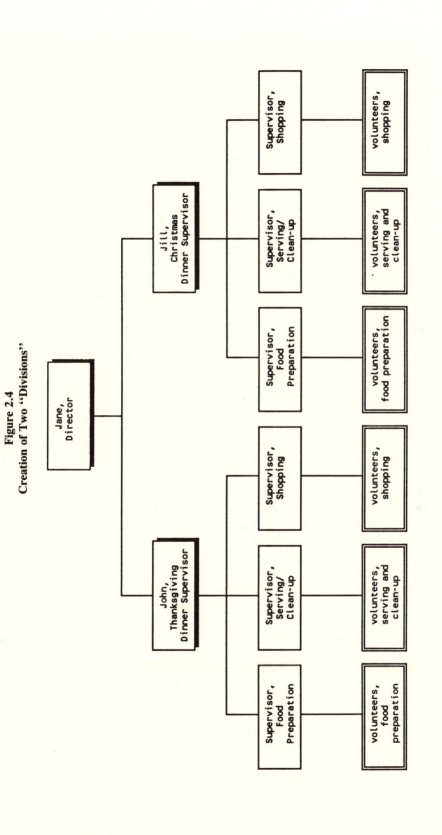

Figure 2.5
Addition of Adult Literacy Program

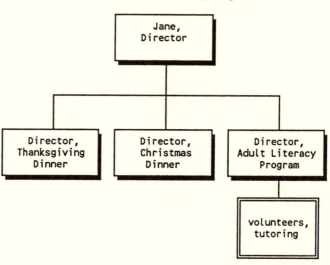

respectively, the Thanksgiving and Christmas dinners, and some newer volunteers managed the specific functions John and Jill formerly had supervised.

The form of organization for Jane's dinners shown in Figure 2.4 is what is usually referred to as a divisional structure, in which the individuals who report directly to the head of the organization are in charge of some region, product, market, clientele, or service (in this case, one of the two annual dinners). This is usually contrasted with a functional structure, in which those reporting to the chief executive direct some specific task such as marketing or finance. Figure 2.3, which shows the organization form in use prior to the decision to expand to two dinners each year, illustrates the functional form. Note that the change from functional to divisional structure occurring from Figure 2.3 to Figure 2.4 created, in a sense, two small functional structures—each supervised by a divisional director—having the same functions as those in the earlier, functional structure.

This rearrangement worked out so well that Jane and her associates felt encouraged to tackle additional problems among the poor in the community. They believed that the poverty in which many of their dinner guests found themselves was in part due to the inadequacy of their basic, job-related skills, and the group decided to institute an adult literacy program. A local middle school agreed to allow them to use their facilities two evenings each week, and Jane convinced a friend of hers, a teacher, to direct the project. When the project began, the director supervised twelve volunteer tutors and reported directly to Jane (see Figure 2.5).

The increasing number of applicants for spaces in the program led to the

Figure 2.6
Growth of Adult Literacy Program

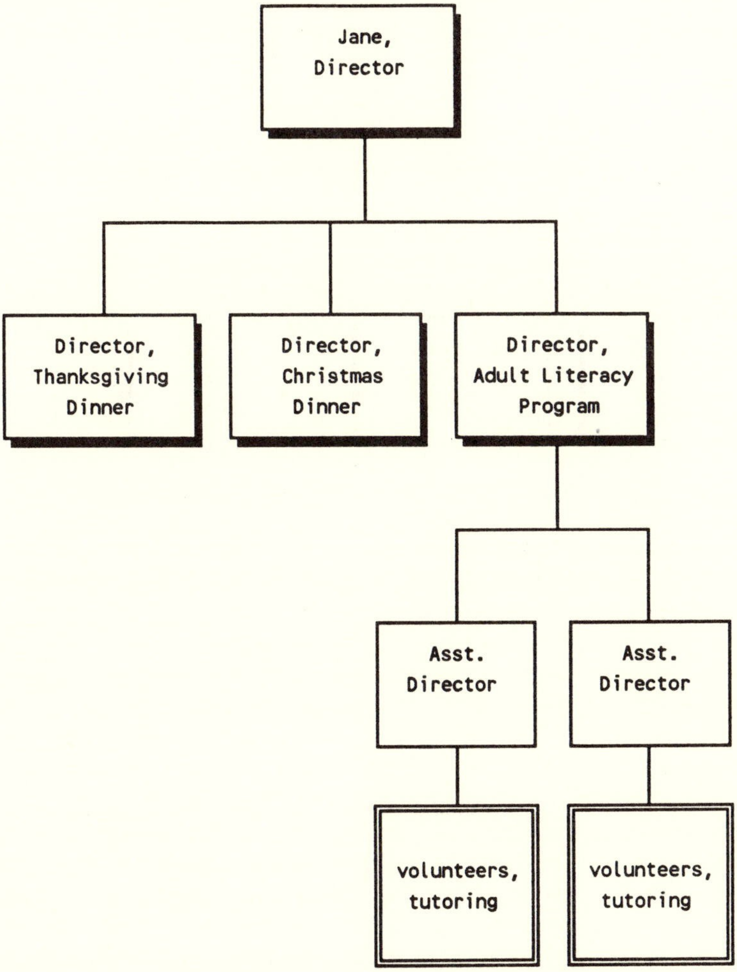

continual recruitment of additional tutors, until eventually, as had happened in this group's earlier activities, a large span of control for the program director led to things becoming somewhat unwieldy. Rather than continuing to attempt directly to supervise the roughly two dozen volunteer tutors herself, the director appointed two of the most experienced tutors as assistant directors, each of whom worked with a dozen tutors (see Figure 2.6). This structure worked well, with the two assistant directors having sufficient time to work in a consultative relationship with the less experienced tutors, and the program director freed to handle administrative duties.

Figure 2.7
Continuing Growth of Adult Literacy Program

```
                        ┌─────────────┐
                        │   Jane,     │
                        │  Director   │
                        └─────────────┘
                               │
         ┌─────────────────────┼─────────────────────┐
         │                     │                     │
  ┌─────────────┐       ┌─────────────┐       ┌─────────────┐
  │  Director,  │       │  Director,  │       │  Director,  │
  │Thanksgiving │       │  Christmas  │       │Adult Literacy│
  │   Dinner    │       │   Dinner    │       │   Program   │
  └─────────────┘       └─────────────┘       └─────────────┘
                                                     │
                            ┌────────────────────────┼────────────────────────┐
                            │                        │                        │
                     ┌─────────────┐          ┌─────────────┐          ┌─────────────┐
                     │    Asst.    │          │    Asst.    │          │    Asst.    │
                     │  Director   │          │  Director   │          │  Director   │
                     └─────────────┘          └─────────────┘          └─────────────┘
                            │                        │                        │
                     ┌─────────────┐          ┌─────────────┐          ┌─────────────┐
                     │ volunteers, │          │ volunteers, │          │ volunteers, │
                     │  tutoring   │          │  tutoring   │          │  tutoring   │
                     └─────────────┘          └─────────────┘          └─────────────┘
```

As new tutors volunteered, they initially were assigned to either of the assistant directors' units. Eventually, however, their spans of control became so large that rather than having the time to sit down and work with individual tutors to iron out problems, they tended to have only enough time for one-way communication. Figure 2.7 shows how the literacy project changed its structure once again to manage this dilemma, creating a third assistant director's position that reported to the project director.

The literacy project eventually needed more physical space than the middle school could spare, and this immediate dilemma precipitated frequent discussions

about the future directions that this group should take. Having worked successfully with the school board in operating the literacy program out of one of their
facilities, they were offered the opportunity to sign a lease with the school board
(for one dollar per year) for an elementary school building that was not in use
due to a decline in the number of children in that age cohort. The group decided
to take the lease and expand their programs by incorporating—as the Northside
Community Services Center (NCSC)—and applying for nonprofit status, putting
together a board of directors, hiring staff, keeping financial records, and carrying
out a variety of other responsibilities that will be discussed in subsequent chapters
of this book. With support from the local government, Jane became a full-time,
paid employee of the organization and was able to recruit human service professionals to direct the major projects. John and Jill, meanwhile, became members
of the board of directors.

The first expansion of services in their new facility was to serve a dinner each
Sunday night, rather than only twice a year. Subsequently, having instituted the
literacy project out of concern for developing the employment skills of the
chronically unemployed in the community, they decided to extend their commitment to that goal by instituting a job counseling service. A director was hired
for this new project, who reported to Jane and had five job counselors reporting
directly to her (see Figure 2.8). As her project expanded, she too found that at
a certain point she simply had too many subordinates to allow her to maintain
effective working relationships with each of them. However, the growth in the
number of subordinates in this project was not nearly as great as with the literacy
program. Instead of appointing two assistant directors, the most experienced
counselor was asked to act as assistant to the project director to handle some of
the more routine aspects of the director's role, and the resulting administrative
structure of the job counseling project was as is shown in Figure 2.9.

The literacy and job counseling programs were meeting with substantial success; not surprisingly, however, Jane and the others at NCSC realized that there
was much more work to be done. A particular need was to help unemployed
people gain more marketable job skills so that they could be placed more readily.
With the help of federal and state grants, NCSC was able to establish a program
to train unemployed people for computer-related jobs. As with the projects
established previously, its director reported to Jane.

Just as the pressures of increasingly large spans of control caused the project
directors to reassign some of their supervisory responsibilities, the increasing
number of project directors reporting directly to Jane was causing her to reconsider how to find enough time to carry out her duties. Acting as the organization's
most senior advisor, coordinator, and maker of nonroutine decisions was itself
a reasonably full-time job, yet she also needed to work at maintaining her
agency's relations with constituents, potential funding sources, and so on, outside
the organization. Her initial response was to hire a Director of Public Affairs
and Development to help her manage the organization's continuing growth. This
new addition to the organization was most similar to the position of the assistant

Figure 2.8
Restructuring and Expansion Following Incorporation

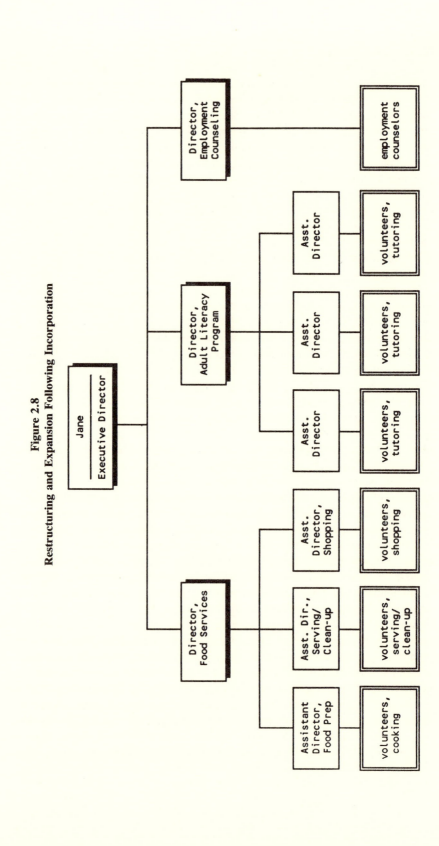

Figure 2.9
Adding an Administrator to the Counseling Program

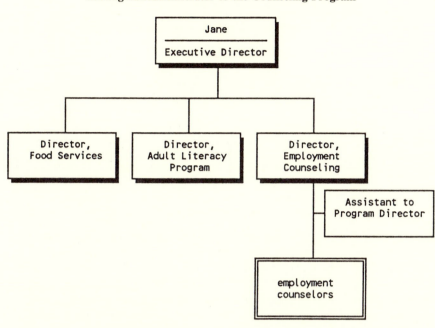

to the counseling project director; that is, the development director did not head a unit in which he supervised subordinates. Rather than being a line manager holding a position in the chain of command somewhere between the executive director and the direct service providers (e.g., tutors and trainers), his position was as sort of an appendage to Jane's—what is referred to as a staff position. His location on the organizational chart is shown in Figure 2.10.

For a while, the addition of this new position enabled Jane to devote more of her time to developing the organization's various projects, rather than to lobbying at the state capital. With the organization's continuing expansion, however, there eventually were too many individuals reporting directly to her to allow her to work effectively with these managers in solving problems, or even for her to have a particularly good sense as to what they were up to. Somewhat reluctantly, she created yet another layer in the organization's managerial hierarchy (see Figure 2.11), creating an Associate Director for Food Services, and an Associate Director for Training and Employment Services, with the appropriate project directors reporting to each of them.

STRUCTURING FOR ORGANIZATIONAL EFFECTIVENESS

Consider the changes that have occurred over the years in the structure of this highly successful nonprofit organization. The increasing demand for services has

Figure 2.10
Adding a Senior Staff Member

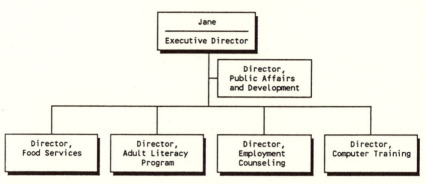

generally led to a need for more members of the organization, either as service providers or as administrators. As obvious as this point may seem, it is not so clearly the case in all organizations. For example, when the demand for petroleum products increases or decreases, refineries do not generally hire or lay off large numbers of employees; increasing or decreasing production is largely a matter of adjusting dials and switches, which requires roughly the same number of employees in either case. Organizations such as that are referred to as capital-intensive, meaning that the more important factor in the cost of providing goods or services is the cost associated with the acquisition and maintenance of capital goods, such as the plant and the equipment in it. The work of the NCSC, on the other hand, is highly labor-intensive, meaning that increases in this organization's output (of services rather than products) necessitate increases in the number of employees and/or volunteers.

As we have seen, the increases in the number of personnel at NCSC put strains on the supervisory spans of control, which led to increases in the number of subunits, and in the number of levels in the administrative hierarchy. These changes seem not to have resulted from a love of bureaucracy or a desire for empire building, but rather from the desire to maintain sufficient time for close relationships between individuals and their immediate supervisors so that their interactions could be two-way exchanges and consultative discussions of problems rather than the quick handing down of orders.

Of course, while maintaining a close relationship with immediate supervisors, the effect of these changes has been to make the individual volunteer tutor or turkey stuffer increasingly distant from Jane. This trend bothers her, not only because she would personally prefer to be involved with service delivery rather than with paperwork, but because she knows that not everyone in the organization has her level of experience, cleverness, and commitment. Back in the days when each of the people in the organization reported directly to her, she was fairly confident that things would be done pretty much as she wanted them to be done. That is, she could look right over the shoulder of the person stirring gravy, and if it was not being stirred sufficiently, she could simply say, "Please stir the gravy some more." But with all the kettles the organization now has in the fire, Jane is no longer able personally to make the very large number of decisions that need to be made. She is left with little choice but to delegate at least the routine decision making down to lower-level supervisory personnel. Of course, while delegating decision-making authority to others may solve the dilemma of having too many people doing too many things for one individual to supervise, the original dilemma of ensuring that the decisions are made as well as they would be if Jane was making them herself is still not resolved.

One way that organizations respond to this problem is for the person on top who wishes to standardize what she feels is the best way for certain tasks to be performed to put in writing the instructions that she would give if she had the time to look over each individual's shoulder. For example, at some point, Jane may have written down the specific steps in her recipes for turkey and gravy. With a clear set of rules in place, Jane does not necessarily need to find supervisors who have roasted as many turkeys as she has; their job is to see that subordinates are following rules that represent an effort to crystallize and transmit the skill Jane has developed from her years of experience.

However, there are many kinds of tasks in organizations for which a standard set of written rules would not be very useful. For example, a supervisor asked by a literacy training volunteer for assistance in dealing with a difficult client might find that the manual for tutor supervisors does not provide clear guidelines for deciding whether this particular client has a cognitive disability, a visual problem, a lack of motivation, or some combination of these or other factors. A manual of written rules tends not to be especially good for dealing with all of the wide variety of exceptional cases that might come up in an organization—if such a manual could be written, it would have to be very lengthy (and, consequently, rather unlikely to be read). Therefore, for tasks that might require the application of a complex body of knowledge to a set of highly variable circumstances, organizations often hire individuals who come to the organization with the rules of the job already built in. For example, much as law firms have their most complex work done by individuals who have had years of formal training in the law and have passed examinations certifying their expertness, dealing with the problems of adult learners might best be facilitated by hiring individuals with relevant formal training, such as a degree in adult education.

The example provided here, of the fictional NCSC, has been offered as an illustration of the findings of decades of research on organizational structure. Not surprisingly, this research consistently has found that organizations with more members tend to be more complex. It appears that increases in size lead to increases in horizontal complexity (the number of different departments or

Figure 2.11
NCSC Today

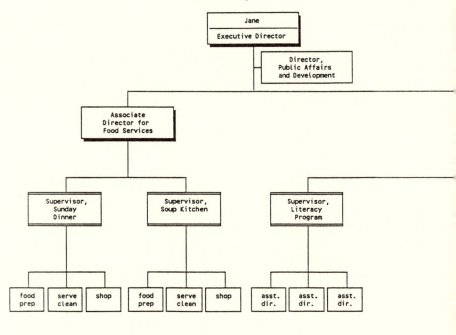

Figure 2.11 (Continued)

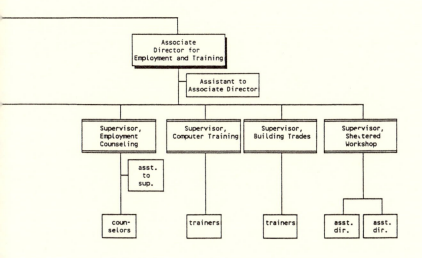

35

divisions), which then cause increases in vertical complexity (the number of levels in the administrative hierarchy) (Beyer and Trice, 1979).

The research evidence also offers an indication of what organizations do to compensate for the loss of direct control experienced by leaders as they find themselves separated from their work force by the increasing differentiation of functions and proliferation of layers of administrators. The inability of the person at the top of the organization to continue to make all the decisions that are necessary in a large and complex undertaking leads to a decrease in the degree of centralization (that is, the extent to which decisions are made at the top of the organization). As was illustrated in the account of NCSC, however, organizations' founders and leaders generally do not allow subordinates simply to "do their own thing." Rather, organizations' members typically report directly to someone whose guidance and decision making is based on their referring to a set of rules that embody the intentions of the person or persons at the top of the organization, and which may be either informal, written (which is more likely as the organization becomes larger), or trained into the individual prior to joining the organization.

Substituting formal rules for the issuance of directives from the organization's leaders is not an equally effective response to the difficulties of "bigness" under all conditions. Although it serves well in routine circumstances, situations that call for rapid responses to highly variable conditions are best served by employing individuals who come into the organization with the rules for carrying out their jobs already ingrained into them and allowing them a great deal of independence in decision making.

The type of organization structure that has been discussed here, in which close attention to rules and a narrow supervisory span of control are emphasized, might seem rather contrary to the sorts of humanistic, democratic values that administrators of voluntary-sector human service agencies are likely to hold and likely would wish to have reflected in the functioning of their own organization. And clearly, to a certain extent these notions reflect the concern that most organizations are likely to have some individuals who are a bit less knowledgeable, caring, and sensitive to the needs of their clientele than others. For the sake of that clientele, it is appropriate to have an organizational structure that can enhance the performance of those individuals.

More important, however, upon closer examination, the features of bureaucratic organization discussed here do not function simply as authoritarian means of control. Although a well-known study of department stores (Worthy, 1950) reported that operating with a very large span of control allowed subordinates more autonomy and resulted in greater satisfaction and productivity, numerous studies have since reported rather opposite results (see Blau, 1968; Meyer, 1968; Moeller and Charters, 1966). They suggest that, more typically, reporting to someone who supervises twenty rather than ten others translates to less access to that supervisor for detailed exchanges of views. Instead, the supervisor has just enough time to tell a subordinate what to do, but not enough to listen to suggestions or offer advice on problems. Indeed, this research evidence indicates that narrow spans of control are especially prevalent in organizations of highly trained professionals in which the individual in the supervisory position is less an order giver than a more experienced colleague available for consultation.

Similarly, written codification of the particular tasks associated with a job and how they are to be carried out is not simply an indication of mistrust of employees. Actually, members of organizations generally like to know what is expected of them and appreciate information that clarifies the roles they are to carry out and the rules they are to heed in doing so (Organ and Greene, 1981).

Nor does bureaucratic structuring of organizations necessarily shortchange creativity. Organizations engaged in routine activities are said to be most appropriately structured with high levels of centralization and formalization, whereas those engaged in nonroutine activities are advised to adopt low centralization and formalization (Lawrence and Lorsch, 1967). There is evidence that the structural characteristics said to be more conducive to organizational effectiveness in a particular environment also contribute to innovativeness (see Kimberly, 1981). Thus, a highly bureaucratized organization would be the recommended structure for eliciting innovation among organizations carrying out routine activities.

Nevertheless, the idea of arranging an organization such that each member is told that he or she may do only a certain, strictly delimited range of things and only in a strictly prescribed way seems inconsistent with the concern for the dignity of each individual that is likely to characterize the values held by managers in human service agencies. Certainly there are a great many "dysfunctions of bureaucracy," a notion around which an entire body of academic literature was focused during the 1950s. One such study identified the dysfunctional consequence of a rule requiring that the performance of employment interviewers be appraised on the sole criterion of the number of job placements made (Blau, 1955). Apparently, this motivated interviewers to send out whomever was being interviewed for whatever job was available, rather than pursue the agency's policy of finding the best possible match between employer and employee (indeed, the rule motivated interviewers to make the worst possible match, so that clients would be fired and then return to the agency to be placed once again). Another study found that establishing a formal rule regarding the precise number of employee absences that would trigger disciplinary action caused an increase rather than the intended decrease in absenteeism (Gouldner, 1954). Prior to the rule's existence employees were unaware of how much—or how little—absenteeism would land them in trouble, and this uncertainty moderated whatever impulses they might have had to go fishing rather than show up for work on Monday morning. The new rule, however, was worded such that there clearly was no adverse consequence of taking off exactly one day fewer than the number that would lead to action—and everyone did just that.

However, the lesson of these studies need not be that making rules, defining roles, assigning clear responsibility for decision making, and so forth are necessarily bad ideas. Rather, they point out that doing so without sufficient fore-thought into their possible consequences is a bad idea. It is under those circumstances that we are likely to hear complaints about "all the darned red tape and bureaucracy around here." When rules are used to make sure that clients' needs are served in the best possible way, when roles are structured so that qualified individuals are carrying them out, and when the hierarchy has enough administrators so that those trying to do the job of delivering the agency's service can get the support they deserve, then rather than anyone mentioning the word "bureaucracy," we are more likely to hear, "I'm glad they finally got things organized around here."

REFERENCES

Beyer, J. M., and H. M. Trice (1979). A reexamination of the relations between size and various components of organizational complexity. *Administrative Science Quarterly* 24, 48–64.

Blau, P. M. (1955). *The dynamics of bureaucracy*. Chicago: University of Chicago Press.
———. (1968). The hierarchy of authority in organizations. *American Journal of Sociology* 73, 453–57.

Gouldner, A. (1954). *Patterns of industrial bureaucracy*. New York: Free Press.

Kimberly, J. R. (1981). Managerial innovation. In P. C. Nystrom and W. H. Starbuck, eds., *Handbook of organizational design* (pp. 84–104). New York: Oxford.

Lawrence, R. R., and J. W. Lorsch (1967). *Organization and environment*. Boston: Graduate School of Business Administration, Harvard University.

Meyer, M. (1968). Expertness and the span of control. *American Sociological Review* 33, 944–51.

Moeller, G. H., and W. W. Charters (1966). Relation of bureaucratization to sense of power among teachers. *Administrative Science Quarterly* 10, 457–72.

Organ, D. W., and C. N. Greene (1981). The effects of formalization on professional involvement: A compensatory process approach. *Administrative Science Quarterly* 26, 237–52.

Worthy, J. C. (1950). Organizational structure and employee morale. *American Sociological Review* 15, 169–79.

3
Developing an Effective Leadership Style

JOSEPH SELTZER

The topic of leadership has been widely studied and many, many theories have been developed to explain or suggest ways of improving an individual's effectiveness as a leader. Although some of these theories offer useful frameworks for analyzing one's leadership style in a broad sense, they cannot hope to provide the specific guidance that many managers would like regarding how to interact with their particular subordinates in the various unique circumstances that arise during the course of a day. As Bradford and Cohen (1984) recently wrote,

Despite the millions of words on leadership that have assaulted managers, little has been written that truly reflects the world of work. Many theories are too simple for the complexity of dealing in real time with resistant subordinates, changing needs and conflicting demands. (p. viii)

Our view is that the most useful theory of leadership is one that the individual builds for himself or herself. This suggestion is that you, the reader, should create your own theory as it relates to yourself and your organization. To do so, we recommend several steps, as follows:

1. Examine your own leadership style in terms of a framework or theory.
2. Analyze your organizational setting to see how your style fits with the constraints imposed by the situation, structure, and staff.

3. Identify your own leadership successes and failures and use that to modify your approach to leadership.

4. Think about the future. What changes do you want to make in your leadership style? How will you accomplish this?

While there is no single best way to be a leader, a variety of behaviors have been shown to be effective in particular situations. The key is to behave in a way that is an appropriate match to the situation. The purpose of this chapter is to assist you in going through the above four steps.

First, we will present two frameworks to help you think about aspects of your leadership style, that is, that integrated set of behaviors that you frequently adopt when in a leadership role. It is important to have a conceptual basis for looking at your own leadership style so that as you build your own theory of leadership, it reflects more than just your own biases and perceptions.

Second, we will provide a series of questions to help you analyze and consider in depth the setting where you are a leader. Many perspectives on leadership suggest that the choice of which style is most effective is dependent on the constraints of the situation. For example, an agency director may choose to deal quite differently with a newly hired clerical worker, a second clerk who has worked for the agency for several years, and a social worker who has recently graduated with an M.S.W. Thus a critical skill for a leader is the ability to understand or diagnose a situation. Factors to consider (often called "contingencies") include

- one's subordinates and their interests, abilities and needs;

- one's superior and his or her style, demands, interests, and needs;

- one's organization—its structures, rules, climate, history, and culture and the external conditions that face it; and

- the nature of the tasks to be performed and the time pressures to do so.

The third step involves a reflective consideration of one's own experiences as a leader to answer the question, What aspects of your current style are effective or ineffective? We will provide a format to assist in this introspective exercise. You may want to modify and refine your own theory. We will also describe methods for discussing leadership with others and obtaining feedback on your leadership style. The goal is to build an individual theory that is both appropriate (in an objective sense) and personally useful.

Finally, we will ask you to integrate your theory of your own style and your diagnosis of the setting. To what extent is there a match between the two? What might you change to improve the fit? We will include a section on how one can change his or her style of leadership if that is appropriate. We will also ask you to consider how your current style will work in the future. How successfully will you be able to create the necessary changes in your organization?

FRAMEWORKS FOR LEADERSHIP: INFLUENCE

The first framework of leadership concerns influence. A central task of a leader is to influence his or her subordinates, peers, and, at times, superiors. This includes influencing people to follow orders and suggestions, to listen to and be persuaded by ideas and opinions, to do tasks or do them differently, to put forth more effort, and to act or not act in a certain manner. A leader must be able to exert influence in order to be effective as a manager.

In any situation, there are a variety of types of influence that are potentially available to the leader. We will identify seven types and suggest where each is appropriate (see Yukl, 1989).

1. Legitimate influence. In organizations, individuals have roles or positions. In addition to a job title, the position helps define the authority of the person who holds that role. Legitimate influence is the use of the authority system in the organization. For example, a caseworker might have the authority to make a referral for a client while a member of the office staff might not. In a discussion between the two, the caseworker might use his or her authority to request that the office worker prepare some paperwork on the referral. The latter would likely view this request as reasonable and ''part of the job'' and would allow himself or herself to be influenced.

   The use of authority as a means of influence is available in almost every situation in which one is clearly subordinate to the other in the organization's hierarchy. It is also a reasonable ''backup'' or second style to use if the first attempt to influence fails. It is less effective among peers or in situations in which the authority system is ambiguous. For example, a project director might have difficulty getting a person who works for a different project to cooperate on a task unless that request is seen as legitimate.

2. Coercive. The threat or action of the loss of a privilege or prerogative or another form of punishment would be needed to attempt to influence someone through coercive power. For example, a director attempting to get a subordinate to arrive on time might threaten to suspend the individual if he were again late. We should note that while the use of coercion often changes behavior, there can also be substantial adverse effects. The subordinate may feel that he or she is being treated unfairly and will thus arrive on time, but not do any work. On the other hand, it is important to use punishment in certain situations. For example, if a staff member were found to be stealing, it would be critical to take action. Also, punishment is reasonable as a last resort if other forms of influence fail and it is important to change the behavior. The most effective way to use punishment is to follow the ''hot stove rule'' (Dowling and Sayles, 1971). If you touch a hot stove, you get burned and you quickly learn not to touch hot stoves. In other words, you change your behavior, which is the major purpose of punishment. The elements of this experience are as follows:

   a. It is immediate. Punishment is best when clearly connected to the offending behavior.

   b. It is consistent. Any time you behave in a certain way (touch the stove) you will be punished.

c. It is impersonal. It doesn't matter if the stove likes you or not, you get burned. Thus the punishment is seen as fair rather than biased.

d. It is strong enough to change the behavior.

3. Reward. An individual can attempt to influence behavior through the use of rewards. Expectancy theory helps explain how this is accomplished by suggesting that people are motivated to behave in a particular way to the extent they believe the behavior will lead to valued outcomes (rewards). That is, the expectation of future rewards will encourage current behavior. These expectations can be influenced by factors such as having been rewarded in the past, knowing that others have been rewarded for the action, or simply being promised a future reward. The choice between several actions will be determined by the person's beliefs about how likely it is that each action will lead to various rewards and how valuable those rewards are.

We suggest, then, that you can influence another by increasing the person's expectation that he or she will be rewarded or, at times, by increasing the perceived importance of that reward. For example, a director who is attempting to get her staff to use a new computer system to retrieve information might occasionally praise those individuals who are making use of it. This would encourage those people to continue or increase their use and also would provide an expectation in the minds of other staff that they too could get praise if they used the system.

A variety of rewards is sometimes available to a leader, including more money, a more desirable task, a better work schedule, some formal recognition (e.g., a commendation in the personnel file), praise or appreciation for a job well done, informal recognition (e.g., letting other subordinates know about an accomplishment), feedback that lets the individuals know about their own successful performance, and some symbol of increased status (e.g., better job title). One difficulty with the use of rewards is that many of the above options are not feasible in or allowed by some organizations. Experience suggests, though, that even available rewards such as sincere appreciation for extra effort are often not used in many agencies.

Rewards are most effective if the individuals can see clearly the relationship of their effort and performance to rewards. It is also important to recognize that individuals are sensitive to the reward systems in organizations. For example, if a new office space becomes available, the assignment of that office may be seen by subordinates as rewarding (or punishing).

Since there are limits to the number of different behaviors that can be rewarded (or punished) it is important to use rewards thoughtfully so as to reward (and thus encourage) behaviors that you really want to have repeated. For example, in one family services agency, the director wanted to increase the amount of time the caseworkers spent in contact with the clients, so he began to monitor the telephone records for length of calls. The perception of the caseworkers, however, was that the director was rewarding those people who had the most calls. This led to a tendency to make more but shorter calls and fewer visits.

4. Expertise. To the extent that someone is seen as more experienced or knowledgeable, that individual is afforded more influence in issues relating to that expertise. From a previous example, a staff member who used the new computer extensively was often asked for advice and assistance and was listened to by other staff members (even by those people who had more expertise in other areas). This is obviously an appropriate

and highly effective type of influence for a leader to use but only if the individual is perceived as having expertise related to the task at hand.

5. Referent power. There seem to be several different forms of influence that have been variously included under this term. One has to do with having charisma and being able to influence others because of your personal magnetism or persuasive power. A second form involves the identification with a leader or his goals or philosophy. It is the beliefs of the followers that create the influence for the leader. A third form involves a sense of loyalty to the individual leader or to the organization. A leader can foster loyalty by being supportive and "going to bat" for subordinates and by making requests (not giving orders) on a personal basis. For example, Frank, a project director, asked Nancy (a subordinate) to write a report by telling her how important the report was and by indicating that he was depending on her. Of course, rewarding people for acting loyally reinforces one's referent power.

All three forms are related, although it is easier to prescribe how to build loyalty than how to become more charismatic. On the other hand, there are many examples of charismatic leaders, and many of them have been affiliated with human service organizations. The reader may be familiar with people like the Rev. James Smith, who saw a need for a recreation center in his neighborhood and worked tirelessly to establish one. He collected money from local businesses, recruited volunteers from his parish and the neighborhood, solicited equipment from sports teams, and acquired an unused building from the school board. The community was amazed at how much he was able to accomplish by himself.

6. Participation. The opportunity to participate in decision making has the effect of better informing an individual or group about the problem and developing a sense of ownership in the solution. Thus a leader can use the need for decision making as an opportunity for influence through participation.

In a decision-making situation, a leader can choose from a variety of options in terms of participation (Vroom and Yetton, 1973). The leader may make the decision based on information that he or she currently has, ask others for information or advice, bring people together to discuss the decision and make a decision as a group, or delegate the decision to others. The choice of which approach to use should be considered on the basis of the nature of the problem, whether either the leader or the subordinates have sufficient information, and how important acceptance by subordinates is in effective implementation. If the decision is to delegate, the leader must be able to do so effectively.

7. Communications. There are several ways that influence grows from communications. It has been said that information is power. One way to influence is to be a source of special information that is useful to others. Over time, a person who is seen as having access to critical information will be afforded more respect and influence. A related way of having influence is to withhold (rather than share) information. For example, in one agency a project director who was related to a board member did not tell other project directors that the board had agreed to fund new programs for the elderly, but not expand child care. While her peers worked on ideas for new child-care programs, she developed a proposal for hot lunches for the elderly. Her proposal was accepted and the director praised her "forward thinking and compassion."

One means of gaining communications influence is to become central in a network of communications. For example, in one agency, anyone with a question on procedures would "ask Alice." Alice was a secretary with many years of experience and was regarded as "the glue that holds the agency together." Needless to say, she was influential, largely because she knew about all parts of the agency and talked with so many different people on a regular basis. Further, once she developed this reputation, more people talked to her first, making her even more important as a source of information.

It should be noted that this is a longer term approach to influence because much time is required to collect and disseminate information. It is, however, an approach that does not require formal authority or the power to reward or punish.

These seven approaches to influence can be used in a variety of different ways, but only some are available in most situations. A leader must choose which method to use to deal with specific incidents, but that is often done reflexively. We recommend that managers think about which methods they use most frequently in order to better understand that aspect of their leadership style. For example, an office manager in one agency was seen as only using coercion and authority (legitimate influence) and as withholding most information. A result of her leadership style (and also a relatively low pay scale) was high turnover in her department. There was little incentive for people to want to stay.

FRAMEWORKS FOR LEADERSHIP: PATH-GOAL THEORY

Although to a great extent leadership involves direct influencing, which can take any of the forms described above, it involves much more as well. The path-goal theory of leadership (House and Mitchell, 1974) provides a framework that helps us understand some of the other roles of a leader. Like expectancy theory, path-goal theory assumes that a leader can motivate subordinates by making the satisfaction of subordinate needs contingent on effective performance. In addition, however, path-goal theory explicitly argues that a major role of the leader in motivating employees is to reduce barriers to goal attainment by providing the coaching, guidance, and support (as well as the rewards) necessary to help subordinates perform effectively.

Path-goal theory suggests that four leadership styles can be useful—depending on the particular circumstances.

1. Supportive leadership includes giving consideration to the needs of subordinates, displaying concern for their well-being, and creating a friendly climate in the work unit.

2. Directive leadership includes letting subordinates know what they are expected to do, giving specific guidance, asking subordinates to follow rules and procedures, and scheduling and coordinating their work.

3. Participative leadership entails consulting with subordinates and taking their opinions and suggestions into account when making decisions.

4. Achievement-oriented leadership entails setting challenging goals, seeking performance improvements, emphasizing excellence in performance, and showing confidence that subordinates will attain high standards. (Yukl, 1989, p. 100)

Factors believed to be especially important determinants of which of these
four styles to use in different situations are the nature of the tasks to be performed,
the goals and rewards available for task accomplishment, and the needs and
desires of the subordinates. One important aspect of the task is the extent to
which it offers role ambiguity versus role clarity. If an individual feels that there
is little chance (even with effort) of doing the task effectively—perhaps because
he or she is inexperienced at that task, because the task does not have standard
rules and methods, or because there is no clear and detailed expectation regarding
the end result—we can say that he or she faces role ambiguity. On the other
hand, repetitive tasks, tasks with standard operating procedures or routines, tasks
for which performance can be monitored easily by the leader, and tasks that are
well structured have role clarity.

If a subordinate feels uncomfortable with the amount of role ambiguity, a
directive leadership style that helps to define the task or gives information on
how to do the task will lead to greater effort and satisfaction by the subordinate.
However, if the subordinate feels that the task provides role clarity, directive
leadership may have little positive effect and may even result in reduced satisfaction if it causes the subordinate to see the leader as overly controlling.

Similarly, an achievement-oriented style may lead to satisfaction and effort
if there is role ambiguity, but will have less impact if there is role clarity.
Behaviors of achievement-oriented leaders, such as setting clear goals and providing feedback on their accomplishments, have been noted to be motivating
for subordinates. To some extent, a participative style can reduce role ambiguity
by providing more information about the task. In a situation of role clarity, it
should have less effect.

A second important aspect of the task is the extent to which it is unpleasant
to the subordinate. A routine, boring, tedious, stressful, or frustrating task may
be a source of dissatisfaction and reduced motivation to some persons. In that
case, a supportive leadership style will be important for increasing satisfaction.
It should be noted that not all people find such tasks to be unpleasant. For those
individuals and for those with more pleasant tasks, a supportive style will have
less impact.

The needs and personality of the subordinate also have an impact on which
leadership styles are most appropriate. To the extent that subordinates have high
needs for autonomy and achievement, participative and achievement-oriented
styles can meet these needs and lead to greater effort and satisfaction. A high
need for achievement implies that the individual is motivated to overcome problems to meet challenging goals. These individuals generally desire feedback and
a feeling of being in control of the task and individual accomplishment. Greater
participation provides better opportunities to satisfy this need. For a person with

low needs for achievement or autonomy, a participative leadership style will
have less impact.

If the individual is not highly internally motivated (not self-directed), then
directive behaviors by the leader that ensure consistent rewards for task accomplishment or increase the value or importance of the rewards to the individual
will increase satisfaction and effort. If the individual is more self-directed, this
style will have less effect.

If the individual has little self-confidence, a supportive style can result in
greater effort and more satisfaction. For the subordinate with high self-confidence, this style has less effect.

DIAGNOSIS OF ORGANIZATIONAL CONTINGENCIES

In the description of path-goal theory, several organizational contingencies
are identified: the clarity of the task, the extent to which the task is unpleasant
or stressful, the subordinate's needs for autonomy and achievement, and the
subordinate's personality. It might be possible to add to that list other factors
that are important contingencies in your particular organization, such as time
pressures; your own style and needs; your superior and his or her style, demands,
interests, and needs; and the structures, rules, climate, history, and culture of
your organization and the external conditions that face it.

While there are many contingency factors listed above, the key is to be able
to specify which of these are most crucial to your organization and to you as a
leader. You can do this by listing the factors that most affect your choice of a
leadership style. You should discuss the list with other people who are familiar
with you and your agency. These might include people in the organization and/
or people outside the organization. Review your list and see if you can identify
specific situations where these factors are important. While reflection and discussion with others will take some time, the goal is to refine your list to a few
factors that should be the critical determinants of your leadership approach.

IDENTIFYING YOUR LEADERSHIP STYLE

Part I

In addition to identifying the key contingencies of your organization, you
should consider your leadership style. We defined a person's leadership style as
that collection of behaviors that an individual frequently uses in a leadership
situation. You can think about the sets of behaviors that you feel comfortable
with. A good starting point is the set of four styles defined in the path-goal
theory. Review the styles and rate each on the scale "I DO A LOT OF THIS——I
DO A LITTLE OF THIS——I DON'T DO THIS AT ALL." What is (are) your primary
style(s)?

How effective has this style been? Do you think there are one or more other styles that you should use more often? It would be helpful if you kept written notes of these reflections and the conclusions you reached.

Now return to the framework of influence. For each of the seven types of influence rate yourself on the scale "I DO A LOT OF THIS———I DO A LITTLE OF THIS———I DON'T DO THIS MUCH AT ALL." What type of influence do I use most often? How effective is this approach? Are there negative side effects? Should I use a different type more often? Again, keep written notes.

Finally, review both the path-goal and influence frameworks and identify whether you typically do not use or feel comfortable with one (or more) style or type. That is, do you underutilize any of these styles or types?

These questions are intended to encourage you to be reflective and to consider your own style in terms of the two frameworks we have presented. You should have written out a summary for yourself of your own leadership style and type of influence that shows what you do most and least often.

Part II

A second approach to understanding your own leadership style is to identify incidents in which you felt that you were very successful or very unsuccessful as a leader. We suggest that you identify at least two of each type, although more would give you more data for your analysis. After you have thought about the incidents and written notes for yourself, see how your behavior fits with the descriptions of the leadership styles and types of influence. The idea is to be able to use your own past experiences to build on the theoretical frameworks and to identify areas in which you might improve.

Part III

The third approach to understanding your own style is to get feedback from others. This is easier to say than to do, so we will present several possible methods. Remember that your own self-assessment is not a purely objective indicator of your behavior because it is simply your perception and open to bias. By asking others for feedback, you are collecting information in a different way. At the same time, people may tell you what they think you want to hear rather than what they have observed. You need to be clear in explaining that you are open to both positive and negative information. Another potential problem is that the feedback will reflect what others (especially subordinates) would like you to do, rather than what would be most effective. You will need to listen to the feedback but make decisions on action for yourself. However, this does raise an associated concern. If you ask people for feedback, you are likely to create expectations that you will act on that feedback. If you aren't willing to change, don't ask for feedback.

One method for getting feedback is to talk with subordinates, peers, or superiors and tell them that you would like some information from them to help you learn more about your own leadership style. Ask specific questions about incidents where they had an opportunity to observe you and ask them to try to focus just on descriptions of behaviors. The most important thing for you to do is to LISTEN. Decide for yourself that you will not respond (other than to say "thank you") no matter what the other person says. Remember that you are asking them to do something that is likely to be very uncomfortable for them (especially if they have negative information). To the extent that there is trust in your relationship, they may be willing to give accurate information, but it is still difficult. You should take notes immediately after the discussion. An alternative is to ask a group of people to discuss you and than have one person give you the feedback. We would suggest that you not use this technique unless you personally feel entirely confident of your response to any feedback.

Another method is to prepare a questionnaire that asks for feedback and have it returned anonymously. Be sure to explain to the people what you are trying to accomplish and write questions that are specific about your behaviors and situation. You might also ask another person to receive these questionnaires and prepare a summary for you.

A final method is to ask another person to interview others and collect feedback for you. We would recommend using an outside party such as a consultant to prepare and present this summary to you. This is our preferred method because the outsider is a neutral party and is most likely to get accurate information.

As you collect information, you may want to revise your own assessment of your current leadership style and influence type. Your written record will provide a summary that you can use in the final part of this process.

MATCHING LEADERSHIP STYLE AND SITUATION

Now that you have diagnosed your leadership situation to find the most important contingency factors and have identified your leadership style and influence type, see how well they match. You might use the path-goal theory and influence models as a starting point, but recognize that the key question is, What is effective in my organization? If there are areas of mismatch, consider whether you would be more effective if your style was as predicted by the theory. What additions or refinements can you make so that your own theory is more relevant to your situation? What are the areas of mismatch that could change so you would be more effective?

If you have found answers to the last question, you can approach change in one of two ways: (1) change your leadership style, or (2) change the situation. We will discuss each below.

Changing Your Leadership Style

One option is to change which leadership style you use most frequently, or in particular situations. To the extent that you can change your style, you can better match the demands of the situation. For some people, changing their behavior may be rather difficult, and it might be easier to change the situation. However, it is possible for most people to substantially change their style. The following process is suggested:

1. Identify your own style and the style to which you want to change.
2. Identify specific behaviors of the new style. You can do this by observing others who use that style.
3. Try the new style. It is best to do so in a relatively low-risk situation. Observe yourself and reflect on what worked and how you felt. Get feedback from others. It helps to explain what you are trying to do and to solicit specific feedback about what behavior the other person(s) observed and how they reacted to it.
4. Reflect on your experiment and decide what other experiments you can conduct for further practice.
5. Repeat steps 3 and 4 until the new style becomes a comfortable and integrated part of your leadership. Don't get discouraged if everything isn't perfect the first time you try it; remember how much experience you have with other parts of your leadership style. See how you feel about the change.

How well does your style match the contingencies now? Do you see changes in your leadership effectiveness?

Changing the Situation

Another approach is to change the situation. This may mean finding a different role within the organization (or a different job) or altering some aspect of the contingencies. For example, a key contingency for one project director was the time pressure that caused her to make many decisions with little consultation with other staff. By discussing this problem with the executive director, they reached an agreement that he would give her more initial information about deadlines and priorities so that she could better plan her time. While this took some effort on both their parts, she found that she was able to use the participative style she was comfortable with on many tasks.

Ask yourself, What contingencies can be changed that would make my current style more effective? At first, don't limit the range of possibilities by considering what you think is feasible to change. Instead identify what would make a difference if it could be changed. Then explore the limitations and opportunities. Weigh the benefits of more effective leadership against the costs of the change, and if the balance is positive, try to make the change.

REFERENCES

Bradford, D., and A. R. Cohen (1984). *Managing for excellence*. New York: John Wiley.
Dowling, W. F., and L. R. Sayles (1971). *How managers motivate: The imperatives of supervision*. New York: McGraw-Hill.

House, R. J., and T. R. Mitchell (1974). Path-goal theory of leadership. *Contemporary Business* 3 (Fall), 81–98.

Vroom, V. H., and P. W. Yetton (1973). *Leadership and decision-making*. Pittsburgh: University of Pittsburgh Press.

Yukl, G. A. (1989). *Leadership in organizations*. 2nd ed., Englewood Cliffs, NJ: Prentice-Hall.

ANNOTATED BIBLIOGRAPHY

Bradford, D. and A. R. Cohen (1984). *Managing for excellence*. New York: John Wiley. A theory of two styles of leadership. Very helpful and pragmatic on how to become a more participative leader.

Tannenbaum, R., and W. H. Schmidt (1959). How to choose a leadership pattern. *Harvard Business Review* 36 (March–April), 95–101. The classic article on participation, yet still quite timely.

Vroom, V. H. (1976). Can leaders learn to lead? *Organizational Dynamics* 4 (Winter), 17–28. Description of the Vroom and Yetton model that discusses different types of participation.

Yukl, G. A. (1989). *Leadership in organizations*. 2nd ed., Englewood Cliffs, NJ: Prentice-Hall. A good summary of various theories of leadership. A bit technical.

4

The Nonprofit Board of Directors

BRUCE V. MacLEOD

This chapter is about managing the responsibilities of governance. We will focus on governance by examining the functions of the board through each of four lenses: legal foundations, characteristics and activities, organization and management, and board performance and development.

LEGAL FOUNDATIONS

The organization and appointment of a nonprofit board of directors is part of the legal process involved when an organization seeks to incorporate under state law. The preliminary steps for incorporation include the filing of articles of incorporation with the state and the preparation of bylaws. When these steps are complete, the organization holds its first formal meeting for the purposes of appointing directors, accepting the articles of incorporation, approving the bylaws, appointing officers of the corporation, and conducting other start-up business transactions required to begin operations as a corporation. Additional steps in the case of a nonprofit organization seeking tax exemption and approval as a charitable organization include authorization of the submission of applications for federal and state tax-exemption status and filing as an organization for charitable purposes structured to benefit the public. Once the board of directors is created, the legal responsibility for the organization transfers from the founders to the newly appointed board members, who then have the oversight responsibility for insuring that the public's interest is served.

State laws regarding incorporation do not require that the specific functions of the officers of the corporation be spelled out in the articles of incorporation or the bylaws; instead, there is usually a provision that the corporation shall be, for example, managed by a board of at least three directors or an executive and the board. A typical article of incorporation in this regard may read "The management of affairs of the organization shall be vested in a Board of Trustees," with the number of trustees specified in another article. There is no common understanding from judicial opinions regarding what board members are responsible for in carrying out the function of managing the organization (Mace, 1971); nevertheless, Streett (1985) recommends that board members be familiar with the legal principles or standards, such as the standard of "ordinary and reasonable care," in their service on nonprofit boards.

The legal process to incorporate takes a considerable amount of time and money, estimated to involve a minimum of six months to a year for the legal and regulatory approvals and $500 to $1500 in legal fees for consultation with an attorney familiar with nonprofit law (Southern California Center for Nonprofit Management, 1987).

Oversight Role of the Board

The oversight role is directly related to the several concessions and immunities granted to a nonprofit organization by the federal and state governments, especially if the organization has achieved tax-exempt status from the state taxing authority and the Internal Revenue Service. A tax exemption is a concession by the federal and state governments to give up their right to tax. Another concession is that a tax-exempt organization can receive gifts from individuals and other organizations that the donors can claim as tax deductions under Internal Revenue Service regulations. These provisions of the law constitute a generous subsidy, because they indirectly provide substantial financial assistance and other benefits to the nonprofit that are not available to profit-making organizations. They are based on the rationale that a nonprofit organization serves the public as opposed to anyone's personal financial gain.

This perspective of a nonprofit board calls for directors to thoroughly understand the organization's mission and the contents of its incorporation papers. The board also should have one or more members who have an understanding, for example, of state and federal government regulations pertaining to financial activities, requirements in regard to standardized fund accounting practice for nonprofit organizations that must be adhered to in some states, and any recent legislation passed regarding the welfare of nonprofit organizations. All of this indicates that board membership is a serious responsibility, to say the least, that requires some knowledge of legal and financial affairs or the willingness to obtain it, a considerable commitment of time, and a willingness to be a proactive participant at board meetings and committee meetings of the board on behalf of the public's interest.

Exhibit 4.1
Example of Bylaw Amendment Limiting Board Member Liability

Members of the Executive Board shall not be personally liable for monetary damages as such for any action taken, or any failure to take action unless:

(1) The member has breached or failed to perform the duties of his office under Section 8363 of the Pennsylvania Corporation law (relating to standard of care and justifiable reliance); and

(2) The breach or failure to perform constitutes self-dealing, willful misconduct or recklessness.

Another way to look at the oversight role is to think of the board as the legitimate source for assurance that the organization remains needed and wanted—a source of management expertise crucial to the success of the organization. The Southern California Center for Nonprofit Management (1987) states the prevailing view of the board of directors today as follows:

The Board of Directors is critical to the success of a nonprofit organization. It can provide clear direction, access to resources, and credibility to the community. It can ensure that the organization will provide effective service now, and in the future. Without an effective Board of Directors, an organization will never achieve its full success. (p. 13)

Legal Implications of the Oversight Responsibility

The board's role as guardian of the public trust has legal implications for individual board members. Because board members are charged with the responsibility to make sure that the public purpose is in fact being served, individual board members can be held liable under most state laws if someone sues the organization in the belief that the organization's activities are not serving the public. Recent increases in litigation involving boards have caused people to be reluctant to serve on nonprofit boards. To deal with this problem, some states have passed laws to limit liability to gross negligence, and boards have been quick to amend their bylaws to take advantage of that change. An example of such a bylaw amendment for a nonprofit organization incorporated in the State of Pennsylvania is shown in Exhibit 4.1. Because board members' responsibilities are ill-defined and the possibility of board members being held liable exists even with a bylaw amendment limiting liability, it is important to understand the oversight role fully and, if necessary, seek legal counsel regarding the extent of individual board member liability.

The remainder of this chapter is written for nonprofit human service organizations, including membership organizations, that are incorporated as public benefit organizations and are structured and approved for charitable purposes under the Internal Revenue Code and a state taxation code. The guidelines and recommendations offered here are based on (1) the results of recent survey research that we conducted at La Salle University to study the composition, activities, and organizational outcomes of boards of human service agencies in the Philadelphia area, (2) recommendations offered in the literature on nonprofit management, and (3) the author's experience as a participant on and observer of boards for several years.

CHARACTERISTICS AND ACTIVITIES OF THE BOARD

What are the characteristics of the typical board of directors, and how are boards structured to carry out their oversight responsibilities? What activities do nonprofit boards perform? The nonprofit management literature provides some guidance in answering these questions; however, very little information is available about the basic characteristics of boards, such as how many members serve on a typical board. Further, much of the information is quite prescriptive in nature; yet, based on the author's experience as a board member, boards frequently do not follow the prescriptions recommended in the literature.

We will present information on the typical human service agency board below—characteristics of the boards, how board members carry out their responsibilities, especially in regard to board meetings, and the functional activities of boards. Each nonprofit organization is different in terms of a number of organizational characteristics such as size, structure, and composition. Accordingly, one might also expect differences at the board level along the same lines. Knowledge of what the typical board looks like and how it acts should be instructive in considering appropriate structures and organization for individual circumstances.

Board Composition

Our research on nonprofit boards focused on 184 relatively traditional human service agencies—"hot line" services, homes for delinquent youths, services for retarded, handicapped, and addicted individuals, and family counseling centers. These agencies had an average of 13 full-time employees and a $70,000 budget.

The results of our research show that the boards of the agencies in the sample have the following membership characteristics:

- An average of 18 directors, with over 40 percent having served on the board for more than five years.
- Eighty-three percent of the directors are considered active by the organization's executive director.

- The typical board has a rich mixture of (1) technical expertise—in accounting, personnel management, legal matters, fund raising and marketing—and (2) community representation—board members from other nonprofit organizations, government officials, program experts, representatives of the client population, and so forth.

These results suggest that an active board of about 18 directors and an overall balance of skills from each of the two major categories of technical expertise and community representation are perceived as being called for in structuring a board.

Appointments to boards are most commonly for three-year terms, with one-third of the members of the board rotating off each year. Those rotated off can be reappointed for one or two more three-year terms if the quality of their service on the board warrants it. These conditions allow for the rotation of the so-called deadwood off the board, the addition of new board members on a regular basis who may be able to offer needed new perspectives and contributions, and the possibility of retaining valued board members through reappointment.

Board Meetings

On average, board meetings are held monthly, except for the summer months, on a weekday evening. The meetings are two hours long and attendance is generally good with 70 percent of the members attending on a regular basis. In some nonprofit organizations, it is not uncommon to have meetings of standing committees before the board meeting. Accepted guidelines for managing a meeting are usually followed.

An agenda is generally mailed to the board members well in advance of the meeting, and supplementary documentation may be included with the agenda to help clarify a particular agenda item, such as would be the case with a proposed budget for a fiscal year. See Exhibit 4.2 for an example of agenda items for a typical, regularly scheduled board meeting.

The minutes of the previous meeting are generally approved first, usually followed by a review of program operations. This is presented by the executive director with a staff member occasionally present to explain a particular program further or to answer questions. Committee chairs may report for their areas next, which may include an executive committee report of actions taken since the last board meeting. These reports may be followed by any one or more of a wide range of items such as a new program proposal, approval of capital expenditures, reports of events or circumstances in the environment that have a bearing on the organization, or a discussion of future concerns.

The board meeting ends when the president or a board member calls for adjournment. If there are board members rotating off the board, staff members leaving the organization, or other ending relationships or events happening, the board members will often adjourn to a brief reception to socialize before returning home.

Exhibit 4.2
Example of an Agenda for a Typical Board Meeting

---

1. Approval of the minutes of the last meeting.
2. Executive Director's report.
3. Report of special Executive Committee meeting.
4. Report of the Personnel Committee on staff handbook changes.
5. Finance Committee report.
6. Development Committee report.
7. Future meeting dates.
8. Other.

    Attachments: Minutes of the special Executive
                   Committee meeting
                   Report of the Personnel Committee

The results reported here might well serve as basic parameters in regard to the management of meetings. They are the logical outcome of experience and thus provide guidance in an area that is fundamental to effective board performance (see Ware, 1977, for further information on the management of meetings).

Board Functions

A common approach to identifying the functions of the board of directors is to list specific responsibilities and duties for board members to carry out and then to explain each of them. These responsibilities and duties tend to be prescriptive in nature, and reflect an active participant role. The typical list of responsibilities includes these six areas: determining the organization's mission and policies, financial control, fund raising, appointment and evaluation of the executive director, public relations, and auditing the organization's activities to ensure the law and the organization's charter are being followed (see Wolf, 1984).

While lists of responsibilities and duties are helpful in identifying the role of the board in general, they are usually stated in such broad terms that they are not as useful as one would hope in guiding board members to deal with the variety of experiences they face. Also, they tend to be applicable only to some boards, perhaps larger boards that have been in existence for some time.

One approach to understanding the functions of boards is to find out what boards do in practice, that is, the kinds of activities boards emphasize today. In our research on human service agencies, we obtained information in this regard by finding out how active boards were in each of eleven typical board activities, such as long-term and short-term planning, overseeing policy and practice regarding the agency's programs or services, providing advice in regard to a variety

Exhibit 4.3
Activities of Nonprofit Boards

Ratings were made on scales from 1 to 7, where 1 = NOT AT ALL ACTIVE and 7 = EXTREMELY ACTIVE. The average ratings for the activities are presented in rank order from high to low.

	Average rating
Long-term planning for future directions of agency	4.4
Determining and overseeing personnel practices and policies	4.2
Short-term budget planning	4.2
Determining and overseeing practices and policies regarding the agency's programs or services	4.0
Working to improve the agency's image in the community	3.9
Financial advising (for example, on matters concerning loans, investments or taxes)	3.8
Short-term program or service planning	3.8
Legal advising	3.6
Fund-raising	3.5
Exercising political influence on behalf of the agency	3.1
Working to attract new clients, members or program participants	3.0

of agency activities, fund-raising, and so forth (see Exhibit 4.3). By rephrasing and expanding these activities and grouping them under appropriate functional headings, an approximation of the functional activities that boards perform today is possible. They are as follows:

1. Setting directions and approving policies: Planning the long-term and short-term directions for the organization and modifying them when necessary; approving precedent-setting policies and establishing boundaries for the organization's operation that are consistent with the established direction.
2. Advising and counseling: Serving as a source of advice and counsel to the executive director and staff of the organization, especially regarding the law, ethics, technical areas, and fiscal accountability.

3. Developing and maintaining external relations: Representing the organization to the community and exercising influence where possible on behalf of the organization.

4. Providing resource assistance: Assisting the organization to obtain an appropriate level of resources to carry out program objectives, which includes establishing stable sources of funding (e.g., revenue for services when appropriate and personal contributions by board members), competent executive personnel, and adequate physical facilities.

These activities suggest that a change in the role of the nonprofit board has taken place—a change from the legalistic, passive role that was common in the past to a more strategic, active role today. They emphasize active involvement in long-range planning rather than narrowly focusing on operational matters with a legalistic perspective; advice and counsel that centers on accountability, ethical concerns, and fiscal responsibility; sharper articulation of mission by identifying an organization's constituency and influencing representatives of that constituency; and an integrated approach to allocation of resources to achieve an appropriate balance between program size and rate of growth, physical facilities, executive capability, and funding base. This perspective of a board's role is of considerable importance to the executives and board members who are concerned with the future direction and development of the public service they oversee— leading an organization to achieve its full success.

BOARD ORGANIZATION AND MANAGEMENT

While detailed coverage of the many guidelines available regarding board organization is beyond the scope of this chapter, we will highlight the main ones and refer the reader to other source material for further information.

Board Member Recruitment, Selection, and Orientation

Although not all boards use nominating committees, the creation of a nominating committee can be a very effective way to organize and plan for obtaining the specific skills needed on the board. When a nominating committee is not in place, this responsibility is often handled by the board as a whole, which may already be burdened with other matters.

The search for qualified board members, with or without a nominating committee, usually leads to the acquaintances of existing board members and the staff, local business persons, large corporations, universities, other nonprofit agencies in the area, or organizations that provide a service of matching board members to nonprofit organizations. Whatever the source, skilled prospective board members are recruited by asking them to serve—a direct appeal by a person whom the prospective board member can respect and who offers a personal statement of commitment to the organization. What follows is a series of steps involving an exchange of information, which is often informal but nevertheless effective in building on initial interest.

From the perspective of the nonprofit organization, there is a need to find out if the prospective board member has the skills and expertise needed (asking for a resume is a good beginning), is willing to spend the time to serve on the board, and is compatible with the general backgrounds of other board members (this criterion is often not a conscious consideration, but is just as real as the others). The Nonprofit Management Association (1985) suggests that some additional specific considerations might include whether the person has potentially useful local, regional, or national contacts, whether the person can deal appropriately with potential conflicts of interest, and whether the person has shown successful leadership and commitment in past involvements with community organizations.

From the perspective of the candidate for board membership, he or she needs information about the organization to decide on whether to join the board. This may be accomplished by reviewing the contents of a trustee manual with the candidate. The trustee manual could include information such as the organization's mission statement, articles of incorporation, and bylaws; a list of current board members and committees; a history of the organization and list of employees; and copies of recent minutes of board meetings and the most recent annual report (Wolf, 1984).

The major goals of these steps are to screen the prospective board member and to achieve his or her commitment to the organization's purpose—to provide a foundation for the initial interest of the prospective board member to grow into a firm commitment to contribute to the organization for many years.

Officers

Once the board is assembled and functioning, it is appropriate to look at the board as an organization in its own right with needs for appropriate leadership positions and organizational structure. State laws generally specify that nonprofit organizations have at least a board president (or chairperson), a treasurer, and a secretary (or clerk). Most bylaws of the organization include the titles of the officers, their duties and authority, and the frequency and method of electing the officers (usually at the annual meeting by majority vote). This is a skeletal framework, and if it becomes outdated (as it sometimes does), it may be changed to accommodate, for example, the need for a vice president or an assistant treasurer. These positions are not honorary; considerations such as length of service, "moving up the ladder," and friendships should not be weighed heavily if at all in the election process. Instead, the need for a high level of skill and firm commitment to the organization's goals and purposes is of major importance. Assigning the task of preparing a slate of officers for election to the board to a group of independent-minded nominating committee members can help reduce the possibilities of "good-old-boy" or "good-old-girl" networks from taking over the leadership of the board.

Committees of the Board

Structuring committees of the board—as opposed to having the board function as a committee of the whole—offers a special opportunity for board development that may not be possible in any other way. Board committees, organized to correspond with functional areas of management such as resource development or program, have these advantages:

- Board members are provided an opportunity to get directly involved in areas of interest and/or expertise, thus creating an outlet for their motivation for volunteer service.

- Board members' interest and ability to contribute to the organization can be assessed.

- The principle of specialization is put into practice, which can contribute substantially to getting board work done expeditiously. For example, more thorough study of issues facing the organization can be done by committees, thus saving the whole board a considerable amount of time. Further, recommendations are likely to be approved more readily because of prior committee work.

- When a staff member serves on a board committee, communication between board and staff members is facilitated. Also, staff participation on board committees can foster improved board-staff relationships and more effective decision making for the organization.

The number and type of committees that a board has will depend upon how large the board is, how long the organization has been in existence, and the particular needs of the organization (Miller, 1986). For the sample of 184 social service agencies mentioned before, the six most frequently established standing committees were executive, budget or finance, personnel, program (or program-related), marketing (or public relations and/or membership), and nominating. In addition, for about one-third of the organizations sampled in our research, advisory boards supplement and expand board expertise and community influence. These groups usually have a liaison with the board of directors and perform an advisory role only, not a decision-making role.

A structure of four standing committees backed up by an executive committee was typical for the boards of the types of organizations we studied. Suggested descriptions of these five committees, which combine the responsibilities of some of the committees noted above as the most frequent, are shown in Exhibit 4.4.

Although board committees are normally chaired by a member of the board, individuals who are not on the board may be included as committee members. Organization staff and outside resource people are sometimes added to fill specific gaps in knowledge and experience. Committee meetings, like board meetings, are planned in advance, and an agenda is sent to the committee members before the meeting is held or an outline of the agenda is presented at the meeting. These meetings are conducted more informally than the meetings of the entire board.

Exhibit 4.4
Descriptions for Suggested Committees

- Resource Development Committee: Concerned with resource development, fund-raising, and marketing for the organization.

- Operations Committee: Responsible for the management oversight of the organization including finance/accounting, personnel, legal issues, and facility concerns.

- Program Committee: Concerned with the service effectiveness of the organization including service delivery, client satisfaction, strategic planning, and regulatory requirements.

- Nominating Committee: Responsible for periodic assessment of the board's composition and its particular needs, and for recruiting and screening potential board members.

- Executive Committee: Serves as a representative of the full board regarding any emergency decisions between board meetings, sets agenda for regular board meetings, and reviews periodically the overall direction and development of the organization including the board.

Adapted from Get Ready--Get Set *(Southern California Center for Nonprofit Management, 1987), pp. 18-19.*

Board-Staff Relationships

The type of relationship between the board of directors and the executive director and staff is a major determinant of the quality of governance possible. When there is a good working relationship, the chances for a board contributing to organizational growth and development are good; when the relationship is bad, the prognosis for the board functioning in its prescribed oversight role is likely to be only marginally possible or nonexistent. The void created in this latter case could well lead to "serious illness" for the organization in the long run. So much rides on the kind of relationship; yet the inherent nature of it creates a paradox.

Both executives and board members are team members—both are dependent on one another's performance; yet the less-than-equal authority of executives is an incentive to be less than candid, which can block effective teamwork. Also, board members in their oversight role have the responsibility to approve plans and projects; yet once executives have prepared detailed plans and budgets and recruited staff, board members can do little but approve, often without questioning, because any other action may be perceived as not being supportive of a team member.

There is also a potential danger that in board meetings or committee service, board members will overstep the bounds of the areas of work that are best left to staff. This may be a problem; however, in some organizations the overlapping roles may be a necessity. In small organizations, for example, board members often wear two "hats"—a board hat and a staff hat—because there are not enough staff members to carry out all the essential functions that will ensure the organization's survival.

These problems are often dealt with by distinguishing the board's responsibilities from the staff's responsibilities, which is sometimes stated in summary fashion as, The board has the responsibility for policy-making and the staff has the responsibility for implementation. While distinctions along these lines help clarify roles, Setterberg and Schulman (1985) suggest that:

For years the notion of *the staff* setting policy was considered rank heresy. Policy was the realm of the Board. In fact, this is a popular old saw, but somehow misstated. The Board can check to make certain that a counseling agency does not metamorphose overnight into a recycling project or fast food outlet. It can approve or reject plans and projects. It can even reorient the organization's very purpose. But once the agency's broad goals and specific strategies have been gathered together within the framework of a long-range plan, then the Board can only sit back and make certain that the manager's policies for operations are safe, sane, appropriate, and productive. (p. 15)

These tensions create a strain on the best of intentions, so much so that managing the relationship with the executive director and the staff has to be a top priority. Without constant attention, apathy, conflict, or organizational politics can rule the day. Prescriptions to treat these potential maladies, however, are not readily available in the nonprofit management literature—an area where further research is needed.

BOARD PERFORMANCE AND DEVELOPMENT

In the sections above concerned with board characteristics, activities, organization, and management, we presented some research results regarding typical boards of human service organizations. One is struck in looking at these and the results of other studies by the large number of active, well-organized boards with well-qualified board members who spend many hours volunteering their own time for the public benefit. The record is impressive given the difficulty of the job and the responsibilities that go with it. These results show that the necessary machinery is in place and the commitment of a large number of people is available to make it work.

Furthermore, our research results regarding the performance of those boards suggest that the oversight responsibility of insuring that the public's interest is being served is being carried out by these boards. In Exhibit 4.5, the responses by the 184 executive directors to questions about their board and agency on different organizational outcomes are shown. While the last two measures in the exhibit may or may not be related to board activities, the ratings overall in the

Exhibit 4.5

Views of Executive Directors about Their Boards and Their Organizations

Executive directors were asked to rate their boards and their organizations on the items listed below. The rating scales ranged from 1 = DEFINITELY FALSE to 7 = DEFINITELY TRUE. The average response and the breakdown according to the percentages of respondents who gave each rating are listed for each item.

	Average Rating	Percentage for each rating						
		1	2	3	4	5	6	7
Board members have helped plan for the future of the agency	5.0	4%	5%	3%	14%	24%	13%	27%
I can trust the board members to help make important decisions	5.6	1	4	7	12	12	27	37
The board members provide me with encouragement and support	5.6	1	3	9	11	11	28	38
The board members keep me aware of events in the environment of relevance to the agency	4.3	6	13	15	16	22	17	9
The agency has been able to adapt well to changes in the environment	5.3	2	3	6	12	25	30	22
I feel secure about the agency's future	5.5	1	6	5	11	17	30	31

Exhibit 4.6
Board Development Indicator

Performance Criterion	Average Rating	Your Rating
Helping make important decisions	(5.6)	____
Providing encouragement and support	(5.6)	____
Securing the organization's future	(5.5)	____
Adapting well to changes in the environment	(5.3)	____
Planning for the future of the organization	(5.0)	____
Keeping the organization informed about events in the environment	(4.3)	____

exhibit lend support to the conclusion that these boards of directors are fulfilling their governance roles quite well. However, the exhibit also shows that some boards are viewed as quite actively involved in the exercise of their governance responsibilities and others are not; that is, not all boards perform equally well.

With that conclusion in mind, the six criteria that were used as an overall measure of organizational outcomes in Exhibit 4.5 may be used also as a rough approach to assess the need for board development in your organization. This can be accomplished by extracting key phrases from each of the items and presenting them for your subjective evaluation of your board's performance on each of the items (1 = DEFINITELY FALSE to 7 = DEFINITELY TRUE) as shown in Exhibit 4.6. Then compare your ratings with the averages shown to determine if your board and organization are performing above or below average. The results of such an evaluation would help to indicate whether board developmental activities might be needed to improve performance.

A major emphasis of this chapter has been the change in the role of nonprofit boards in carrying out their oversight responsibilities today—a change from the traditional role of satisfying legal requirements. When the board's role is viewed this way, it tends to function mainly as a legal entity acting to review proposed actions to be taken by executives in a somewhat cursory way. The board is not actively involved in the decision making of the organization nor the long-term development of the organization.

A more active decision-making role focuses on the future development of the organization. The board assumes an active participant role with the executive director in the management of the enterprise and the future-oriented purposeful development of the organization. The board is active in reviewing major strategic, financial, and resource decisions.

This change in role has come about in part because of the abrupt cutback in support for a large number of nonprofit organizations caused by changes in public policy in the 1980s under the Reagan administration, and partly because the education and training of nonprofit managers in areas such as strategic management have been receiving increasing attention in the last five years from schools of business and public administration, consultants, and service providers in the nonprofit sector (O'Neill and Young, 1986).

Both of these trends have contributed to an increasing awareness of the need for boards of directors to provide sharper articulation of direction for nonprofit organizations, greater emphasis on accountability in legal and fiscal affairs, and clearer identification of and communication with representatives of an organization's constituency. Further, there is recognition that nonprofit organizations cannot be all things to all people; community representatives on boards, foundations, state and federal governments, and other funding sources are now asking for better planning in resource allocation and greater involvement by the board in regard to long-term growth and development.

REFERENCES

Mace, M. L. (1971). *Directors: Myth and reality*. Cambridge, MA: Harvard University Press.

Miller, L. E. (1986). Determinants and consequences of board committee structures. *Proceedings of the Fourteenth Annual Meeting of the Association of Voluntary Action Scholars*, 19–32.

Nonprofit Management Association (1985). *Board management tapes: Client self-analysis program combining audio tapes and manual*. Minneapolis: Nonprofit Management Association.

O'Neill, M. and D. R. Young (1986, November). Educating managers of nonprofit organizations: A background paper. Paper presented at the National Conference on University-Based Education for Nonprofit Education Managers, San Francisco.

Setterberg, F. and M. Schulman (1985). *Beyond profit: The complete guide to managing the nonprofit organization*. New York: Harper & Row.

Southern California Center for Nonprofit Management (1987). *Get ready—get set*. Los Angeles, CA: Southern California Center for Nonprofit Management.

Streett, S. C. (1985). Board powers, responsibilities and liabilities. In E. Anthes, J. Cronin, and M. Jackson, eds., *The nonprofit board book: Strategies for organizational success* (pp. 9–22). Hampton, AR: Independent Community Consultants.

Ware, J. (1977). *A note on how to run a meeting* (No. 9–478–003). Boston, MA: Intercollegiate Case Clearing House.

Wolf, T. (1984). *The nonprofit organization*. Englewood Cliffs, NJ: Prentice-Hall.

PART II
FISCAL MANAGEMENT AND ADMINISTRATION

5
A Framework of Accounting for Human Service Agencies

PAUL R. BRAZINA

The ultimate responsibility for an agency's financial status lies in the hands of the top administrators and the board of directors. Although bookkeepers and professional accountants may record the agency's finances, prepare and interpret financial statements, and offer financial advice, managers should have at least a fundamental understanding of these matters. This chapter differentiates the various accounting specializations with which managers should be familiar and discusses how accounting principles are developed. It then explains the basic objectives of accounting information and some important issues regarding accounting in human service agencies, including the important distinction between accounting on a cash basis and on an accrual basis.

ACCOUNTING SPECIALIZATIONS

There are four major specializations in accounting that are of importance to the nonprofit community: financial accounting, managerial accounting, auditing, and taxation.

Financial accounting concerns the recording of business transactions, preparation of financial statements, analysis of financial information, and interpretation of that information for management. The basic recording is usually performed by the bookkeeping department. Bookkeepers maintain the daily journals, post the summary general ledger, reconcile the bank accounts, and so forth. Many of the basic financial summaries are also prepared by bookkeepers; however, preparation of fully adjusted financial statements normally is done by an accountant. Chapter 6 provides a more detailed discussion of financial reporting for human service organizations.

Managerial accounting in the nonprofit organization deals with the planning and control of financial information. Whereas the financial accountant records the history of the agency, the managerial accountant uses the past results to look into the future. This area of accounting includes comprehensive budgeting and cost analysis. The comprehensive budget encompasses the budgeted statements of revenues and expenses, balance sheet, cash flow, and capital acquisitions. Managerial accountants are actively involved in determining the cost to provide a service, contribution margin analysis (excess revenue over the variable costs of a program), breakeven analysis, and cost allocation procedures. Chapter 7 offers suggestions for how accounting information can be used to aid the decision making of human service organization managers.

Auditing deals with the verification of financial information and the development, implementation, and testing of internal controls to safeguard the organization's assets and ensure the integrity of the financial records. As human service managers are well aware, auditors can be employees of the agency, outside CPA's, individuals sent by funding sources, or auditors who work for the government. To the chagrin of most managers, auditors can originate from a variety of sources and come in all sizes, shapes, and temperaments.

An agency can have several types of audits depending on the requirements of outside organizations and the internal sophistication of management. Financial statement audits are required by state bureaus for charitable organizations. Each state monitors charities soliciting donations within its jurisdiction. One method used to monitor the activities of nonprofits is to require submission of an annual audited financial statement from the agency.

Operational audits are not an examination of the financial statements but rather an evaluation of the effectiveness and efficiency of management's policies. For example, an auditor may perform an operational audit of a meals program to feed the homeless. In performing the review the auditor would document the flow of the work, summarize the costs of providing service, and then determine whether management's objectives are being met in a cost-efficient manner.

Compliance audits determine whether an agency is in compliance with a law or an agreement. If an agency received a state grant to study drug and alcohol abuse on college campuses, a compliance audit may be required to determine if the agency performed the study in conformity with the contract.

Many people are under the impression that nonprofit implies no tax. However, the taxation of nonprofits is a very technical area; nonprofit agencies are subject to payroll taxes, sales tax, and tax on unrelated business income. It is perhaps the least understood and most overlooked specialty in nonprofit accounting.

In order to be tax-exempt, solicit tax-deductible contributions, and obtain grants, human service organizations apply for exemption under Internal Revenue Code Section 501(c)(3). Application for this status must be filed (Form 1023) within 15 months from the month of the incorporation. An exempt organization must file an annual information return (Form 990) with the IRS if it has gross receipts exceeding $25,000.

Even though a nonprofit organization does not pay tax on an operating surplus, certain activities of the agency may be subject to tax as unrelated business income.The first $1,000 of unrelated business income is not subject to tax, but earnings in excess of this amount are subject to regular corporate tax rates. Examples of unrelated business income would be income received from the sale of advertising in a magazine the agency publishes, from the sale of goods (such as stuffed toy animals from a zoological society gift shop), and from services provided that compete with for-profit organizations. Many social service agencies walk a fine line between for-profit activities and activities that qualify their organization as tax-exempt.

In states that impose sales tax, many nonprofit organizations are sales–tax-exempt. Some jurisdictions have a very narrow definition for the exemption including only health care and educational institutions. A human service agency should not assume sales-tax exemption until filing with the proper state bureau.

THE DEVELOPMENT OF GENERALLY ACCEPTED ACCOUNTING PRINCIPLES

Financial accounting is sometimes described as the language of business. Over the years, accountants have developed specialized terminology with which they communicate information between themselves and the nonaccounting community. Many times, terms used by accountants have different meanings to the general public. For example, if a director of an agency develops a new procedure for implementing a program or raising funds for a program, we might compliment that person by calling him or her a creative administrator. In the accounting discipline, a ''creative accountant'' implies a dishonest person who circumvents accepted accounting procedures to the detriment of the general public. In the film *The Producers*, Gene Wilder plays an accountant who devises a plan to turn a profit for the producers of a play that is a total flop for the investors. The artistic creativity of the cast of this play is significantly different from the accounting creativity of the producers.

In order to have uniform terminology and procedures in accounting, the profession has established an independent standard-setting organization known as the Financial Accounting Foundation (FAF). This foundation has eleven board members from six sponsoring organizations: the American Accounting Association (AAA–Accounting Educators), The American Institute of Certified Public Accountants (AICPA–CPA practitioners), the Financial Analysis Federation (FAF), the Financial Executives Institute (FEI), the National Association of Accountants (NAA–Private Industry), and the Security Industry Association (SIA).

The most visible unit of the FAF is the Financial Accounting Standards Board (FASB). This organization is primarily responsible for establishing financial accounting and reporting standards. Its pronouncements are adopted by the accounting profession as generally accepted accounting principles (GAAP) and are applied to the reporting of financial accounting information to the general public. As groundwork for issuing pronouncements on specific procedures, the FASB develops Statements of Financial Accounting Concepts (SFAC). These monographs look at objectives of reporting, qualitative characteristics of accounting information, and elements of financial statements.

Of particular relevance to human service organizations is the Statement of Financial Accounting Concepts No. 4, which compares the objectives of financial reporting by nonbusiness organizations with those of business enterprises. An important feature of this statement is the recognition by the accounting profession that information needed by the nonprofit organization is different from that needed by the business community. The FASB issued this statement in December 1980 and is still in the process of developing alternative reporting formats for nonprofits. Perhaps the most significant stumbling block is determining meaningful financial criteria to evaluate the success of an organization. The for-profit community has used net income, earnings per share, return on investment, debt to equity ratio, cash flow, and so forth to evaluate performance. These measures do not seem especially meaningful in the nonprofit setting. Thus, the inability to communicate financial information to the general public is not a weakness of nonprofit managers but rather a weakness of the accounting profession in developing a meaningful reporting system for nonprofit organizations.

BASIC QUALITATIVE OBJECTIVES OF ACCOUNTING INFORMATION

Relevance

The information presented in the financial statements should help the reader make economic decisions to the extent possible. For example, when an agency presents its financial statements to a foundation as part of the grant proposal package, the information should help the funding source decide whether to make the grant. On the other hand, small human service agencies are not expected to generate substantial surplus, so that the limitations in using historical information to predict the future financial success of an organization must be recognized.

Understandability

An educated reader should be able to comprehend the information presented in financial statements. Financial statements of nonprofit organizations are specialized, complicated documents including a balance sheet with separate funds, a statement of support, revenue, and expenses showing fund activity, and a statement of functional expenses by program. The form and content of these statements are explained in chapter 6, but just from the general description of these statements, it is obvious that understandability is not easily achieved.

Verifiability

Accounting information should be traceable from the statements back to the general ledger, to the journals, and finally to the source documents. This is commonly referred to as the audit trail. Since most social service agencies are required to have audited financial statements, it is the responsibility of management to keep clear, organized records with supporting source documents. The nonprofit organization is accountable to the funding sources, general public, and government agencies (e.g., the IRS and the State Commission on Charitable Organizations). Proper documentation includes receipts, cancelled checks, authorizations for expenditures, and copies of grants. Many small human service agencies maintain their books on the cash basis using the cash receipts journal to record revenue and the cash disbursements journal to record expenses. At the end of the reporting period, the accountant will make adjusting entries to accrue revenue and expenses in the proper time period. It is important that the agency obtain copies of all adjustments made by the accountant.

Neutrality

Accounting information should not favor any particular party. The information should be unbiased. One criticism of the accounting profession is that accountants reflect the will of management. For example, if an agency is having a bad year and has the potential for a large operating deficit, some managers feel that the accountants can make entries to eliminate the current deficit and show a more favorable picture. It is the responsibility of the accountant to remain independent in attitude and independent in fact.

Timeliness

Accounting information should be available to management before it loses its capacity to influence decisions. A financial statement that is issued six months after year end loses its value to the organization as a management tool for planning and evaluation.

Comparability

Accounting information is more meaningful to the organization if it can be compared with similar information of other agencies or with financial statements from different time periods for the same organization. In order to achieve comparability, agencies must use similar accounting principles applied on a consistent basis. If one agency records grant revenue on the accrual basis while another agency uses the cash basis, it may be difficult to compare the financial statements for a particular year. The Financial Accounting Standards Board issues statements on particular accounting problems to achieve comparability among organizations and consistency in application of these principles.

Completeness

Financial statements should include all the necessary information relevant to the reader. In some instances an agency may feel that it is only necessary to prepare an income statement for an outside party, leaving off the balance sheet and supplementary schedules. However, the balance sheet could contain information on equipment, liabilities, and so forth that might influence the decision of the funding sources.

ISSUES IN FINANCIAL ACCOUNTING

Cash Basis versus Accrual Basis

With a cash basis of accounting, transactions are recorded when dollars are either received or paid out. For example, when an agency receives a check for $20,000 from a foundation, revenue is recorded. When the agency pays for an insurance policy or pays the telephone bill, expenses would be recorded on the cash basis.

In contrast, the accrual basis of accounting matches revenue and expenses to the proper time period. Therefore, when an agency receives a $20,000 check for a foundation grant, revenue is not recorded until, according to the terms of the grant, the required services have been performed. Similarly, expenses of the agency would be matched to the corresponding revenue or to the proper time period. For example, fees paid to consultants for work performed on a specific grant would be matched to the performance of the service instead of being charged to expense when paid to the consultant. Also, a May telephone bill paid in June would be recorded as a May expense rather than a June expense.

Historically, the accounting profession has recognized the accrual method of accounting as the legitimate basis for financial statement presentation. Accountants generally feel that the accrual basis shows a more accurate picture of revenue and expense for a period, while the cash basis only shows the flow of cash through the organization. If funds are received by an agency but not earned, the organization has a liability to the funding source to either perform on the contract or return the funds to the foundation. The cash basis does not show the liability of the agency for funds advanced by the foundation, but instead, simply shows the funds received as revenue.

For most nonprofit managers, a report of cash flow is extremely important. Many agencies are more concerned about the ability to meet their bills than they are with the kind of information they can obtain by accounting on an accrual basis. The managers prefer a monthly budget and income statement on the cash basis to track the flow of money through the agency. In fact, many small agencies prepare statements for funding sources on the cash basis and do not prepare accrual basis statements. Financial statements prepared on the accrual basis of accounting showing receivables, prepaid expenses, payables, and unearned revenue are more difficult to prepare, take additional sophistication to read, and are not always viewed as meaningful to the nonprofit manager. Aware of the additional expertise needed to prepare financial statements on the accrual basis, many funding sources and state agencies will allow the human services organization to submit financial statements on the cash basis. However, when financial statements are prepared in accordance with generally accepted accounting principles, the accrual basis is used with a statement of cash flows.

Conservatism

Some people feel that conservatism in accounting means that accountants should wear white shirts and dark suits; however, this term refers to prudence in reporting financial information. At one time, conservatism meant that assets should never be overstated nor liabilities understated. Therefore, accountants had a tendency to deliberately understate the assets and overstate the liabilities. Today, this concept of intentionally misstating assets and liabilities is rejected. Conservatism in financial reporting should no longer connote deliberate, consistent understatement of assets and profits. Accountants are now charged with the task of ensuring that uncertainties and risk inherent in business situations are adequately considered while showing a realistic picture of the organization's financial position.

Continuity of Life

Accounting is based on the "going concern" concept. That is, it is assumed that the organization will remain in existence. In order to continue in existence, an organization must build financial strength. In the past, nonprofit organizations were supposed to plan for revenues to meet expenses. The idea of a budgeted surplus was absurd. Therefore, with imposed depression economics, it was difficult to state that many social service agencies had future viability. In recent years, many funding sources recognize that to continue in business, nonprofit organizations should accumulate an adequate general fund surplus.

Entity Concept

We normally account for the business unit. In most cases that would mean a separate accounting system and set of financial statements for each organization. If an organization is a member of a central fund-raising group such as the United Way, we would still account for the individual agency. However, the American

Institute of Certified Public Accountants (AICPA) has stated that when organizations are closely affiliated or financially related the auditor should consider whether combined financial statements are necessary.

Historical Cost

Generally, transactions are recorded at original cost. This is normally the invoice price for an item. There are some very specific problems in nonprofit accounting concerning the valuation of donated property and donated services. The AICPA (1981) has stated that

donations of securities, materials, facilities, and other nonmonetary items generally are recorded at fair value when received, provided the organization has a clearly measurable and objective basis for determining the value. If values are not reasonably determinable, the donations are not recorded. (p. 23)

Receiving donated property places the nonprofit manager in the position of acting as a valuation expert. The donor is usually looking for an inflated value for the property. If the nonprofit manager systematically overvalues the assets, however, it will result in misleading financial statements and potential problems with the Internal Revenue Service.

Donated services are a particular problem for social service agencies. The AICPA has stated that such service should not be recorded as an expense, with a corresponding amount recorded as contributions or support, unless all of the following criteria exist:

a. The services performed are significant and form an integral part of the efforts of the organization as it is presently constituted; the services would be performed by salaried personnel if donated or contributed services were not available for the organization to accomplish its purpose; and the organization would continue this program or activity.

b. The organization controls the employment and duties of the services donors. The organization is able to influence their activities in a way comparable to the control it would exercise over employees with similar responsibilities. This includes control over time, location, nature, and performance of donated or contributed services.

c. The organization has a clearly measurable basis for the amount to be recorded.

d. The services of the reporting organization are not principally intended for its members.

Materiality

Financial statements should not contain any significant misstatement that would affect the economic decision of the reader. Materiality has been an elusive concept. Many have tried to develop a quantifiable, objective measure for materiality. Some have recommended a percent of net income; others have suggested a percent of total assets. However, when put to the test, these arbitrary measures do not hold up. The identification of a material misstatement of financial data is left to the judgment of the accountant to anticipate the effect of the error on the economic decision of the intended reader. If the amount would influence the decision of the educated reader, it is considered material.

Quantifiability

Financial statements reflect dollar amounts. At this point, it is difficult to incorporate qualitative results in accounting information. A criticism of accounting for human service agencies is this inability to report the results of programs in a balance sheet and income statement. The Financial Accounting Standards Board (1980) observed in Statement of Financial Accounting Concepts No. 4:

Financial reporting is but one source of information needed by those who make economic decisions about nonbusiness organizations. The need exists to combine information provided by financial reporting with relevant social, economic and political information from other sources. (para. 26)

Stable Monetary Measure

In nonprofit organizations, assets remain at original cost adjusted only for depreciation charges on property and equipment. Large for-profit businesses show supplemental current values for assets; however, nonprofit organizations still maintain the strict historical cost approach. Therefore, the human services agency that acquired land and buildings twenty years ago will show this property on its financial statement at original cost less accumulated depreciation. Current market values are not reflected in the basic financial statements.

In the following chapters, this basic framework of financial accounting will be used to develop the reporting system for human service agencies and give insight into the principles used to develop the financial data base for management planning and control.

REFERENCES

American Institute of Certified Public Accountants. (1981). *Audits of certain nonprofit organizations*. New York: American Institute of Certified Public Accountants.
Anthony, R. N., and D. W. Young (1984). *Management control in nonprofit organizations*. Homewood, IL: Irwin.
Commerce Clearing House. (1987). *U.S. master tax guide 1988*. Chicago: Commerce Clearing House.
Financial Accounting Standards Board (1980). *Statement of financial accounting concepts no. 4, objectives of financial reporting by nonbusiness organizations*. Stamford, CT: Financial Accounting Standards Board.

Hay, L. E. (1985). *Accounting for government and nonprofit entities*. Homewood, IL:
    Irwin.
Henke, E. O. (1986).*Accounting for nonprofit organizations*. Boston: Kent.
Herbert, L., L. N. Killough, and A. W. Steiss. (1987). *Accounting and control for
    governmental and other nonbusiness organizations*. New York: McGraw-Hill.

6
Developing a Financial Reporting System
JOHN D. ZOOK

The purpose of this chapter is to provide the manager of a not-for-profit organization with an overview of a financial reporting system. The chapter is not intended to be a "nuts and bolts" sequence of accounting, but rather a focus on those items that are essential to providing a sound reporting system. The chart of accounts—that is, the underlying foundation of the organization's financial records—forms the primary basis of an accounting system. Consequently, this chapter emphasizes the development of a chart of accounts that provides the level of detail needed by the organization for decision-making and budgeting purposes.

Of course, organizations do not all require the same types of information or level of detail. The needs of the ultimate users of the information should play a key role in shaping the characteristics of the reporting system. Too often we find that accounting systems are designed for everyone but the people who will be reading the financial statements and making decisions based upon the information contained in those statements. Therefore, this chapter emphasizes the importance of thoroughly evaluating the needs of potential users prior to the development of an organization's financial system.

ACCOUNTING SYSTEMS: WHAT SHOULD THEY DO?

Let us consider for a moment that an organization's accounting system is set up like an assembly line for a manufacturing operation. The raw materials to be processed are various business transactions that result from financial events and are to be placed into our manufacturing operation. Those transactions are then converted into various statistical and formatted bits of information, they are adjusted and summarized, and then they are formalized into a finished product—a financial statement.

This analogy attempts to convey the purpose of an accounting system and what it should do. The accounting system and the accounting function provide relevant information for internal and external users of an organization so that they are able to make rational decisions regarding the direction and objectives of the entity. The accounting system should be user-oriented and should provide the final product in a format that is both meaningful and practical.

An accounting system should be designed and implemented in such a way that it is able to record all of the business transactions that are meaningful to the organization's business purpose. It should be designed in such a way that all relevant financial events are captured by the system, which will then trigger the conversion process of each transaction into financial information. To accomplish these ends, we must have a system that is both flexible and practical to operate. The system must be able to grow as the organization grows and must be built on a solid foundation such that the expansion process or development of new areas is a minor task and provides proper continuity with the system of the past.

A PROPER SYSTEM OF INTERNAL CONTROL

The foundation of any sound accounting system should be a proper system of internal control. Internal control can consist of both accounting controls and administrative controls. Accounting controls are generally concerned with the safeguarding of assets and the reliability of financial records, whereas administrative controls are concerned mainly with operational efficiency and adherence to managerial policies. The necessity of strong accounting controls can be enjoined with the stewardship responsibility that management has in directing the organization to comply with its stated objectives.

A strong system of internal control is dependent upon the proper personnel and a proper plan of organization. It consists of a series of checks and balances, which ensures that transactions are recorded on a proper and timely basis and that the safeguarding of assets is done to prevent intentional and unintentional errors. This system generally requires a significant number of qualified personnel who are performing functions independent of each other within the organization. For example, you would not want an individual who is responsible for the record-keeping function of a particular area to also be responsible for the custodial function of that area. The individual who is the custodian of the supplies inventory should not also record the increases and decreases to such inventory; performing both functions would give that person the ability to alter the records. Therefore, it is desirable to have proper segregation of duties by employing one person to be in charge of the custodial function and another person to be in charge of the record-keeping function.

To set up this type of organization requires a strong commitment of resources that ensures the checks and balances are in place. It should be noted that an organization must always look at the costs versus the benefits of providing proper controls. Consequently, a small not-for-profit organization may find that a proper accounting control system would be too costly for the benefits that it would yield. Yet a larger organization may find that the cost of the system and the additional personnel required to maintain it would be well worth the potential safeguarding of assets and reliable financial reporting that may result.

THE USERS: WHAT ARE THEIR NEEDS?

The most important aspect of an accounting system is that its design should be directed towards the end result. The product that it produces should meet the needs of the users. The users of financial statements can be classified into two general groupings, internal users and external users. Internal users are the management of the organization. It is essential that they have very detailed and timely information in order to make meaningful decisions about expending resources, acquiring assets, incurring additional debt, and general planning and controlling within the objectives and policies of the organization. The external users, by contrast, generally receive much less detailed information than the internal users. They often receive the information at a much later date than the internal users, which may affect their ability to make decisions.

Let us look at the types of external users that exist. These types may not apply to all not-for-profit organizations, but are involved in many. For instance, there is a governing body—the board of trustees or board of directors—which has the fiscal responsibility for overseeing the general direction and major decision making of the organization. A second group of external users is the investors and creditors, who are responsible for lending money to the organization or extending credit for purchases of necessary supplies and equipment. A third group is the resource providers—the contributors, whose dollars are necessary for the organization to provide its services. A fourth organization is an oversight body such as a governmental agency or legislative body. The oversight body is that body that is responsible for reviewing the organization's compliance with its objectives and guidelines. The final group of external users is the constituents who use and benefit from the services rendered by the organization. These external users need information in order to function in their respective capacities. The financial statements must provide them with the required information in a format that is usable and readily understandable for their purposes (Anthony, 1978).

Now that we have discussed the users, let's address their needs. The internal users need expanded data relating to each expense category, whereas the external user only needs to see the expense category as a total amount. For instance, an external user may see the total expense for insurance for the current fiscal year as a program or supporting service expense. This tells the external user which percentage or portion of the funds available for that particular program was spent for insurance. The internal user needs details regarding the types of insurance and the related amounts for each of those types that make up the total. This may, and should, influence the decision-making process for future periods by directing management to review coverages, deductibles, and additional quotes from other insurance brokers and to evaluate whether to continue certain organizational programs in light of the related insurance costs.

This same type of analysis could be extended to any other expense category within the organization. In addition, the detailed information provided to the internal user regarding the various subaccounts provides a sound basis for budgeting the organization's expenditures in future periods. Therefore, when designing an accounting system, we must attempt to develop a system that will produce a useful product for all users concerned.

RECORDING FUNCTION: A FINANCIAL HISTORY

The accounting cycle encompasses the accounting function from the inception of a transaction to its ultimate disposition on the financial statement. The financial records and the underlying books of accounts of an organization are often thought of as a financial history of the organization. They tell a story of how the organization progressed from day to day, month to month, year to year, and from its inception through its most recent balance sheet date. Through this process of summarization of financial events, we are able to derive meaningful financial information about an organization's past performance from which we can evaluate its current position and make important decisions as to its future.

A CHART OF ACCOUNTS AND THE RECORDING PROCESS

In order to accomplish this recording of the financial history of an organization, we have to employ certain books of record. These books of record consist of various journals that capture the day-to-day transactions which are then summarized on a monthly basis, and finally entered into a general ledger. In most organizations, the day-to-day activities are somewhat repetitive and can be recorded in separate sets of journals. For instance, a cash receipts journal can record all cash that is received by the organization and classify it as to its respective source. Thus, every day as cash is received it is recorded in the cash receipts journal. There are similar journals for cash disbursements, purchases, payroll, and billings.

In addition to these journals, there is the general journal where we record journal entries that are not found in the repetitive journals described above. These entries generally consist of nonrecurring or unusual financial transactions.

From the general ledger we prepare a trial balance. The trial balance is a sequential listing of all general ledger accounts, which ensures us that the total debit balances equal the total credit balances for all accounts. Once we have these in balance, we must then analyze the makeup of each account in order to review the accuracy and propriety of the data. This may result in adjusting journal entries to provide for the proper inclusion of revenue and expense items for the current period and/or adjust balance sheet account balances to their proper amount. Once the trial balance has been adjusted to make sure that we have properly stated all balances for the period and as of the balance sheet date, we then proceed to preparing the financial statements that are our end product.

The underlying structure of an accounting system is a well-thought-out and properly detailed chart of accounts. The chart of accounts provides the necessary classifications for which we detail information for ultimate inclusion in our financial statements. The chart of accounts may be thought of as a number of accumulators for the financial events of a business. These accumulators either accumulate the financial transactions for a given period of time, which results in an income statement, or they accumulate the financial transactions from the organization's inception to a point in time, which results in a balance sheet. It is necessary to have a strong chart of accounts, since it eliminates any confusion in classifying a particular disbursement or revenue item. When dealing with not-for-profit organizations, the need to provide detailed expense information is paramount. Therefore, it is in the organization's best interest to properly establish a chart of accounts whose accumulation and summarization result in meaningful captions for the financial statements and thus for the intended users of those statements.

Returning to our earlier example of insurance expense, let us provide a sample of what the chart of accounts should do for this particular expense category. In general terms, the chart of accounts should consist of a description and a numerical format. In most accounting systems, the numerical format is from three to nine digits. The sequencing and separation of these digits provides the user with the necessary level of detail. For example, let us assume a nine-digit sequence for insurance expense. The breakdown is as follows:

XXX	XXX	XXX
General	Program	Type of Insurance

The general category represents insurance expense. This is the summary account. The program digits specify the particular program account or management and general account that is covered by the insurance. The final subaccounts for type of insurance identify whether it was for workmen's compensation, liability, auto, umbrella, and so forth.

Using the data from Exhibit 7.6, let us show a breakdown of this information.

GENERAL	839 =	Insurance
PROGRAM	100 =	Camp
	200 =	Day Care
	300 =	Settlements
	400 =	Management and General
INSURANCE	01 =	Workmen's Compensation Insurance
	002 =	Liability Insurance
	003 =	Umbrella Insurance

The general designations above show the breakdown that is available within the chart of accounts for this nine-digit sequence. If we were to build the general ledger accounts, in order to arrive at the final data provided in Exhibit 7.6, we might see something like the following:

839 - 100 - 001	$1,752	
- 002	5,207	
- 003	612	
839 - 100		$7,571
839 - 200 - 001	1,680	
- 002	4,602	
- 003	507	
839 - 200		6,789
839 - 300 - 001	322	
- 002	945	
- 003	127	
839 - 300		1,394
839 - 400 - 001	27	
- 002	262	
- 003	82	
839 - 400		371
839		$16,125

As seen from the example above, the external user can see total dollars spent for insurance by program as well as information regarding the portion of revenues that were expended on each particular expense category for a particular program. The internal user can see the makeup of the types of insurance and the amount expended for each. This provides the management of the organization with a basis for decision making and budgeting in the future.

THE FINANCIAL STATEMENTS: AN OVERVIEW

With the financial statements being the end result of the accounting cycle, we must now turn to the purpose that these statements are to serve. It could be said that the objectives of financial statements are a reflection of the needs of the users of those statements.

Let us review the primary objectives that financial statements should satisfy. Listed below are those objectives that appear to be the most significant when considering the environment in which a not-for-profit organization operates.

Probably one of the most significant objectives is for the financial statements to show how well the organization's officers and directors have performed in their stewardship capacity. This involves a review of the allocation of the organization's resources in order to properly provide the necessary services and comply with the organization's chartered objectives. A second objective is to depict the performance of the organization for the most recent period of time. That is, the statements should reflect the net change in resources that has occurred during the previous year and the balance that is remaining for use in future years.

A third objective, which is closely related to the second objective, is to review the financial position of the organization as it enters a new fiscal year. An evaluation must be made of the resources that remain and the corresponding obligations that must be met within the next fiscal period. In connection with this objective is the review of the use of dollars and their availability for certain restricted services and objectives.

As noted earlier, financial statements that are available for external purposes usually have certain limitations within them that restrict the availability of detailed information for all users. However, we also have to meet the needs of internal managers, who look at financial statements from an internal standpoint. These individuals need much more detail in order to assess an organization's performance and the achievability of its objectives in a much closer perspective.

Let us now proceed to the types of financial statements that are presented for a not-for-profit organization.

THE BALANCE SHEET

The balance sheet represents the organization's resources, obligations, and fund balance at a specific point in time. Sometimes it may be thought of as a snapshot of an organization at the end of its fiscal month, quarter or year. It should be noted that this picture will change the next day just as it is different from the previous day, due to the ongoing process of financial transactions. Every balance sheet contains resources (assets), obligations (liabilities), and revenues that are retained for use in the business (fund balance). Assets are considered to be the resources of a business expressed in monetary terms, including cash, receivables, land, building, equipment, and investments. Liabilities are obligations of the organization that must be paid at some point in the future, such as accounts payable, notes payable, and accrued expenses. In effect, they represent the creditors' claims against the assets of the organization. The fund balance represents the residual claims of the organization against its assets. The fund balance is an accumulation of the excess of revenues over expenses that has resulted from the organization's inception to the date of the balance sheet.

The balance sheet of a profit-making enterprise is classified by current and noncurrent positions, representing the order of asset conversion and consumption, or the priority of liquidating the liabilities. In either event, however, the total resources that are available for the company's use are contained within the organization as a whole. Therefore, we derive what we consider the single entity concept. That is, the resources are all applied toward satisfying the set of needs of a single operating entity.

When considering a not-for-profit organization, however, certain assets have been "designated" (contain donor restrictions) or are needed to accomplish certain objectives. The segregation of these assets is required to properly present what resources are available for their intended objectives. Consequently, a not-for-profit organization requires a multiple-entity concept. That is, there are several funds operating within the organization.

In order to provide this presentation, certain funds are established. The most commonly used funds are the following:

Current funds—unrestricted and restricted

Land, building, and equipment

Endowment fund

As Exhibit 7.2 shows, the current funds are presented in unrestricted and restricted format. The assets contained in the unrestricted section are available for the general operations of the not-for-profit organization in accordance with its charter and bylaws. These assets come under the discretionary control of the board of trustees of the not-for-profit organization. Consequently, they may be referred to as board-designated. The unrestricted funds may contain the fixed assets and related accounts of the particular organization, or the fixed assets may be contained in a separate fund as described later in this chapter.

Unlike unrestricted funds, restricted funds are donor-designated and must be expended in accordance with the donors' requests. The donor-designated funds cannot be changed, as compared to board-designated funds, which may be changed at the board's discretion.

Unrestricted land, building, and equipment is often accounted for in a separate fund, referred to as the plant fund. Contained within this fund are the long-lived assets (e.g., land, building, equipment) used for the operation of the organization. This fund also contains the related debt obligations connected with the fixed assets, which may be in the form of a mortgage or notes payable. If these amounts are not significant, then they usually are contained within the current unrestricted funds.

The endowment fund contains funds received by the organization from donors who have requested that the principal remain intact in perpetuity until the occurrence of a specified event, or for a specified period, and that only the income from the investment thereof be expended either for general purposes or for purposes specified by the donor. If the income is unrestricted, then it is available for use in the unrestricted funds. If there is a donor restriction for the use, then it should be transferred to the appropriate restricted fund.

THE STATEMENT OF SUPPORT, REVENUES, AND EXPENSES AND CHANGES IN FUND BALANCES

In a profit-making enterprise, the income statement is the statement that is regarded as having the highest level of importance due to its emphasis on earnings, profitability, growth, and the ability of the entity to pay its debts. These are all dependent upon the earning process.

In a not-for-profit organization, the Statement of Support, Revenue, and Expenses and Changes in Fund Balances is also regarded as the statement with the highest level of importance. However, the emphasis is different. Like the balance sheet, the income statement for the not-for-profit organization should reflect the total activity of each fund for the current period. Our concern regarding the balance sheet is to separate the resources and obligations into various funds. Similarly, for the income statement our objective is to present separately the inflows and outflows of resources for each fund; thus the users can determine total activity within that fund for the respective period. To accomplish this objective, a columnar presentation is provided.

The presentation shows the activity for each fund and the total activity or "total picture" for all the funds presented for the respective accounting period. At the bottom of the statement are the changes in fund balance for the year, which represent the excess or the deficiencies of revenues over expenses.

As can be seen from Exhibit 7.5, the support, revenue, and expense of each fund are separately presented. The total of all fund activity is summarized in the next to the last column to the far right, with comparative totals for the previous year adjacent to it.

Generally, all that is required is totals for revenues and expenses. There is no requirement to present the total of the "excess (deficiency) of revenues over expenses" at the far right, since this may cause confusion for the user of the financial statement. However, there is nothing prohibiting these totals, and they have been presented here for illustrative purposes.

THE STATEMENT OF FUNCTIONAL EXPENSES

The third statement required for voluntary health and welfare organizations is the "Statement of Functional Expenses" (see Exhibit 7.6). This statement may be thought of as an extension of the "Statement of Support, Revenue, and Expenses and Changes in Fund Balances." In effect, it represents an external reporting of the actual results of internally budgeted expense. Unlike the income statement of a profit-making enterprise, which is presented for external use and emphasizes brevity, here we see a detailed analysis of the expenses of "Program Services" for each program as well as "Supporting Services."

The purpose of this statement is to satisfy the needs of the various user groups in order to review the disposition of the funds as required by the organization's policies and objectives. Each program should be segregated in a columnar format with functional expense categories detailed as necessary to provide a meaningful understanding of the expenses of running each program. The defining and gathering of these functional expense categories by program will vary from one organization to another. An important step toward arriving at the final product is the development of an accurate and rational approach to allocating common expenses that apply to more than one program service. This may require the organization to establish a system of internal distribution of payroll, employee benefits, utilities, supplies, and various overhead expenditures in order to provide a meaningful financial statement presentation. As mentioned earlier, a strong system of internal control requires proper accounting classification as part of its basic structure. This ensures reliable financial reporting. It should also be mentioned that the costs versus the benefits of such requirements should be reviewed.

As noted earlier, expenses for supporting services should be segregated from those for program services. These would include expenditures for management and general and fund raising. The management and general expenditures include expenses for the "overall direction" of the organization. These costs should also include the cost of disseminating information to inform the public about the organization. There are those expenses that cannot be directly connected with a specific program or fund-raising activity. If a direct relationship exists, then a proper allocation should be made among the respective functions.

The example contained in Exhibit 7.6 does not reflect a separate column for fund-raising expenditures. In most voluntary health and welfare organizations these expenditures constitute a significant amount, and would require a separate column within the supporting services category. These expenditures may include payroll, printed material, mailing costs, and so forth. Once again, the origin of these costs may cover several programs or support services, and a proper allocation would be needed.

One additional point that should be made concerns the isolation of depreciation expense as the final item of the functional expense statement. Depreciation expense is a necessary cost in providing a service. It reflects the allocation of the assets cost over its estimated useful life. This provides for a proper measurement of the expenditures toward the value of the service rendered. Not-for-profit organizations argue that depreciation charges are based upon replacement accounting, and that the replacement of an asset is a decision to be made by the board of trustees and not directly applied to the cost of a program.

Addressing this controversy, the Financial Accounting Standards Board issued Statement of Financial Accounting Standards No. 93, "Recognition of Depreciation by Not-for-Profit Organizations," in August of 1987. This concluded that "not-for-profit organizations shall recognize the cost of using up the future economic benefits or service potentials of their long-lived tangible assets—depreciation" (FASB, 1987). This was to be effective for all financial statements issued for fiscal years beginning after May 5, 1988. However, the Financial Accounting Standards Board issued Statement of Financial Accounting Standards No. 99, "Deferral of the Effective Date of Recognition of Depreciation by Not-for-Profit Organizations," which changed the effective date to fiscal years beginning on or after January 1, 1990.

DISCUSSION OF A STATEMENT OF CASH FLOWS

The financial statements of a profit-making enterprise require the presentation of a Statement of Cash Flows when both a balance sheet and an income statement are present. The Statement of Cash Flows is presented as a basic financial statement and is necessary in order for the financial statements to be in conformity with generally accepted accounting principles. These requirements are established by the Statement of Financial Accounting Standards No. 95, "Statement of Cash Flows" (1987). However, this statement does not include not-for-profit organizations within its scope.

Since the statement of cash flows is not yet required for nonprofit organizations, we will not describe here the format and the manner of presentation. But the statement is of significance in that it presents to the user the operating, financing, and investing activities of the organization. The advantages of this statement are described more fully in chapter 7.

It should be noted that at this time the Financial Accounting Standards Board is still in the process of evaluating whether not-for-profit organizations should be required to provide statements of cash flows.

The manager of a not-for-profit organization must measure his or her own performance and the organization's performance in a number of ways. One of those measures is the organization's financial statements.

Therefore, it is essential that the manager be able to understand and interpret those statements so that the appropriate courses of action may be taken to maintain and improve the organization's operations. Managers should take an active role in the development and modification of their accounting system to ensure that they are receiving financial information that fulfills their needs as well as the needs of other users. A primary factor in this development is the underlying foundation of the accounting system—the chart of accounts. Proper attention to this foundation will ensure the resulting financial reporting structure and the satisfaction of the needs of all users.

REFERENCES

Anthony, R. N. (1978). *Financial accounting in nonbusiness organizations: An exploratory study of conceptual issues*. Stamford, CT: Financial Accounting Standards Board.

"Financial Accounting Standards Board." (1987a). *Statement of financial accounting standards no. 93, Recognition of depreciation by not-for-profit organizations*. Stamford, CT: Financial Accounting Standards Board.

————. (1987b). *Statement of financial accounting standards no. 95, Statement of cash flows*. Stamford, CT: Financial Accounting Standards Board.

————. (1988). *Statement of Financial Accounting Standards No. 99, Deferral of effective date of recognition of depreciation by not-for-profit organizations*. Stamford, CT: Financial Accounting Standards Board.

BIBLIOGRAPHY

American Institute of Certified Public Accountants, Accounting Standards Division (1978). *Statement of position 78–10, Accounting principles and reporting practices of certain nonprofit organizations*. New York: American Institute of Certified Public Accountants.

American Institute of Certified Public Accountants, Committee on Voluntary Health and Welfare Organizations (1974). *Audits of voluntary health and welfare organizations*. New York: American Institute of Certified Public Accountants.

American Institute of Certified Public Accountants, Subcommittee on Nonprofit Organizations (1981). *Audits of certain nonprofit organizations*. New York: American Institute of Certified Public Accountants.

Financial Accounting Standards Board (FASB; 1980). *Statement of financial accounting concepts no. 4, Objectives of financial reporting by nonbusiness organizations*. Stamford, CT: Financial Accounting Standards Board.

Haller, L. (1982). *Financial resource management for nonprofit organizations*. Englewood Cliffs, NJ: Prentice-Hall.

Hay, L. (1980). *Accounting for governmental and nonprofit entities*. Homewood, IL: Irwin.

Henke, E. O. (1983). *Accounting for nonprofit organizations*. Boston: Kent.

7
Accounting Data as a Management Tool

LESTER BARENBAUM
AND THOMAS MONAHAN

The previous chapter discussed the rationale and format of traditional financial statements required for health and welfare agencies. The standards followed in developing these statements were issued by the American Institute of Certified Public Accountants (AICPA) and the Financial Accounting Standards Board (FASB). These formal accounting rules have evolved to ensure that external users of these statements can evaluate various agencies based on their stewardship role in managing assets.

As the financial statements presented in the last chapter demonstrate, the balance sheet, the statement of support, revenue, and expenses and changes in fund balance, and the statement of functional expenses are prepared and organized based on traditional formats utilized in financial reporting. In many cases, however, these formats hide information that would be extremely useful to both management and external users in evaluating the financial position and performance of the agency.

This chapter will evaluate the use of the accounting data as a management tool. It will also demonstrate that reorganizing each of the primary financial statements can significantly increase their information content with virtually no increase in the cost of preparation.

THE BALANCE SHEET

The traditional balance sheet format utilized in Exhibit 7.1 does not treat each fund as an individual entity, but merely groups each fund's assets, liabilities,

Exhibit 7.1
Balance Sheet (as of June 30, 1987)

ASSETS	1987	1986
CURRENT FUNDS		
UNRESTRICTED		
Cash	$ 29,279	$
Receivables	220	1,000
Other assets	11,691	9,421
	41,190	10,421
RESTRICTED		
Cash	1,877	2,279
Grants receivable	47,866	98,345
Other assets	6,073	12,051
Interfund advances	12,576	
	68,392	112,675
LAND, BUILDING AND EQUIPMENT FUND		
Cash	419	396
Land, buildings and equipment	696,054	712,858
Construction plans	3,725	3,725
Interfund advances	82,556	75,376
	782,754	792,355
ENDOWMENT FUND		
Cash	519	422
Investments - at fair market value	56,746	65,086
Accrued Interest	1,119	1,099
	58,384	66,607
TOTAL ASSETS		
(exclusive of interfund advances)	$855,588	$906,682

Exhibit 7.1 (Continued)

LIABILITIES AND FUND BALANCES	1987	1986
CURRENT FUNDS		
UNRESTRICTED		
Cash payable	$	$ 1,530
Notes payable	4,000	75,000
Accounts payable	71,847	49,146
Accrued expenses	16,060	15,948
Interfund advances	94,635	19,794
Total liabilities	186,542	161,418
Fund (deficit)	(145,352)	(150,997)
	41,190	10,421
RESTRICTED		
Accounts payable		644
Other liabilities	25,271	25,271
Public support and revenue designated		
for future periods	43,121	31,544
Interfund advances		55,216
Total liabilities and deferred revenues	68,392	112,675
Fund balance	0	0
	68,392	112,675
LAND, BUILDING AND EQUIPMENT FUND		
Unexpended plant funds designated for		
future construction	17,611	8,611
Fund balance	765,143	783,744
	782,754	792,355
ENDOWMENT FUND		
Accrued expenses	60	74
Interfund advances	497	366
Fund balance	57,827	66,167
	58,384	66,607
TOTAL LIABILITIES AND FUND BALANCES		
(exclusive of interfund advances)	$855,588	$906,682

Note: For Exhibits 7.1 to 7.6, 7.9, and 7.10, certain accounts and details have been consolidated in order to provide anonymity of the agency.

Exhibit 7.2
Balance Sheet in Columnar Format (as of June 30, 1987)

ASSETS	Unrestricted Fund	Restricted Fund
Cash	29,279	1,877
Receivables	220	
Other Assets	11,691	6,073
Grants Receivables		47,866
Land & Equipment		
Investments		
Accrued Interest		
TOTAL ASSETS	41,190	55,816
LIABILITIES & FUND BALANCE		
Notes Payable	4,000	
Accounts Payable	71,847	
Accrued Expenses	16,060	
Other Liabilities		25,271
Deferred Income		43,121
Fund Balance	-145,352	
Interfund Transfers	94,635	-12,576
TOTAL LIABILITIES & FUND BALANCE	41,190	55,816

Exhibit 7.2 (Continued)

Plant Fund	Endowment Fund	TOTAL 1987	TOTAL 1986
419	519	32,094	3,097
		220	1,000
		17,764	21,472
		47,866	98,345
699,799		699,779	716,583
	56,746	56,746	65,086
	1,119	1,119	1,099
700,198	58,384	855,588	906,682
		4,000	76,530
		71,847	49,790
	60	16,120	16,022
		25,271	25,271
		43,121	31,544
782,754	57,827	695,229	707,525
-82,556	497	0	0
700,198	58,384	855,588	906,682

and fund balance under the appropriate headings. By including interfund advances under both asset and liability categories and not segregating balances for each account across funds, this format makes analysis of financial statements much more difficult. Utilizing a columnar format such as that presented in Exhibit 7.2 provides additional information on the financial position of both individual funds and the total agency. To further clarify the advantages of this columnar format one only has to compare Exhibits 7.1 and 7.2.

As noted in the previous chapter, the balance sheet simply represents the financial position of an organization at a point in time. By isolating a firm's resources (assets), obligations (liabilities), and fund balances, however, the traditional format presented in Exhibit 7.1 can be misleading. For example, although total resources available to the agency are of interest to financial statement users, the multiple-entity concept must be emphasized to determine the true financial position of each fund within the agency. By breaking the total entity down into funds, one can better determine how efficiently management is carrying out its stewardship responsibility.

The traditional balance sheet lists each fund individually without any functional classification of account totals across funds. For example, it is obvious in Exhibit 7.1 that the unrestricted funds has a cash balance of $29,279. To determine the total amount of cash within the agency, however, one must add the cash balances from each individual fund. The same is true for all other account balances. By utilizing the columnar format in Exhibit 7.2, these functional totals are automatically derived (e.g., cash = $32,094) without sacrificing the breakdown by responsibility center or fund.

Consequently, common size statements can be generated for each individual fund as well as for the agency in its entirety. Common size statements use percentages to show the relationship of each item on the balance sheet to total assets. Comparisons of common size statements over time reveal how balance sheet items are increasing or decreasing relative to the entire entity. As a common size statement, Exhibit 7.3 indicates that the $29,279 cash balance in the unrestricted fund represents 3.4 percent of the agency's total assets. Standards could be established to help employees efficiently manage assets within each fund as well as to help determine how assets of the total agency should be distributed among funds. With the development of electronic spreadsheets this type of analysis could be handled easily once the columnar balance sheet was developed.

Another major advantage of this columnar format is the increased clarity of presentation when reporting interfund advances. In Exhibit 7.1 these advances are included in the balances of the appropriate asset or liability account, yet are not carried down to the totals since they offset one another. The columnar format utilized in Exhibit 7.2 clearly indicates which fund advanced or received net transfers from other funds and what impact these transfers had on various fund balances. For example, in Exhibit 7.1 the total interfund transfers carried as assets would equal $12,576 in the restricted fund plus $82,556 in the land, building, and equipment fund. These assets are offset by liabilities of $94,635 in the unrestricted fund and $497 in the endowment fund. Obviously, both the asset and liability totals for these interfund advances equal $95,132 and consequently they wash. The total assets and liability and fund balances, however, do not include these transfers. It would be relatively easy, therefore, given the confusion of including transfers as assets or liabilities within each fund but not carrying these balances down to the total fund, to initiate a transfer to improve the standing of a particular fund. With the columnar format these interfund transfers are not carried as assets or liabilities, but involve elimination entries under the fund balance account (see Exhibit 7.2).

Overall, therefore, this columnar format provides analysts with additional insight into the financial position of the agency without increasing the agency's accounting costs.

STATEMENT OF CASH FLOWS

Overview

As noted in chapter 6, the statement of cash flows (SCF) is not a required financial statement of health and welfare agencies. As a component of an accounting system used to promote efficiency, however, this statement is invaluable. Since the balance sheet merely relates which segment of an agency holds wealth at the end of a period, additional information is needed concerning sources of cash within the agency and how this cash was used. The statement of changes provides exactly this type of information.

Since the balance sheet and income statement are utilized in developing the SCF, the AICPA committee on voluntary health and welfare agencies did not require it as a formal statement.

Opinion 19 permitted but did not require enterprises to report cash flow information in the statement of changes in financial position. Since that opinion was issued, the significance of information about an enterprise's cash flows has increasingly been recognized. "A full set of financial statements for a period should show: Cash Flows during the period" (AICPA, 1971).

This attitude concerning the importance of the SCF has been reinforced in the accounting literature and Wall Street (Largay and Stickney, 1980). In health and welfare agencies, which depend so heavily on outside funding and grants, control over cash flow becomes even more important. The SCF enables management (and analysts) to determine exactly what caused a liquidity crunch or surplus during an operating period. Corrective action can then be taken to insure that the agency has sufficient liquidity to meet its social goals.

Preparing the Statement of Cash Flows

In identifying the sources and uses of cash in the SCF, funds are generally defined as either cash or cash plus cash equivalents (marketable securities). In

ASSETS	Unrestricted Fund	Restricted Fund	Plant Fund
Cash	3.4%	0.2%	0.0%
Receivables	0.0%		
Other Assets	1.4%	0.7%	
Grants Receivables		5.6%	
Land & Equipment			81.8%
Investments			
Accrued Interest			
TOTAL ASSETS	4.8%	6.5%	81.8%

LIABILITIES & FUND BALANCE

Notes Payable	0.5%		
Accounts Payable	8.4%		
Accrued Expenses	1.9%		
Other Liabilities		3.0%	
Deferred Income		5.0%	
Fund Balance	-17.0%		91.5%
Inter-fund Transfers	11.1%	-1.5%	-9.6%
TOTAL LIABILITIES & FUND BALANCE	4.8%	6.5%	81.8%

Exhibit 7.3 (Continued)

Endowment Fund	TOTAL 1987	TOTAL 1986
0.1%	3.8%	0.4%
	0.0%	0.1%
	2.1%	2.5%
	5.6%	11.5%
	81.8%	83.8%
6.6%	6.6%	7.6%
0.1%	0.1%	0.1%
6.8%	100.0%	106.0%
	0.5%	8.9%
	8.4%	5.8%
0.0%	1.9%	1.9%
	3.0%	3.0%
	5.0%	3.7%
6.8%	81.3%	82.7%
0.1%		
6.8%	100.0%	106.0%

Exhibit 7.4
Statement of Changes in Financial Position (for the Year Ending June 30, 1987)

OPERATIONS

Deficit of Revenue over Expenses from Operations	($12,296)	
Plus Depreciation	52,008	
Funds Provided by Operation	$39, 712	
Changes In Working Capital		
Decrease in Accounts Receivable	780	
Decrease in Grants Receivable	50,479	
Decrease in Other Assets	3,708	
Increase in Accounts Payable	22,057	
Increase in Accrued Investment Expense	98	
Deferred Revenue	11,577	
Increase in Accrued Interest	(20)	
Net Change in Working Capital	$88,679	
Cash Provided by Operations		$128, 391

INVESTING ACTIVITIES

Less: Increase in Fixed Assets	(35,204)	
Add: Decrease in Investments	8,340	
Increase (Decrease) in Cash from Investing		(26,864)

FINANCING ACTIVITIES

Decrease in Notes Payable		(72,530)
INCREASE IN CASH BALANCE		$28,997

recent years there has been a movement toward using a cash plus cash equivalent definition of funds since equivalents can be immediately turned into cash at the agency's discretion. When funds are defined as cash plus cash equivalents the agency would simply be describing the reason for a change in its cash position over the year. Since there is no conjecture involved, the cash definition of funds is considered to be more objective than the previously popular working capital (current assets – current liabilities) definition of funds.

The basic format used in developing an SCF is presented in Exhibit 7.4. Note that it starts off by identifying the ($12,296) loss as a reduction in funds during 1987. This loss is taken directly from the income statement (Total All Funds Column) presented in Exhibit 7.5. This is not a cash figure since the accrual accounting system has been used in its derivation. To derive operating cash flows from this income figure, a number of adjustments must be made. First, all noncash expense in the statement of support, revenue, and expenses must be added back to the deficit. Since depreciation expense is not paid out each year and merely represents the allocation of the cost of an asset over its useful life, it must be added back to the deficit in measuring cash flow from operations. This depreciation charge is not readily apparent in Exhibit 7.5 but is broken out in Exhibit 7.6, the statement of functional expenses.

Once depreciation has been added back to the agency's income (deficit), the funds from operations has been derived. To identify cash from operations, all changes in working capital accounts must be assessed to determine their impact on cash flow. For example, a sales transaction would be recorded as revenue before cash flowed into the firm through increasing accounts receivable. Also, purchasing inventory reduces cash, yet the current asset account inventory increases. As a general rule, therefore, all increases in current asset accounts would be viewed as uses of cash in adjusting funds from operations. In contrast, all decreases in current assets would be considered sources of cash. Most analysts agree that the cash provided from operations is the key figure in the SCF, since an agency must provide positive cash flow from operations if it is to remain a going concern over the long run.

In Exhibit 7.4 of our sample set of financial statements, grants receivable went down by $50,479. Based on the discussion above, this amount of cash must have flowed into the agency this period even though it was booked as revenue last period. In contrast, accrued interest increased $20, which indicates the agency recorded this amount as revenue on the accrual basis without receiving it in cash. After adjusting the funds flow for all these changes in working capital, the net cash flow from operations totaled $128,391.

Once cash flow from operations is determined, all changes in long term accounts are assessed to determine sources and uses of cash from investing and financing activities. As with current assets, any increases in noncurrent assets are viewed as sources of cash and decreases as uses of cash. The reverse naturally holds true with liabilities, i.e., increases are sources and decreases represent payments of cash or uses. Exhibit 7.4 also indicates the investment activity of this agency during the year. The agency sold $8,340 worth of assets during 1987. This $8,340 is viewed as nonoperational since it is not likely to be repeated continuously in the future. In addition, the agency used $35,204 to purchase fixed assets, leaving a net decrease in cash from investment activities of $26,864. Finally, the agency paid off $72,530 of notes payable, representing a use of cash to change its capital financing plan. All of these changes in cash due to operating, investing, and financing activities tie into the change in the cash account in Exhibit 7.2's balance sheet. This represents the net increase in cash that was generated by the agency in 1987, with explanations as to the exact sources and uses of cash leading to that net change.

Before leaving the statement of cash flows, a final note comparing cash flow

Exhibit 7.5
Statement of Support, Revenue, and Expenses and Changes in Fund Balances
(for the Year Ending June 30, 1987)

| | Current Funds | | Unexpended Plant Funds Designated for Future Construction |
	Unrestricted	Restricted	
PUBLIC SUPPORT AND REVENUE:			
Public support:			
Government agencies	$	$919,585	$
United Way	240,165	47,644	
Other contributions	14,270	70,719	9,000
Total public support	254,435	1,037,948	9,000
Revenue:			
Program service fees		90,458	
Investment income		4,975	
Unrealized loss on investments			
Miscellaneous	9,982	6,611	
Total revenue	9,982	102,044	
Total public support and revenue	264,417	1,139,992	9,000
EXPENSES:			
Program services:			
Camp		203,467	
Day Care		999,215	
Settlements	_____	69,108	
		1,271,790	
Supporting services:			
Management and general	102,515	_____	
Total expenses	102,515	1,271,790	
Excess (deficiency) of public support and revenue over expenses	161,902	(131,798)	9,000
OTHER CHANGES IN FUND BALANCES:			
Property and equipment acquisitions from Restricted Funds		(24,459)	
Transfer to meet deficit in Restricted Funds	(156,257)	156,257	_____
Excess (deficiency) of revenue over expenses after transfer	5,645	0	9,000
FUND BALANCES (DEFICIT), BEGINNING OF YEAR:	(150,997)	0	8,611
FUND BALANCES (DEFICIT), END OF YEAR	$ 145,352	$ 0	$17,611

102

Exhibit 7.5 (Continued)

Land, Building and Equipment Fund	Endowment Fund	Total All Funds	
		1987	1986
$	$	$919,585	$967,922
		287,809	271,300
8,834	_____	102,823	102,620
8,834	_____	1,310,217	1,341,842
		90,458	51,462
		4,975	4,894
	(8,340)	(8,340)	(1,125)
273	_____	16,866	4,473
273	(8,340)	103,959	59,704
9,107	(8,340)	1,414,176	1,401,546
12,382		215,849	203,928
38,277		1,037,492	1,045,147
664		69,772	69,005
51,323		1,323,113	1,318,080
844		103,359	97,945
52,167		1,426,472	1,416,025
(43,060)	(8,340)	(12,296)'	(14,479)
24,459			
_____	_____	_____	_____
(18,601)	(8,340)	(12,296)	(14,479)
783,744	66,167	707,525	722,004
$765,143	$57,827	$695,229	$707,525

Exhibit 7.6

Statement of Functional Expenses (for the Year Ending June 30, 1987)

| | PROGRAM SERVICES | | |
	Camp	Day Care	Settlements
Salaries	$82,971	$598,851	$44,524
Employee health and retirement benefits	2,659	67,106	4,741
Payroll taxes, etc.	9,918	62,843	4,206
Total salaries and related expenses	95,548	728,800	53,471
Professional fees and contract service payments	4,629	22,555	50
Supplies	42,955	126,887	5,911
Occupancy	15,599	83,466	5,895
Repair and maintenance	19,705	7,932	144
Local transportation	7,212	8,535	1,173
Insurance	7,571	6,789	1,394
Interest			
Telephone	3,604	6,719	628
Rental of equipment	3,351	6,737	90
Miscellaneous	3,293	954	352
Total expenses before depreciation	203,467	999,374	69,108
Depreciation of buildings and equipment	12,382	38,118	664
TOTAL FUNCTIONAL EXPENSES	$215,849	$1,037,492	$69,772

Exhibit 7.6 (Continued)

	SUPPORTING SERVICES	TOTAL	
Total	Management and General	1987	1986
$726,346	$28,330	$754,676	$754,393
74,506	3,215	77,721	73,794
76,967	2,823	79,790	88,099
877,819	34,368	912,187	916,286
27,234	7,966	35,200	50,183
175,753	8,510	184,263	167,148
104,960	19,401	124,361	117,376
27,781	1,736	29,517	9,880
16,920	1,125	18,045	21,583
15,754	371	16,125	21,685
	1,033	1,033	8,377
10,951	2,832	13,783	14,159
10,178	4,231	14,409	15,031
4,599	20,942	25,541	26,040
1,271,949	102,515	1,374,464	1,367,748
51,164	844	52,008	48,277
$1,323,113	$103,359	$1,426,472	$1,416,025

and income flow is in order. Exhibit 7.5 demonstrated that the agency actually lost $12,296 from operations in 1987. This identifies the change in wealth of the agency during 1987. Exhibit 7.4 indicates, however, that over the short run (1987) the agency actually generated more cash flow than it spent. From a short-run liquidity standpoint, therefore, the agency has increased its strength. However, over the long run the agency cannot continue to lose wealth and hope to remain a viable enterprise.

OPERATIONAL PLANNING

Operational plans can be stated in many ways. Traditionally, the budget is a financial representation of an agency's plan for the coming year. This budget is based upon expected output and the resources necessary to support that output. When its components are understood, the budget can become a potent management tool rather than a dreaded annual chore. Agency management is continually faced with difficult choices among alternative courses of action. Each action has some cost attached to it and also offers potential benefits to the community. One function of management is to weigh the costs and benefits of pursuing various paths of action. The budget and the budgeting process can help provide managers with a mechanism to both develop the best course of action and monitor progress over time.

The complexities involved in running agencies often prevent managers from setting aside adequate time for systematic planning. There are always immediate issues that require attention. The budgeting process is critical to breaking this reactive cycle by focusing management's attention on future planning issues. This in itself is valuable, but the budgeting process goes further by providing a planning structure to convert operational goals into dollars.

Once a budget has been prepared, feedback on the agency's performance is necessary. Agencies, unlike for-profit enterprises, must prepare a statement of functional expenses. This statement represents a detailed look at how resources were allocated (expensed) across programs and expense categories during the year. Essentially, it details what happened, whereas the budget relates what is expected to happen. The statement of functional expenses, therefore, should be used as a feedback mechanism to the budgeting process.

To generate maximum use of the agency budget, a clear understanding of cost classification and the concept of contribution margin is necessary. A discussion of these concepts follows and is supported by a detailed example.

Cost Structure

The most straightforward and useful classification of costs separates them into two basic types, fixed and variable. Fixed costs are those that will be unaffected by variations in service or sales volume in a given time period and over a given range of sales levels. That is, fixed costs are constant throughout the specified time period and independent of the level of services provided in that period. Typical examples of fixed costs include executive salaries, rent, and depreciation.

Fixed costs can and do change over time, but these changes should not be attributed to changes in sales volume within a given time period. For instance, an increase in executive salaries will cause fixed expenses to change, but changes are not directly tied to an increase or decrease in sales volume. Fixed costs, therefore, do not represent those costs that never change, but rather those costs which do not change with output over the relevant range.

Variable costs are those costs that are affected by the level of revenues within a time period. Generally, such costs as wages and materials are classified as variable costs. Direct variable costs reflect the direct relationship between the inputs of materials and labor required to produce a unit of output. Since each unit of output requires specified amounts of materials and labor, increases in output will cause proportionate increases in material and labor costs.

Although there are many refinements and extensions of the fixed and variable cost dichotomy, the basic classification of all costs into these two categories is extremely useful.

Determining Fixed and Variable Costs

There are several methods used to classify fixed and variable costs. They include the engineering approach, the specific accounts method, the high-low method, and regression analysis.

The engineering approach estimates costs through an analysis of the physical inputs necessary to produce a level of output. This approach is best suited to situations where the results of past experiences are unavailable.

The specific accounts method relies on the existence of past accounting records and the judgment of the analyst. The analyst classifies costs as being fixed or variable based upon an understanding of the nature of the cost elements. For instance, utilities could be classified as either fixed or variable, depending upon how sensitive utilities expense is to changes in service volume. A limitation of the specific accounts method is the subjectivity inherent in the process.

The high-low method and regression method are statistical techniques that can be useful in separating costs into fixed and variable components. Both methods determine the incremental change in costs arising from an incremental change in service volume. These techniques are objective in nature, and thus remove the subjectivity bias inherent in the specific accounts method. To employ these techniques, certain key assumptions must be met or the analyses lose their validity. One assumption is that the data used in the analyses all fall within the relevant range of service volume. This assumption is usually met when examining costs over several months, but is rarely met when data span several years.

For social service agencies, we recommend the specific accounts method to classify costs into fixed and variable categories. This is preferred due to its relative ease of use. Any accuracy lost probably does not warrant the time and

Exhibit 7.7
Statement of Support, Revenue, and Expenses (for 1988)

REVENUES

Program Service Fees	$100,000
United Way	300,000
Total Public Support	$400,000

EXPENSES

Program Services	350,000
Management and General	40,000
Total Expenses	390,000

**EXCESS OF PUBLIC SUPPORT
AND REVENUE OVER EXPENSES**   **$10,000**

---

expense involved in generating a more precise classification of costs into fixed and variable categories.

Contribution Margin

Once costs have been separated into fixed and variable components, the traditional income statement format can be reorganized to provide management with additional information. For example, since both revenues and variable costs are proportional to service volume, it is useful to compare them. The difference between total revenue and total variable cost is called the contribution margin.

An understanding of contribution margin is best accomplished through an example. The statement of support, revenue, and expenses for a fictitious agency will be used in this example and is shown in Exhibit 7.7.

What would be the financial impact to the agency if service volume were to increase by 10 percent? One could initially infer that the excess of revenue over expenses relative to revenue is proportional. That is, a 10 percent increase in

Exhibit 7.8
Statement of Support, Revenue, and Expenses in Contribution Margin Format
(for 1988)

REVENUES	OLD	NEW
Program Fees	$100,000	$110,000
United Way	300,000	330,000
Total Revenue	$400,000	$440,000
VARIABLE EXPENSES		
Labor Costs	$200,000	220,000
Material Costs	20,000	22,000
Total Variable Costs	$220,000	$242,000
Contribution Margin	180,000	$198,000
Contribution Margin per $	$.45	$.45
FIXED COSTS		
Labor Costs	$140,000	$140,000
Material Costs	30,000	30,000
Total Fixed Costs	$170,000	$170,000
EXCESS OF REVENUE OVER EXPENSES	$10,000	$28,000

service revenue would result in a 10 percent increase in the agency bottom line. This would result in an additional $1,000 for the agency. This analysis misses the point that certain costs are fixed and will not change with increases or decreases in service volume. To show this, we can recast Exhibit 7.7 in a contribution margin format, as shown in Exhibit 7.8.

The 10 percent increase in volume results in a 180 percent increase in funds for the agency, since many of their expenses are fixed. We can see the $40,000 increase in revenue results in income increasing by $18,000 or $.45 × the

Exhibit 7.9

Proposed Budget by Service (for the Year Ending June 30, 1987)

	1 TOTAL (Col. 2 & 5)	2 TOTAL Supporting Services (Col 3. & 4)	3 Management & General
EXPENDITURES FOR CURRENT SERVICE OPERATIONS			
Salaries	808,844	34,011	21,997
Employee Health and Retirement Benefits	90,040	13,170	10,125
Payroll Taxes, etc.	82,779	3,476	2,242
Professional Fees and Contract Service Payments	26,015	12,315	5,740
Supplies	175,520	6,300	5,250
Telephone and Telegraph	13,832	3,675	2,625
Postage and Shipping	2,570	1,680	1,365
Occupancy	173,216	24,129	21,609
Rental & Maintenance of Equipment	16,970	6,825	6,825
Outside Printing and Publications	3,361	1,761	1,341
Local Transportation	29,382	2,782	2,572
Conference, Conventions, etc.	7,381	2,310	2,310
Specific Assistance to Individuals	7,000		
Organizations Dues	3,150	3,150	3,150
Awards and Grants			
Repairs and Replacements not Capitalized			
Miscellaneous	13,898	10,798	10,798
Amortization			
National Dues			
Fixed Asset Purchases–Capitalized			
Total Expenses for all Activities			
(Line 7 form 1)	1,453,958	126,382	97,949

TOTAL SUPPORTING SERVICES (LINE A – Col. 2) Distribution
1. TOTAL PROGRAM COST
2. SERVICE VOLUME AND UNIT COST: NO. UNITS OF SERVICE
Total Average Cost Per Unit, $^{(1)}/_{(2)}$

Note: This table represents a United Way budget form.

110

Exhibit 7.9 Continued)

4 Fund Raising	5 Total Services (Col. A, B, & C)	PROGRAM A	PROGRAM B	PROGRAM C
12,014	774,833	636,361	61,278	77,194
3,045	76,870	68,526	4,931	3,413
1,234	79,303	63,865	6,527	8,911
6,575	13,700	4,500	5,700	3,500
1,050	169,220	127,645	12,200	29,375
1,050	10,157	5,502	1,055	3,600
315	890	200	140	550
2,520	149,087	103,289	13,240	32,558
	10,145	8,690	1,105	350
420	1,600	400	50	1,150
210	26,600	15,400	2,200	9,000
	5,071	4,171	900	
	7,000		7,000	
	3,100	1,000	1,600	500
28,433	1,327,576	1,039,549	117,926	170,101
	126.382	98.957	11.248	16.177
	1,453,958	1,138,506	129,174	186,278
		260,832	10,250	18,082
		4.36	12.60	10.30

111

$40,000 increase in revenue. The agency's contribution margin represents funds that are available to cover fixed costs and then contribute to the agency's bottom line. Stated another way, variable costs consume $.55 of each sales dollar. The remaining $.45 per sales dollar goes to profit after all the fixed costs have been covered.

On a more pragmatic level, we know that agencies do not relish the idea of showing too healthy a financial position, since that may impair their ability to raise funds in the future based on need. Therefore, published financial statements are often "manicured" to show a small surplus, if any. Additionally, agency public support is not always responsive to changes in service activity in the short run. Finally, agency income statements in general do not contain the level of detail necessary to classify costs into fixed and variable components. All of these conditions, however, do not negate the agency's need to develop an understanding of fixed and variable costs for decision making. This understanding should enable an agency to increase the scope of its services without impairing its fiscal solvency.

Using the Budget

The agency budget is an appropriate financial statement that can be utilized to maximize information for management decision making. As noted earlier, agencies operationalize their plans through a budget. The budget represents a plan for how agency resources are to be utilized over the coming year. Helping an agency cope with the financial impact of a change in plans is one important role the budget plays.

Exhibit 7.9 is a direct abstract from the United Way budget of the agency represented in Exhibits 7.1 through 7.6. We will confine our comments to Program A. We see that this agency is poised to offer 260,832 units of service at a total cost of $1,128,506. This results in an average cost of $4.36 as shown. Suppose this agency is offered the opportunity to provide an additional 5000 units of service, but will only receive $3.00 a unit. Should the agency accept this offer? On first inspection, it appears that this agency cannot afford to undertake this venture. To adequately answer this question, however, we must first develop a better understanding of this agency's cost structure.

Given the above discussion of cost classification, agency costs can now be segmented into their fixed and variable components. It is important to recognize that many of the costs are difficult to classify; however, prudent management judgment is generally sufficient in developing a classification scheme that works. This agency's costs were classified into fixed and variable components based upon the information shown in Exhibit 7.9 and a more detailed breakdown of salary expense supplied to us by agency management.

We see in Exhibit 7.10 that the variable cost of providing a unit of service is only $2.51 as opposed to a total average cost of $4.36. That is, a one-unit

Exhibit 7.10
Cost Behavior Patterns (for the Year Ending June 30, 1987)

COST CATEGORY	FIXED COMPONENT	VARIABLE COMPONENT	
SALARIES			
Executive Salaries	$41,419		
Program Director	43,840		
Assistant Director	35,802		
Teachers		$214,835	
Teachers Aides		102,350	
Substitutes		50,683	
Clericals	49,584		
Social Service		25,168	
Maintenance Director	35,914		
Maintenance Staff		36,766	
Total Salaries		$206,559	$429,802
OTHER EXPENSES			
Benefits & Payroll Taxes	50,309	82,082	
Professional Fees	4,500		
Supplies		127,645	
Telephone & Telegraph	5,502		
Postage & Shipping	200		
Occupancy	103,289		
Equip. Rental & Maintenance	8,690		
Outside Printing	400		
Local Transportation	15,400		
Conferences	4,171		
Miscellaneous	1,000		
Supporting Services	83,124	15,833	
Total Other Expenses		276,585	225,560
Total Expenses		$483,144	$665,362

Total Fixed Plus Variable Expenses = $1,138,506
Total Units of Service = 260,832 hours
AVERAGE VARIABLE COST PER UNIT OF SERVICE; $2.51 = ($665,362)/260,832

increase or decrease in units of services provided should only add $2.51 in costs. Clearly, this agency would be financially able to handle the proposed 5000 units of service with a reimbursement of $3.00 a unit. Of course, this is premised on the assumption that the agency's normal market will not be affected by this discounting of services.

REFERENCES

American Institute of Certified Public Accountants, Accounting Principles Board (AICPA; 1971). *Reporting changes in financial position, No. 19.* New York: American Institute of Certified Public Accountants.

Darlin, D. (1983, September 29). Picking a loser. *Wall Street Journal*, 1.

Financial Accounting Standards Board (1987). *Statement of financial accounting standards no. 95, statement of cash flows.* Stamford, CT: Financial Accounting Standards Board.

Largay, A., III, and C. Stickney (1980, July–August). Cash flows, ration analysis, and the W. T. Grant Company Bankruptcy. *Financial Analysts Journal* 36, 51–54.

PART III
OPERATIONAL FUNCTIONS

8
Adapting and Adopting a Marketing Perspective for the Community Service Agency

JUSTIN FINK

The 1980s have not been easy years for nonprofits. Cuts in public support for human service programs began in the late seventies, which was also a time of rising inflation. Severe cuts imposed at the federal level beginning in 1981 saw many programs curtailed. Some agencies went under. For those that managed to survive, there were new pressures for diversified revenues, but also for heightened accountability and management procedures that were "more businesslike." One result was that the sector began to turn its attention to applying concepts and methods of marketing that had long been used in the business world. Indeed, this has been a decade of marketing for nonprofits, and given the financial squeeze voluntary organizations have faced, it is easy to understand why nonprofit marketing has caught on so rapidly.

Previously, the language and values of marketing had found acceptance only in larger, more institutionalized nonprofit organizations such as universities, hospitals, large cultural organizations, and others with well-organized development programs. But from the early eighties on, journal articles, books, seminars, and training workshops have exhorted all nonprofit managers to look toward the marketing of programs and services as a means to bolster income. Marketing techniques have been especially focused on attracting members, patrons, and clients to boost revenues from dues and fees for service and on applying direct mail, telemarketing, and other techniques to acquire and retain donors. Thick textbooks by Kotler (1975), Lovelock and Weinberg (1984), Lauffer (1984), and others pioneered the application of sophisticated marketing concepts to the nonprofit arena in ways that were previously unimagined. Publications such as *Fund Raising Management* and *Harvard Business Review* have documented the ascendency of the marketing perspective, particularly that of direct marketing.

Large numbers of smaller community service organizations, however, operate with limited staffing and budgets well under a million dollars or even less than half a million dollars. Many agencies whose clients cannot pay and who also lack viable donor constituencies support their service programs primarily through grants and contracts. They sustain themselves in this way instead of raising monies through annual funds, planned giving, or capital campaigns. The latter are the kinds of fund-raising or development efforts that have best utilized the tools of the marketer's trade. But what nonprofit marketing has largely failed to do is speak to the realities of life in these smaller nonprofits. This is not terribly surprising; neither the fields of social work, public management, nor nonprofit management have given sufficient recognition to the important role community-based organizations, or CBOs, play in meeting human service needs at the local level.

In fact, smaller nonprofits are playing an increasingly important role in providing human services in local areas all across the United States. Spurred on by the expansion of government and private funding during the 1960s and 1970s, community-based organizations active in social service, civic action, community development, and the arts numbered about 80,000 in the 1981 Federal Census. They accounted for more than $21 billion of expenditures and employed well over 10 million persons. Small, locally based voluntary organizations have a long tradition in American communities, and they have been recognized as having "distinctive competencies" in delivering certain kinds of personal human services (Kramer, 1987).

Communities all over the country benefit from a broad array of programs offered by thousands of relatively small, locally based human service organizations. These agencies provide services in program areas such as adult basic education; children and youth services; drug and alcohol abuse prevention and treatment; crime prevention; employment and training; services for the elderly; emergency food, clothing, and shelter; energy assistance; housing and community development; information and referral; rape crisis intervention and other specialized services for women; social casework and counseling; and transportation. Community service agencies are often crucial in filling gaps in local service networks, and many of those who benefit from their programs are of low or moderate income status.

This chapter is intended to advance the field of nonprofit marketing by adapting and applying its basic concepts to smaller, community-based human service organizations. These are agencies that most often have multiple goals and mixed income, a significant portion of which is derived through submitting proposals for funding grants and contracts. The overall goal will be to provide a pragmatic orientation to strategic marketing that is directly applicable to community service organizations. Specifically, the chapter will attempt to

1. foster an understanding of the nonprofit as a market-like entity;
2. clarify the economic basis of community service organizations by using a framework of exchange and transaction, and related ideas such as mediated exchange and the "bifurcated market";
3. introduce the concept of nonprofit or "community agency enterprise," which entails an appropriate matching of client and community service needs with donor and funder needs, as well as other revenue opportunities; and
4. introduce adaptations of marketing tools and techniques such as the analysis of resource and service markets, the marketing information system, the market review, and the marketing mix.

In proceeding it is important to underscore what will not be addressed. This chapter is not about the mechanics of fund-raising or grant writing for community-based organizations, about which many others have written (e.g., Kiritz, 1979; Seltzer, 1987). Thus, omitted here are important topics that are commonly discussed under the rubric of "institutional advancement." For those interested, there are many excellent, specialized publications covering topics such as annual and capital solicitation, deferred and planned giving, telemarketing, and special events (for a useful bibliography see Seltzer, 1987). Further, only in passing will popular strategies for earned income be examined. For these the reader is directed to several books that provide thorough treatment of this area of growing interest (Crimmins and Keil, 1983; Skloot, 1988).

THE NONPROFIT AS AN ECONOMIC PHENOMENON

A Marketlike Entity Subject to Economic Forces

One of the most significant developments in the voluntary-sector scholarship in recent years has been the recognition that the sector's representative organizations in both human services and the arts are creatures of the larger economy (Gassler, 1986; Hansmann, 1987; Weisbrod, 1977). Nonprofit activity in the United States has been shown to vary greatly from region to region (Wolch, 1985; and Wolpert and Reiner, 1985). That is, the extent and kind of programming carried out differ by geographic area in response to both community needs and the availability of public and private support.

Thus, despite earlier assertions of some economic theorists that the nonprofit form arose as a response to the failure of the market to provide a response to certain unmet social needs (e.g., see Weisbrod, 1977), managers might more accurately think of the nonprofit organization as a marketlike entity. In this view, the nonprofit is seen from a very different perspective, more like a firm with a unique organizational shape and characteristics.

Mission, Constraint, and Opportunity in a Unique Form of Enterprise

Nonprofits must be recognized as specialized businesses that exist under a distinctive set of opportunities and constraints. These must in turn be understood to be both economic and otherwise. The major constraint to which nonprofit corporations are subject is that stricture prohibiting distribution of any surplus revenues to individuals in the form of dividends or profits. By statutes operative in each state, nonprofit corporate charters are issued to those incorporators whose intended purposes meet stated criteria for enhancing the public good. Exemption from federal income taxation is granted according to criteria established under the U.S. Internal Revenue Code, and any funds contributed or earned must be applied in support of the organization's charitable purpose. Charitable solicitation is usually state-regulated.

Thus both the activities and the income of the nonprofit face one set of constraints imposed by law or regulation. Counterbalancing those constraints is the range of acceptable possibilities open to organizations with regard to supplying needed services and generating resources in any given locale. Options for developing programs and services are partly conditioned by the organization's chosen mission and the extent of demonstrable community need. And as every agency executive director or planner knows, program development is constrained by the ability to generate resources sufficient to cover costs. Despite the fact that their stated purposes and goals are always other than to generate profit, not-for-profits (as tax-exempt organizations are legally termed) remain resource-dependent. They in fact must attract not only the consumers of any programs they might produce, but also enough money, materials, and paid or volunteer staff to support their service efforts.

Although still not well-described in either the research or management literature, the building and sustaining of charitable organizations does thus constitute a unique kind of venture or enterprise. To understand the way voluntary organizations work economically, we must look more carefully at where their resources come from and how they get them. Hansmann (1980) divided the sector into two parts according to derivation of income. He suggested that traditionally, most charity organizations have been donative in nature, receiving support through contributions. Some, such as hospitals, however, have sustained themselves largely through user fees and could be termed commercial. He asserts that "commercial nonprofits" are growing in importance, raising the specter of unfair competition with proprietary service providers.

According to *Giving USA*, published each year by the American Association of Fund Raising Counsel, by far the most support for charitable causes in this country—about \$93.7 billion in 1987—comes from individual donations (AAFRC, 1988). Some two-thirds of this giving is to churches and other religious institutions. According to a study by Salamon (1989), after the exclusion of health, education, and research institutions, nonprofit human service providers averaged well over half of their income from government sources and one quarter or less from private giving. Social services got less than 15 percent of income from fees.

For many agencies whose clients have limited ability to pay, charging a fee for services provided holds only limited income-generating potential. And unlike some organizations that have a base of financial support in a national parent organization and that can identify a clear donor constituency, or that offer significant recognition for philanthropists, many community-based organizations have limited resources for seeking any appreciable contributions from individuals. These agencies tend to have low profiles outside their immediate areas, and are comparatively "unglamorous." Unsolicited donations of any magnitude are a rarity.

Thus most CBOs, especially many that serve low-income populations, cannot benefit significantly from a range of direct marketing techniques and methods that promote individual solicitation or effective competition for fee-paying clients. Extensive fund-raising and advertising campaigns that underlie the mainstays of support for higher education, hospitals, and high-profile cultural institutions will generally be of little or no use to the small agency executive or board member. Instead many, many CBOs exist as creatures of what the economist Kenneth Boulding (1973) first termed "the grants economy." That is, they identify community needs and then seek out and apply for grants or contracts to conduct appropriate programs. Although grants and contracts rarely constitute any agency's entire income, they commonly account for 50 to 90 percent of many CBO budgets.

Undeniably, a marketing perspective can help community agency boards and staff plan strategies and make informed choices about the development of programs and program support. Marketing as a way of thinking about the life of a community agency offers a framework for organizing and integrating program planning and resource development. As such it offers a means for enhancing an organization's ability to generate sufficient resources in order to pursue a chosen mission of service.

Exchange as the Basis for a Marketing Perspective

The man who pioneered the field of nonprofit marketing, Philip Kotler (1975), has defined marketing itself as "the analysis, planning, implementation and control of carefully formulated programs designed to bring about voluntary exchanges of values with target markets for the purpose of achieving organizational objectives" (p. 6). To understand the significance this definition holds for the community service agency, one must first grasp basic concepts of exchange, transaction, and markets.

Much social interaction and the majority of our economic relations are characterized by a process of exchange. Trading goods and services for money has replaced historically earlier arrangements where society depended greatly upon barter. Today we are largely a "money economy."

There are, however, various types of exchanges that serve to accommodate the richness and complexity of our social and economic life. Social scientists have long been aware that some exchanges entail another kind of reciprocity (Mauss, 1954) wherein goods and services are traded for other rewards such as favors, status, gratitude, or personal satisfaction. This has been termed social exchange (Homans, 1958).

Writers in the field of marketing have also understood the complexities of exchange. As defined by Kotler, exchange is a process as opposed to an event. For exchange to occur several conditions must be met. First, there must be at least two parties, each being capable of offering something of perceived value to the other. Further, each must be capable of communicating about and delivering on their offers. Finally, each must be free to accept or reject what is offered. A successful exchange is marked by a transaction.

Sensitive to nuance, Kotler has identified several varieties of exchange, including commercial, employment, civic, religious, and charitable transactions. In a commercial exchange, money is traded for goods or services in a quid pro quo arrangement. In an employment transaction, an employer trades wages and benefits in exchange for an employee's work. Civic transactions are marked by the provision of goods and/or services (e.g., education, police protection, or road maintenance) in exchange for the payment of taxes by citizens.

Other exchanges may be less tangible. Although not often described in these terms, a member of a church congregation may receive spiritual services in return for contributions and/or attendance at religious worship services. Finally, the "charitable transaction" is conceived of primarily in terms of the individual who makes a contribution of time, goods, or money to a charitable cause. In exchange, he or she presumably derives some sense of satisfaction that what has been given is going to support a worthy effort, and perhaps receives a measure of public recognition as well.

Mixed Exchanges, Intangibles, and Value Transactions

The exchange model has been applied to transactions at the organizational level in the nonprofit world (White, Levine, and Vlasak, 1980). Exchanges in the nonprofit arena do tend to have several kinds of special characteristics. For one thing, they often entail social exchange with a mix of the tangible and intangible, as described above. One common example of this is a funder supporting a service program with outcomes that are difficult to measure, such as the teaching of self-esteem to low-income, single mothers. Additionally, the work of voluntary organizations often seeks to provide relief from suffering or to correct perceived social ills. As such, exchanges in the nonprofit arena are heavily influenced by values, especially social, religious, and political ones. Exchanges in the sector can often appear one-sided, as when job placement services are provided to clients free of charge.

Further, exchanges in the nonprofit world are often far more complex than the "tit-for-tat" commercial transactions with which we are most commonly familiar. Consider the following. A woman goes into a grocery store. For a sum of $5 she gets a box of disposable diapers for her baby. Later that day the same woman places a call to staff at a local, United Way-funded agency that provides her with information concerning available subsidized day care slots for children of families meeting income eligibility guidelines. After responding to a few questions concerning her own background, job, and financial status, she schedules an appointment for the following week during which she will receive help in evaluating her options and in filing the necessary application forms that will presumably lead to eventual enrollment.

What do these separate incidents have in common and how are they different? In the first instance, the woman offered a specified amount of money and in return received a specified amount of goods, that is, disposable diapers. It could be said that there was a transaction or direct exchange of money for goods, a quid pro quo. In the second instance, however, she was given information and other help without having to pay, at least in monetary terms.

What, if anything, was she giving in return, and what was the nature of the transaction that occurred? Why was the agency providing her these services in the first place, and what, if anything, was it getting from assisting its client? How could it not charge and still survive as a viable service-providing entity meeting the costs of maintaining its location, staff, telephone, and so forth?

Recall that the woman provided the agency with some personal data about herself and received information as well as counseling and placement assistance for her child. For a United Way-member agency it is likely that at least part of the cost of assisting her would be borne by the charitable contributions of individuals, corporations, and/or foundations that channeled their philanthropic impulses ultimately toward her and her need for child care, but mediated once through the collective auspices of United Way and then again through the agency funded to provide direct services. Although the process through which the agency received that United Way support was undoubtedly a complex one, it is fair to say that the likelihood of the agency continuing to receive funding from it and other sources will be enhanced by being able to report having met the service needs of individuals who fit certain eligibility criteria. Thus we have the client's participation working to help legitimize the agency's claims of beneficial community service. Being able to report that participation and its happy outcome in turn helps the agency justify continued financial support.

Mediated Exchanges

A key marketing concept helps us to understand the roles of various participants in the range of community agency transactions. Kotler's concept of a nonprofit organization's "publics" (1975, pp. 46–55), or what Lovelock and Weinberg term "constituencies" (1984, pp. 57–61), might best be understood in terms of all those individuals and groups both inside and outside the organization who have some interest in the organization's activities.

Kotler categorizes publics according to input publics (e.g., donors, suppliers, and regulatory bodies who provide resources or impose constraints), internal publics (those who work to accomplish the organizational aims, such as management, board, staff, and volunteers), intermediary publics (e.g., merchants, agents, facilitators, and marketing firms who help organizational programs, products, or services), and consuming publics (e.g., clients, local communities and the general public, media, and competitors). Lovelock and Weinberg have a slightly different and somewhat less complete schema of constituencies.

While each of these major contributors to the nonprofit marketing literature does give attention to fund-raising as a marketing issue (Kotler to donors as input publics, and Lovelock and Weinberg to "financial resource suppliers" as a constituency), neither adequately identifies funding sources as consumers. Neither is the exchange concept fully developed as it pertains to grant-funded organizations. If, however, we take the basic concepts of marketing and apply them to the reality of organizational life in CBOs, we find that they provide a way to understand things that also suggests a practical approach to agency development.

Looking at the sequence of interactions in the preceding section, what we have described actually entails several exchanges: between the woman and the agency, between the agency and United Way, and between United Way and its contributors. We see the agency acting as an intermediary or linking agent for those whose philanthropic values and beliefs led them to give donations in support of social services for people like the woman and her child. In a sense, we can talk about it in terms of the community organization having identified and addressed the needs of a particular population with a particular set of problems, but in doing so, also identifying and addressing the priorities of funders or donors.

Like social exchange, this indirect or mediated exchange is a form of social behavior that has been noted by some social scientists (Berger and Neuhaus, 1977; Blau, 1964). However, it has been little studied in the field or talked about in the nonprofit management or fund-raising literature. As a social and economic arrangement, mediated exchange reflects one of the ways we as a society have evolved to meet our individual and collective needs. It is perhaps the primary means by which grant-funded community service organizations participate in the economy at large.

Indirect exchanges can only be completed with the participation of at least three partners—a client, funder or funders, and the agency acting as a go-

Figure 8.1
A Model of Transactions between Client, Community Service Agency, and
Funder/Donor

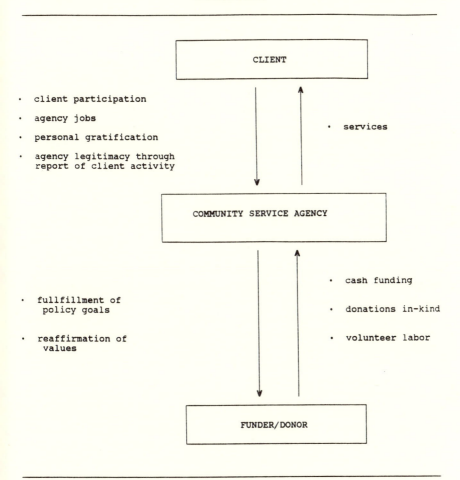

between. As illustrated in Figure 8.1, the agency works to link the needs of the client with the resources of funders and donors according to their acknowledged value preferences, policies, or guidelines. While the woman who went to the employment agency in the example above has not been required to cover the cost of providing the service through a fee, her participation in the program returns several rewards to the service-providing organization: (1) gratification for individual workers involved in service provision, (2) affirmation for individuals and the agency as a whole that their jobs are justified, and (3) a means for the agency to feed back data that serves to legitimize the use of the funders' dollars and verify that their philanthropic goals are being pursued and met through the agency's efforts. The value of these things should not be underestimated.

Similarly, we cannot ignore the value of the agency's role in implementing the policies and goals of organized philanthropy—local, state, and federal funding bodies; foundations and corporations; United Ways; and other federated fundraising efforts. In fact, having to work directly with a targeted client population or service need would likely place an unwanted or impossible burden upon most philanthropic donors, especially institutional philanthropies such as foundations and corporations. In any case, it is something for which most donors are wholly unprepared. While a variety of motives may underlie charitable giving by individuals, foundations, and businesses, in most instances a donor's philanthropic goal is probably to alleviate a social problem, meet a local need, or bring about desired change in community conditions. Should a foundation or business receive favorable publicity for supporting a popular cause, its needs for legitimacy and a favorable image within the community are being met in an even more demonstrable way.

A similar analysis can be applied to public support for voluntary service provision, that is, service provision by private agencies with volunteer boards and/or staff. A 40–year trend of federal, state, and local governments to contract out the provision of many human services to nonprofits—a trend commonly referred to as "privatization"—is evidence that large governmental bureaucracies with their rigid procedures and built-in high overhead also may not be ideally suited to carry out some types of human service programs. When governments support programming through issuing contracts, public policy and political goals are operative. De facto, the work of the nonprofit presumably serves these goals, too. The model of mediated exchange is delineated in detail in Figure 8.2.

Thus, while pure exchange involving both money and other tangible benefits is the "economic glue" that binds us together, mixed, mediated and social exchanges are, to an extent, our "social glue." It is a mechanism fundamental to society's providing certain kinds of programs and services that have been deemed essential to the well-being of individuals, families, and communities. A close look at community service agencies will show that many, if not all of them, derive their very existence from their ability to facilitate these indirect exchanges.

Typically, voluntary service organizations are said to begin because a group of concerned citizens experiences or recognizes a need or set of needs within their community. They seek to do something about it by creating a new organization as a vehicle enabling a response to those perceived needs. This perception of a collective, associational basis for nonprofits constitutes the conventional wisdom and acknowledges the primacy of our long, historical traditions of voluntarism and community-based problem solving. It reflects what one prominent writer has termed "America's voluntary spirit" (O'Connell, 1983). Alternatively, there is evidence emerging to support the contention that at least some nonprofits are largely the product of energetic individuals motivated by a variety

Figure 8.2
An Example of Transactions between Clients and Donors Mediated by the
Community Service Agency

CLIENT/SERVICE MARKET

Clients	Services
ELDERLY YOUTH FAMILY WOMEN -single -unemployed -abused -teen mother	SOCIAL SERVICES TRANSPORTATION RECREATION EMPLOYMENT -job counseling -job preparation -job placement -skill training

Job counseling,
  preparation &
  placement services
  for low-income,
client   unemployed minority
  participation   women
agency
  legtimation

COMMUNITY SERVICE AGENCY

                                   cash   Promotion of
RESOURCE/DONOR MARKET   funding;   self-sufficiency
                                   in-kind   independence,
                                   donations   and equal
                                                 opportunity;
PUBLIC	Fed, State, Local	150 people served each year;
PRIVATE	United Way foundations business church donors individual volunteer in-kind	50 placed in education or skills training placements
SELF- GENERATED	related (fees) unrelated	

of personal factors (Fink, 1989; Milofsky, 1987; Young, 1987). Nonetheless, each of these views places emphasis upon a recognition of community need by civic-minded individuals or groups acting on behalf of the interests of themselves or others.

In fact, it might be argued that over the last 30 years many new nonprofits have come about in response to the availability of funding to support certain types of programs and services felt to be needed by government or institutional philanthropy. Unlike the preceding explanations, this view places the recognition of individual need, that is, the demand for agency services, at the policy level, versus at the local level with either clients, volunteers, or professionals. This policy decision is followed by a dedication of resources, which then spurs the creation of new organizations to achieve the policy's objectives.

THE CHALLENGE OF THE BIFURCATED MARKET

Regardless of the theory we prefer, the nonprofit service organization can be viewed as emerging in response to needs, or as economists would say, demand. These are either the needs of a community for the remediation of problems or provision of services, or the priorities of government or organized philanthropy. In any case, this viewpoint suggests that the nonprofit must be understood as simultaneously serving two masters, the pool of potential service recipients on one hand, and the pool of potential funders on the other. We might say that, because of its unique function in mediating between the needs of a client population and the needs of funders, the market for any community service agency is bifurcated.

Understanding the concept of exchange and the special qualities of transactions in the voluntary sector are first steps toward adapting a marketing perspective to the needs of the community service agency. But if exchange is the medium through which a marketing effort realizes its objectives, it can only come to life in the actions of its participants—the sellers and the buyers.

The basic, critical element in the definition of marketing is the term "market" itself, which invokes the image of those participants; a market is defined as a set of actual and potential consumers of a market offer. We have identified the unique way in which CBOs are sustained by mediated exchanges. No agency can last for long without giving adequate attention to its client population or its prospective sources of support. We would do well to recognize that for the community service agency, both client population *and* funders are actual or potential "consumers," marketlike constituencies for the things an agency has to offer. Clearly, what CBOs "sell" to prospective clients and funders are programs and services, or aspects of them.

How might we more adequately define, identify, and analyze these constituencies in order to assess the prospects for doing business with them? Moreover, how do we face up to the challenge of matching the needs of these seemingly disjointed but potential partners in mediated exchange? Fortunately, there are useful tools for meeting these challenges that can be derived from reinterpretations of basic marketing concepts.

USING MARKET SEGMENTATION

Two of the most powerful analytic concepts from the field of marketing are segmentation and target marketing. These lend themselves nicely to identifying and finding out about the range of opportunities for the community service organization: for meeting the service needs of prospective clients on one hand, and pursuing resource opportunities on the other.

Segmentation is simply the splitting up of any set into subgroups on the basis of commonly held traits, descriptors, or combinations of characteristics. First, we will apply the concept of segmentation to the client/service side of our two-track model.

Segmentation of the Client/Service Market

Human service programs can rarely be accurately described without invoking their prospective beneficiaries, that is, service recipients. Similarly, for a service-providing agency, clients are most often thought of in connection with program activities geared to their service needs. It is therefore useful to think of programs both in terms of client characteristics and service definitions. We might incorporate each of these dimensions into our community agency market schema by referring to this side of things as the client/service market.

To use the example above one more time, the woman who sought child care information and placement assistance might be described as a woman of a certain age and ethnicity; a mother; or a single parent with a given educational background, employment status, income level, and so forth. Her particular human service needs could be seen as a function of any one or any combination of these things that pertain to her, or perhaps none of them. Alternately, her needs might be discussed in terms of certain categories of programming or services, such as social service programs like counseling and information and referral; education programs such as adult or early childhood education; or employment programs such as vocational counseling, training, and job placement.

The client/service market can be extensively segmented, thus giving us a means for examining a range of possibilities for framing programs and services. To do this we combine the range of program categories (i.e., education, employment, health, housing and community development, legal aid, public safety and protection, recreation, social service, transportation, etc.) and the range of client characteristics (e.g., age, sex, marital status, socioeconomic status, educational background, employment status, etc.) to form the overarching concept. We then proceed to break down each of these identifiers into more discrete units of analysis. Thus we might look at the situation of the woman in the example above as representative of a certain segment of the client/service market—the low-income, single mother with a young child and with limited educational background, for whom job training, job readiness, and/or job placement would be beneficial, but only possible with collateral subsidized day care. The analytic scheme would be as indicated in Figure 8.3, labeled "Example of Client/Service Segmentation."

Perhaps the most extensive taxonomy of programs and services is to be found in a publication of United Way of American entitled *UWASIS II* (United Way

Figure 8.3
Example of Client/Service Segmentation

CLIENT TYPE		SERVICE NEEDS
AGE:	27 yrs	EMPLOYMENT
SEX:	woman	Job readiness or training
MARITAL:	single -- mother	Job placement
SOCIOECONOMIC:	low-income	SOCIAL SERVICE
EDUCATIONAL:	H.S. equivalency	Information & Referral
EMPLOYMENT:	unemployed	Day Care (subsidized)
		EDUCATION
		Early Childhood Education
		Placement
		Subsidy

of America, 1976). The effort that resulted in *UWASIS II* was intended to produce an exhaustive schema of services which could form the basis of a standardized system for tracking service delivery in United Way–funded agencies throughout the nation. For the purposes of the present discussion, *UWASIS II* should be noted as the single best segmentation of the service component of the client/ service market, and it can be a very useful reference.

Traditionally, examination of community service issues is handled through a needs assessment. This procedure, developed mainly within the field of social welfare planning and administration, can be based on a formalized process that combines survey research, statistical data, or interviews, or on less rigorous measures of key informant testimony or direct observation. The typical community agency executive responsible for program development rarely has the time or resources to conduct an extensive needs assessment. The most effective agency executives keep in touch with community conditions through their contacts, observations, and ability to secure a range of input from board, staff, and community residents. Experienced agency managers, planners, and grant writers become especially adept at utilizing readily accessible information from public and private sources to justify proposals for programs and services.

However, an important conceptual distinction must be made between the utility of conventional needs assessment and our need to think within a marketing framework. Social service planning has customarily been taught as an activity that should be handled apart from funding considerations. Program planning has often been idealized based upon the results of needs assessment. Thus, in the past, program planning has frequently been done in isolation from financial planning. That might have worked during the 1960s, but it doesn't any longer. Today, limited availability of funding and the common reluctance of funders to underwrite more than just a portion of any agency or program, means that those responsible for agency development must assess community needs and opportunities for covering costs simultaneously. This calls for a means of analyzing the range of possibilities for generating resources of money, volunteers, and in-kind donations.

Segmentation of the Resource/Donor Market

We can also apply segmentation in order to understand the range of possibilities for agency revenue. It is helpful to think of this dimension in the broadest possible terms, as a sort of universe of resource possibilities, a resource/donor market. In theory, any agency has access to only three major categories of potential revenue: government or public funders; private funders such as foundations, United Ways, individuals, and other contributors; and self-generated sources of income from fees, memberships, earned interest, and so forth. For many community agencies, private in-kind donations and contributions of volunteer time are significant sources of support, and these should be retained in our conceptual scheme.

As can be seen in Figure 8.4, the resource/donor market can also be systematically organized and further segmented to identify and examine a range of possibilities for support. Public sources, for instance, can be separated into the three primary categories of federal, state, and local (county or municipal) government. Taking just the state level as an example, we can further analyze its possibilities by developing a series of secondary and even tertiary categories of departments, bureaus, or agencies that offer grants or purchase of service contracts for which nonprofits are eligible to apply or bid. An example of this kind of segmentation of funding opportunities at the state level (for Pennsylvania) appears in Figure 8.5.

Just as we have done for the category of public funding, we can segment other categories. Within the field of private funding, the foundation segment can be broken down into small local or family foundations, community foundations, larger regional foundations, and foundations of national or international standing.

Similarly, business donors run from small businesses to larger businesses of local, regional, national, or multinational orientation. Many large corporations have established foundations as vehicles for corporate philanthropy in addition to what they may contribute out of annual community relations or marketing departmental budgets. Clubs and civic associations can be understood through a similar kind of analysis, as can sectarian philanthropies. Charitable giving within the Catholic Church, for example, can be examined at the level of the parish, diocese, archdiocese, or at the national and international levels.

Federated giving, sectarian and nonsectarian, refers to umbrella fund-raising efforts, such as United Way, the Federation of Jewish Philanthropies, and Catholic Charities. Other federated, workplace solicitation programs are now emerging, such as women's funds, the Black United Fund, and other alternative funds.

The last major category of the resource/donor market is self-generated funds. This entails what the U.S. Bureau of Internal Revenue terms "related" and

Figure 8.4
Segmentation of the Resource/Donor Market

PUBLIC
SOURCES

FEDERAL GOVERNMENT

STATE GOVERNMENT

LOCAL GOVERNMENT
County
Municipal

PRIVATE
SOURCES

(cash &
in-kind)

FEDERATED DONOR ORGANIZATIONS
United Ways (membership; affiliate
grants; donor option)
Black United Fund
Other special federated funds (women's)

FOUNDATIONS
Community, regional, corporate,
national/international

CHURCH-RELATED ORGANIZATIONS
Local churches, dioscesan, regional/national
umbrellas, ecumenical & special funds

CORPORATE DONORS
Local, small businesses, large corporations
(local, regional or home offices)

CLUBS & CIVIC ASSOCIATIONS
Lions, Elks, Rotary, etc.
Professional associations (legal, medical)

INDIVIDUAL DONORS
Annual fund, phonathons, etc.
Volunteer labor

SELF-GENERATED
SOURCES

MEMBERSHIPS
Individual, institutional

FUNDRAISING EVENTS/ACTIVITIES
Benefits, annual dinners, festivals, etc.

ASSETS MANAGEMENT
Space & equipment rentals
Interest bearing accounts

BUSINESSES
Related: fees for service, user fees,
proceeds from program activities, etc.
Unrelated: taxable, for-profit subsidiaries

Figure 8.5
**Segmentation of the Resource/Donor Market in Pennsylvania: The Public
Segment at the State Level**

PUBLIC: FEDERAL

          STATE (Pennsylvania)
             Dept. of Public Welfare
             Dept. of Aging
             Dept. of Education
             Dept. of Energy
             Dept. of Community Affairs
                  Bureau of Recreation
                  Bureau of Housing
                  Bureau of Human Resources
                  (State office of economic opportunity)
                      Div. of Federal Programs
                          Weatherization
                          Community Services (Community Services Act)
                      Div. of State Programs
                          Urban Assistance (Cash Grants)
                          Community Conservation (Cash Grants)
                          Training Employment & Manpower (TEAM)

          LOCAL/COUNTY

          LOCAL/MUNICIPAL

PRIVATE: FOUNDATIONS

          BUSINESS

          FEDERATED

          CHURCH-RELATED/RELIGIOUS

          CLUBS & CIVIC ASSOCIATIONS

          INDIVIDUAL DONORS

SELF-
GENERATED: RELATED BUSINESS
 (earned   member dues
  income)   fees for service
               other

          UNRELATED BUSINESS

"unrelated" earned income. Monies derived from business activities connected with an agency's mission are termed related. These include fees for services, discussed earlier in the chapter; sales that represent relatively minor fund-raising efforts; interest earned on agency bank accounts; and proceeds from business activities that are clearly within the guidelines for nonprofit status. Examples of such business activities include the rental of extra space to another nonprofit, or home repair services provided by agency client-trainees.

Once again, it is important not to overlook either labor donated by volunteers or materials and services donated in kind. Potentially, each of these represents an area of opportunity for generating resources that could play a part in implementing desired service activities. There are, for instance, many community organizations across the country that have substantially improved blighted urban neighborhoods by repairing homes primarily using volunteer power and donated materials.

A MARKETING INFORMATION SYSTEM FOR COMMUNITY AGENCIES

To a great extent, agencies rely on information to formulate viable program and agency development strategies. Kotler has recognized this in formulating a "marketing information system" (1975, chapter 6). Marketing professionals in the commercial sector often employ a formalized system built upon internal records, marketing intelligence, formal market research, and data analysis. Agency managers, planners, and fund-raisers often have an intuitive grasp of community needs, but they especially crave information about funding possibilities. We can adapt the approach and system used in the commercial sector to fit the realities of life in the small, community nonprofit. We should keep in mind that for it to be really useful to us, the system should account for both dimensions of our bifurcated universe of opportunity more fully than does Kotler's scheme in its original form. The four levels of the system described above—records, research, intelligence, and analysis—do have analogs on both the client/service and resource/donor sides.

Internal Records

Records, sometimes called "results data," pertain, on the client/service side, to the previous and current service experience of the agency. Results data can include program case information both in individual and aggregated forms. These data are often summarized in monthly, quarterly, or yearly reports to boards and funders. Along with fiscal information on things like cost per unit of service, cost per placement or cost per client/outcome, this kind of information can be very useful in helping to make a case for new or extended service initiatives.

On the resource/donor side, records consist of old and current program plans and budgets, old and current donor lists and data, previous grant proposals and solicitations (including those that failed), and tabulations of volunteer efforts and prior in-kind contributions. The program files, correspondence file, or Rolodex containing funder contact information are also key elements of the marketing information system's records component.

Marketing Intelligence

Marketing intelligence, also called "happenings data," partially entails client and/or community feedback on agency programming and emergent community needs. Information that surfaces in meetings of agency board or staff members may often pertain to new or unmet needs or qualitative changes in programming that are called for. Needs information can arise from any number of sources inside or outside the agency. It is important to note that, to a considerable degree, community-based organizations along with religious organizations often function as a sort of "early warning system" for society's problems at the local level. The responses of churches, community organizations, and informally organized volunteer groups to such problems as child care, urban blight, and homelessness generally have preceded those of government and institutionalized philanthropy by several years. The ability of smaller, locally based agencies to remain in close touch with community networks through direct personal contact is one of their strongest characteristics. These community ties are a primary source of ideas for new programs and services.

In the category of resources, intelligence can include any sources of information that reveal "what's going on" in a field and among funders. This includes published information, public relations and informational materials, verbal communiqués, and even "scuttlebutt." One can keep in touch with government funding opportunities by looking at federal and state legislative annals and budgets, all of which are available to any good public or university library, or digests of government activity often published by state United Way organizations or associations of human service professionals. Trade publications, books, journals, and newsletters are increasingly available on a specialized industry basis. Further, directories of government, foundation, corporate, and even sectarian funding activities have proliferated during the last ten years.

The next level of written information entails public agency, foundation, corporate, and federated giving indexes and annual reports detailing funding patterns of the previous year. Each of these sources provides the kind of information that can contribute to the creation of a sort of prospectus for funding particular categories of programs identified as potentially responsive to community needs.

The trick, of course, is to stay current and on the "cutting edge." Generally, it is good practice to identify and get on the mailing lists of any government offices, foundations, and corporate donors that fund services related to an agency's basic mission. In this way funding guidelines, requests for proposals, and changes in regulations should be received well in advance of deadlines.

It is often possible to keep in touch with grant programs through periodic discussions with program officers, bureaucrats, politicians, and colleagues. Since block granting became pervasive in 1982, much of the action for CBOs has been at the county or local level. Officials at these levels are often far more accessible than their federal or state counterparts. Federated giving sources such as United Ways and community chests nearly always have an extensive volunteer committee structure. It is good policy to have agency board or staff members participate in some aspect of these activities on a volunteer basis and to know the decision makers. In many instances, public and private funders hold information sessions, seminars, or workshops where funding officers are present, and attendance at these can be quite beneficial. In some locales, a good daily newspaper can also provide invaluable information on trends, shifts, and specific opportunities for public and private funding.

Needless to say, it requires time, dedication, and intensive research to acquire a detailed understanding of each segment of the resource market for CBOs. The nature of the field is such that only constant attention and an ''ear to the ground'' enable one to keep up with new opportunities, changes in eligibility guidelines, emerging priorities, and the inside politics of the world of public and private grants.

Market Research

Market research and analysis go hand in hand. What is emphasized here is an organizational perspective that seeks to rationalize the way in which any organization attends to selecting its exchange partners and structuring its relations with them and other actors in its environment. Thus, according to the accepted wisdom of the field, a marketing orientation adheres to the philosophy that the main task of the organization is to systematically determine the needs and wants of target markets and satisfy them through the design, communication, pricing, and delivery of goods and services in order to fulfill its mission (Kotler, 1975, p. 23). For the community agency, then, this means that the needs of both clients and funders must be well researched and understood, and then matched through the process of program design, budgeting, proposal writing, and program implementation. An analytic marketing system is some technique or combination of techniques that allows us to make sense of the available information in order to come to intelligent decisions about how to formulate a service program that will be of use to an identified, prospective client constituency on one hand, and a prospective funder or set of funders on the other. As preoccupied as we may be with bringing in revenues, it should be remembered that many funded programs have failed because of an inability to interest and engage sufficient numbers of clients.

For the client/service component, research entails gathering either quantitative or qualitative needs assessment data about the nature of community problems and service issues. On the resource side, we must carefully review information obtained from potential funders, essentially their past history, policies, and regulations, as well as their current priorities and guidelines.

ANALYSIS AND TARGET MARKETING

As, it is hoped, we have begun to see, the community service agency exists only insofar as it is able to identify the needs of both market dimensions simultaneously and to marry those needs in its own activities through the medium of mediated or indirect exchange. This, in fact, is about as close as we have come so far to defining the kind of enterprise through which community service agencies sustain themselves and their mission of service. But to help round out the picture, we need to understand in more detail how a community service venture is developed into a program and finally, how an agency uses information to make good, systematic decisions and puts programs together to make a life for itself as an organization.

Recall Kotler's definition of marketing. For both theorists and practitioners the key phrase in this definition is likely to be *voluntary exchanges of values with target markets*. Target marketing is a set of techniques aimed at differentiating and selecting various segments of any market as a basis for focused efforts. We have begun to see how both dimensions of the market for CBOs can be segmented. Once we have redefined our approach to segmenting community agency markets and completed our information gathering, we can go on to do the analyses needed to target particular client and service niches, and to choose appropriate resource providers to target for program and agency support.

A comparatively simple procedure, the market review, can help to identify where the agency stands in relation to the range of possibilities for programming and generating support. This kind of review helps to organize thinking around the current status of programming as compared with new categories of programs and services, which an assessment of community need might suggest. We examine basic categories of service as they emerge from research and compare them with what the agency is now doing and what we are learning about community issues and problems. Like our concept of community agency markets, our review is a two-track process, and the review can be applied to an entire agency or just a single area of service.

First, we look at the kinds of clientele targeted and current service activities, as compared with the array of possible program and client types and their more discrete segments (as in Figures 8.6 and 8.7). Segmentation of clients is by identified characteristics. Client characteristics are primarily demographic and include the things mentioned previously, such as age, sex, marital status, socioeconomic status, and so forth. Additionally, we add such considerations as ethnicity, geographic focus (i.e., urban, suburban, or rural) and program scope (i.e., individual, family, or mixed), since these factors help us to identify discrete client segments that may have been previously overlooked.

At this first level of analysis, services are categorized under higher-order

Figure 8.6
Client/Service Market Review Scheme for a Community Service Agency or Program: Client Segment

---

Agency Review ___
Program Review ___
Title: _____

		CURRENT CLIENT SEGMENT	PROJECTED CLIENT SEGMENT

CLIENT TYPES

AGE GROUP — children / youth / adult / elderly / advanced elderly

SEX — male / female

MARITAL STATUS — single / married

SOCIOECONOMIC STATUS — low income / middle income

EMPLOYMENT STATUS — employed / unemployed / underemployed

EDUCATION STATUS — elementary / middle school / high school/equivalency / vocational/trade or technical / college

SERVICE SCOPE — individual / family / mixed

GEOGRAPHIC SCOPE — urban / suburban / rural / mixed

ETHNIC FOCUS — white/Anglo / white/ethnic / African-American / Latino / Asian-American / Native American / other: _____

Note: Respond by checking off appropriate current and projected client characteristics.

Figure 8.7
Client/Service Market Review Scheme: Program Segment

Agency Review ___		
Program Review ___	**CURRENT**	**PROJECTED**
Title: _____	**CLIENT**	**CLIENT**
	SEGMENT	**SEGMENT**

PROGRAM SEGMENTS

ADVOCACY/EMPOWERMENT/SOCIAL CHANGE
EDUCATION
EMERGENCY SERVICE
EMPLOYMENT
ENERGY
HEALTH
HOUSING & COMMUNITY DEVELOPMENT
LEGAL AID
PUBLIC SAFETY/PROTECTION
RECREATION
SENIOR'S SERVICES
SOCIAL SERVICES
SPECIAL SERVICES FOR WOMEN
TRANSPORTATION

Note: Respond by checking off current and possible program segments.

program categories. Figure 8.7 includes most but not all possible program categories. The breakdown is intended to be logical and generic, but an alternate scheme of categorization would certainly be imaginable. Within each program category are discrete services that will ultimately be pinpointed in program planning. Suffice it to say that each category could be further broken down into any number of possible services. The housing category, for instance, contains services such as housing counseling, housing rehabilitation, home repair, transitional housing, and housing for the elderly and handicapped to name a few. Establishing a viable, fundable array of services for an agency is based upon careful selection of program categories that become something akin to an agency's "product line." This is an important issue for long-term agency development, and is treated more extensively in the concluding section of this chapter.

At the same time, we are concerned with priorities and guidelines for potential funding. Just as we have used a market review format to begin analyzing clients and services, at the same time we can review where the agency is in relation to the universe of possibilities for resource generation. Figure 8.8 shows a simple adaptation of the resource/donor market schema shown earlier applied to an urban agency providing shelter and services for the homeless. Columns have been added for financial data and percentages of an agency budget. The value

Figure 8.8

Analysis of Current Status of an Urban Agency Providing Shelter for the Homeless in Relation to Resource/Donor Opportunities

RESOURCE CATEGORY	SOURCE	CURRENT FUNDING	% OF TOTAL BUDGET
PUBLIC			
Federal Government	• Federal Emergency Management Agency-FEMA • U.S. HUD	$20,000 0	3% 0
State Government	• State Dept. of Community Services • State Dept. of Public Welfare	0 0	0 0
Local Government	• City Dept. of Welfare • City Community Development Block Grant	350,000 0	54% 0
	TOTAL PUBLIC	$370,000	57%
PRIVATE			
Federated Giving	• United Fund • Black United Fund	$80,000 0	12% 0
Corporate	• major corporate donors • professional associations • area small businesses	20,000 0 0	4 0 0

Foundations		
• Do-Good Foundation	5,000	1
• Very rich Family Foundation	60,000	9
• other small local foundations (rec'd)	6,000	1
• other local foundations (projected)	73,000	11
Church-Related Donors		
• area congregations	15,000	2
• national umbrellas	0	0
Civic Organizations	0	0
Individuals		
• Christmas mail solicitations	14,000	2
• special events (concert, dance)	0	0
TOTAL PRIVATE	$273,000	42%

SELF-GENERATED

Related Business		
• interest from reserve	$5,000	1%
• fees for services provided	0	0
• space rental income	0	0
Unrelated Business		
• None	0	0
TOTAL SELF-GENERATED	$5,000	1%
TOTAL	$648,000	100%

Figure 8.9

Analysis of Resource Opportunities by Category for an Urban Agency Providing Shelter for the Homeless

RESOURCE CATEGORY	PROSPECTIVE SOURCES	PROJECTED AMOUNTS
PUBLIC		
Federal Government	• HUD	$ 250,000 (3 year)
State Governmen	• Public Welfare (Bridge Housing)	50-75,000
Local Government	• Community Services (Urban Assist)	20-30,000
	• none	
PRIVATE		
Federated Giving	• United Fund	50-75,000 (new $)
	• Black United Fund	0
Corporate	• 1 major corporate partnership (Megabuxs Intl. Ins. Corp.)	75-100,000
	• 1 professional group (e.g., law firms)	2,000 from 10 firms
	• area businesses	500 from 50

Foundations	• 1 major national foundation, multiyear model program grant Trans. Housing/Services	50-300,000
	• local foundation	100,000 annually
	• other local foundations (projected)	
Church-Related Donors	• area congregations	45,000
	• national umbrellas	???
	(Campaign Human Development, etc.)	
Civic Organizations	• Elks, Lions, Rotary, etc.	10,000
Individuals	• "Friends of the Shelter" (annual giving, direct mail)	50,000
	• planned giving solicitation	N/A
	• annual telephone campaign	N/A
	• special events (concert, dance)	25,000
SELF-GENERATED		
Related Business	• interest from reserves	5,000 annually
	• fees for services provided	N/A
Unrelated	• not recommended now	N/A

143

of this worksheet lies in its identification of where an agency's revenues are concentrated and where new opportunities for diversification may exist.

An integrative analytic approach has us looking simultaneously at both dimensions of prospective agency exchange. In other words, we look at broadly identified categories of community need and general areas of donor interest. We might take the preceding analysis of current status and project what opportunities are open and what level of potential support exists for agency programming. This process is illustrated in Figure 8.9 for the same emergency shelter we examined above. Having matched prospective program categories with one or more possible public or private funders, we then proceed to refine our projected program/client categorization by specifying prospective client characteristics and specific new service types within a program category. This specification is informed by what we know about the parameters of possible sources of support. For example, we might specify a neighborhood chore service for the elderly with the prospect of approaching the state department of services for the aging and a private foundation devoted to supporting programs for seniors but currently interested in promoting independent living.

As the analysis progresses, we are able to begin sketching out program or service plans, moving to greater levels of specificity in terms of program goals, objectives, methods, outcomes, and costs. The results of this process of analysis should be a program plan outline with a basic statement of overall goals, tentative objectives, and projected service outcomes. It should also produce an initial program budget with line item costs roughed out and a best-guess program budget listing likely targets for public, private, and self-generated revenues.

These considerations provide the basis for formulating what marketers call the "marketing mix" (Kotler, 1975, pp. 107–9). Traditionally referred to as "the four Ps" of marketing, the commercial marketing mix is essentially a strategy that carefully blends the elements of product, pricing, placement, and promotion. Product entails the nature and features of the item being offered. Price refers to just that, the cost at which the item will be offered, while placement refers to where and when the product will be available. Finally, promotion entails the efforts that go into stimulating interest on the part of prospective buyers. It can include such activities as advertising and publicity, as well as personal selling.

As with other marketing concepts, the marketing mix concept can be adapted to the concerns of the community-based organization by turning attention to both clients and funders. Key decisions are defining the basic unit of service for any program effort and figuring out just what methods will be used to carry out the program. The concerns of funders are often different or at least cast in different terms. Defining the "product," i.e., service, in such a way as to appeal to both clients and potential funders is one of the most challenging and creative parts of community agency life. A large part of making a good idea reality in this arena lies in the ability to articulate the idea in language that will appeal to both audiences. Even if the service idea is the same, the language used to target clients and funders seldom is identical. Just imagine service recipients trying to make their way through a government or foundation grant proposal!

Pricing of a program and its various cost components is expressed in the costs per participant or per unit of service delivery. It is also apparent in the specific line items any prospective funder is offered in a program budget. Overall program and unit costs should normally be comparable to other similar programs in the field. Research should yield a good feel for the kinds of priorities, guidelines, and restrictions of different funders and donors, and this information should guide decision making. Every line item in every proposal budget submitted should be the result of careful consideration. New programs that combine several sources of potential support—including some of the agency's own funds—prove to be more attractive to funders, and this is a part of pricing, too.

Promotion also applies along both the client and funder/donor dimensions. Promotion of programs within the community is normally called "outreach." Advertising, community meetings, networking with other community institutions (schools, churches, etc.), agency open-house events and other means help to get the word out and interest prospective clients who might benefit from agency service provision. Many funded programs have ultimately failed due to a lack of client interest that might be attributable to a failure to do adequate outreach.

Promotion within the resource market is comprised of several activities. Personal contacts in meetings or on the telephone, correspondence, and other mail contacts utilizing agency brochures, annual reports, news clippings, and program documentation can all help to promote funder interest. Much, of course, rests upon the creation of well-wrought case statement and proposal materials. In some instances influential contacts can make up for a poorly written proposal, but without good support from community leaders, the best proposals are likely to fail.

Finally, placement is no less operative in this field than in any commercial setting. Timing and carefully locating the launching of a new service can make the difference in terms of client participation. Choices must be made as to when the agency is truly ready to take on a new service. Too often these choices are made in a reactive mode. At the same time, learning when to submit requests for funding or donor support—timing proposal submissions—is critical. Information-gathering on funders should help govern these decisions. And even under the constant pressures that typify community agency life, a little time must be devoted to making an annual funding plan and a calendar for grant submission deadlines.

AN EXAMPLE OF THE COMMUNITY AGENCY MARKETING PROCESS

Taking once again the example we have repeatedly used, if we were in the agency that received and served the woman described, we might have observed that she and many others like her in our geographic area of service are poor and unemployed partially as a result of never having developed the self-confidence to face entry into the world of work. In fact, there are almost no available programs in the area that serve this population, which is now facing a tightening of general assistance and child assistance eligibility guidelines. Despite a mandate for able-bodied mothers to seek work, it is clear that employability in this group is comparatively limited. Further, there are few if any available day care slots priced according to ability to pay, so even a woman motivated and qualified to work could not. We might decide that, in order to address the underlying issues, it would be beneficial to attempt a program combining individual counseling, peer sessions, and career motivation workshops with job readiness and placement. Also, perhaps a cooperative day care agreement could be secured. By contacting officials at the local Office of Employment Security and the local Private Industry Council, we learn that the local unemployment rate of 5.4 percent is not shared equally by women or minorities. Black and Hispanic women currently have unemployment rates of 22 percent, not including those who have stopped looking and dropped out of the workforce. A review of census tract figures for our area shows a high proportion of women just like this who live nearby. We have our program staff interview about fifty, using church ministers to help identify them, and find that our theory about low self-confidence appears to be true. We resolve to bring the issue up at the next meeting of the agency's board.

But that is at least two weeks away. Meanwhile, we review the community needs highlighted in the most recent report of the priorities and planning committee of our local United Fund. We see that self-sufficiency of single, low-income mothers on welfare is emphasized along with care for the infirm elderly and health promotion and protective services for children of youth at risk. We also note that a recent mailing from our program officer at the United Fund mentioned participation in United Way of America's Venture Grant program. As a member agency, our current level of funding is modest, covering some of our core budget for salaries and operations costs. However, the most recent campaign exceeded goals, and a well-justified increase might be a possibility.

Next, a call to one of our colleagues working in the school system reveals that the county Office of Employment Services has been allocated Federal Job Training Partnership Act funds, passed down through the state, which are designed to assist the "structurally unemployed" improve their employability. These funds may be spoken for, but that is uncertain. We place a call to that office and request that the most recent annual report and policy and funding guidelines, as well as any requests for proposals (RFPs), be mailed out as quickly as possible.

At this point, we head to our nearest university library's reference section. There, we locate and examine the latest edition of our state's *Guide to Foundation Funding*. Using the index, we locate a cross-section of large and small foundations that have funded programs for women, minorities, and the poor. We note program titles and descriptions, examine eligibility guidelines, and note which agencies were funded and the amounts awarded. Further, we glance at the listings of trustees and record the submission deadlines and requirements. One foundation is a past supporter of women's centers and programs of advocacy for minority women. One or two others appear to be investors in substantive programs of education for low-income populations. Returning to the office, we send out a letter requesting the annual report and guidelines for each of these.

Early the next week, the outline of a possible program plan begins to emerge as shown in Figure 8.10.

During the next few weeks, this plan will be refined to accommodate some specific funder guidelines as they become clearer. Following initial telephone or mail requests for information, the executive director will send letters of inquiry or ask for preliminary meetings to discuss the outlines of the project. For each of these sources, a different proposal will ultimately be drawn up in keeping with the various formats and requirements. Additionally, in making the written case for support, we will make every attempt to focus on the priorities, guidelines, restrictions, and implicit values gleaned from all available sources of information. Proposals to the government sources will give extra attention to internal mechanisms for insuring agency accountability.

To account for some restrictions in what the government sources are willing to cover, proposals will be drawn up with certain line items included in the United Fund and foundation proposals but excluded from others. The state Office of Economic Opportunity provides funding to promote upward mobility in low-income neighborhoods. Its policy priorities are connected to helping the poor adjust to a tightening of state welfare guidelines. It is willing to allow for 25 percent of its funding to cover administrative costs. The county's employment programs are carried out under federal standards and guidelines that are focused on a minimum standard of 60 percent job placements out of all employment program participants. Funding is according to a range of cost per trainee and cost per placement with relative budgetary freedom.

A review of guidelines and other information about private funders reveals another set of concerns. For example, the Do-good Foundation is committed to community self-help through voluntary organizations, but will not pay for any agency overhead at all, just "program costs." In the case of the United Fund, the agency had been receiving $28,300 for general funding of all its programs. The agency will attempt to use the proposed new initiative as a means to increase its annual allocation to $35,500, arguing that the program is in line with identified community need and in keeping with targeted self-sufficiency goals.

In the case of the foundation and United Way, the role of the agency's volunteer board of directors will be emphasized. Exemplifying the role of personal selling in the field, the agency's president and treasurer and the executive director will attend a meeting with the foundation's program officer and try their best to convey the potential for community improvement they feel the program represents. The foundation officer will be invited to visit the agency and its programs in the near future. The board representatives will also speak on behalf of the proposed new program at the agency's annual United Fund Allocations Com-

Figure 8.10
WOMEN IMPROVING NOW Program Plan and Budget (Tentative)

PROGRAM GOAL

To provide services that will result in increased self-esteem and job readiness for low-income, single mothers living in the inner city.

OBJECTIVES

1) Series of 12 weeks of workshops designed to build self-esteem, and foster career exploration and job readiness for 25 women.

2) Weekly peer support group focused on sharing experiences of single parenthood, welfare dependency, status as minority females, etc. Cooperative child care to be organized.

3) Job placement for 15. Placement of 5 others in training or further education.

PROJECT BUDGET (tentative)

EXPENSES

Executive Director (10% @ $27,500)	$ 2,750
Program Coordinator (50% @ $20,000)	10,000
Counselor	16,500
Admin. Asst. (20% @ 14,000)	2,800
Benefits/withholding (18%)	5,769
Fiscal Services ($40/mo.)	480
Rent/Utilities ($75/mo.)	900
Telephone ($30/mo.)	360
Postage	25
Printing/Duplication	50
Travel (200 miles/month @ .205/mile)	492
Insurance ($55/month)	660
TOTAL	**$40,786**

REVENUES

County Office of Employment	18,500
State Office of Economic Opportunity	12,500
United Fund	7,200
Do-good Foundation (or Bigbucks Fund)	2,000
Metropolitan Utility, Inc. (printing/postage in-kind)	75
Board reserve fund	500
Bank interest	101
TOTAL	**$40,786**

mittee hearing. There, the treasurer will emphasize that the effort is intended to be a partnership between the agency, its clients, and the prospective funding sources.

The executive director, who has run the agency for several years now, will modify the budgets of each different proposal, following the 10/8/6 Rule. That rule of conservative agency contingency planning recommends that one "ask for 10, hope for 8, but be prepared to live with 6." This practice helps to mitigate the risk and uncertainty that are endemic to the nonprofit world, but seldom adequately addressed. Thus she will slightly inflate each request for funding and deflate expected support from each other source. She will also have as many alternative funding options as she can identify. Because it is unlikely that major funders other than those already identified will emerge within the agency's locale, she will assess the possibility of funding the program by generating many more small requests if necessary. If the projected primary sources of support are forthcoming, the immediate marketing challenge will have substantially been met. But if the project does get funded and off the ground programmatically, the more daunting challenge of sustaining the program—and the agency—over the long term will remain to be solved.

STRATEGIES FOR INTERIM AND LONG-RANGE ACTIVITY

Committing Adequate Resources to the Marketing Function

In many human service endeavors—and in the preponderance of nonprofit literature—the preeminence of voluntarism is something of an enduring myth. When an organization makes a move into the world of program grants and purchase of service contracts, paid staffing becomes a necessity in order to manage the operation, guarantee a consistency of service delivery and quality, and meet contractual obligations for service provision (Milofsky, 1980).

As research is increasingly revealing (Fink, 1989; Herman and Heimovics, 1986), the executive director is often the central figure in the community-based nonprofit. Much as is commonly found in small businesses, it is that person upon whom the life of the organization depends. It is this writer's experience that, to a great degree, it is the agency executive who provides the vision and the drive for agency development, and who bears the burden of risk and uncertainty that every small nonprofit faces with each impending fiscal year.

In the majority of instances, it is also the agency manager who is responsible for the agency's marketing function, formulating new program ideas and packaging them in such a way as to appeal to clients and funders. Marketers like to emphasize having an adequate level of expenditure to cover the costs of marketing. For the CBO, those costs are primarily expressed in terms of the time required to carry out all of the tasks discussed in the preceding sections. Too often, the overextended executive director is unable to devote sufficient time and energy to handling the various aspects of that function, though it most surely constitutes the basis for continued agency growth and development.

Perhaps the first step toward solving this problem is to acknowledge it for what it is. The marketing function should not be a nonassigned or residual responsibility. Rather, it should be a central part of agency planning and should be reflected in at least one if not more paid staff or volunteer job descriptions. Various tasks can be delegated, and a team effort is optimal, but one person, usually the agency executive, needs to have the overview and to put together the elements of the agency's "market offers" to clients and funders. If an agency is lucky enough to have a board member who is knowledgeable about the grants world and its procedures, that person can be extremely valuable. Agencies that are prosperous enough might have a part-time or full-time planner / grant writer. In any case, agency survival, let alone growth, will be severely constrained without a clear investment in the marketing process.

Diversification of Programs and Revenues over Time

The long-term challenge for the community agency executive and board is to develop and implement a strategy or plan whereby exchange relationships with program recipients and funders will serve to enable the agency to pursue its mission of service from year to year. As with proprietary firms, an agency's potential for growth and sustenance will depend upon its mission and the extent of community need. But it will also depend upon the availability of and competition for funding in its particular geographic locale and an agency's ability to pursue opportunities and overcome constraints.

While many community service agencies start with a single purpose, service, or program based upon start-up money from one source such as an initial donation, foundation seed grant, or government contract, few continue in this fashion for very long. Many or most organizations soon adopt a statement of purpose or mission. Mission provides a basis for agency activity, and from it often spring multiple activities, programs, and/or services. In response to a variety of factors—newly identified needs, a desire for growth, or shifting opportunities for funding support—most nonprofits soon take on multiple goals and acquire multiple sources of support.

Diversification of programs and support in the right combinations can be said to be a desirable goal for the community service organization, in that it strengthens an agency's ability to serve the community and to sustain itself as an entity in order to continue doing so (James, 1983; Seltzer, 1987). Achieving this balance entails finding and sustaining the right mix of programs and support. Therein, a combination of community needs and the multiple "needs" of government and philanthropy are joined through the programmatic activities of the community service agency. This constitutes a kind of enterprise unique to the nonprofit sector. In fact, it is this ongoing choice of activities in relation to mission, constraints, and opportunities described earlier—along with the facilitation of the complex of mediated transactions this choice implies—that lies at the heart of community agency marketing and the nonprofit enterprise.

REFERENCES

American Association of Fund Raising Counsel, Inc. (1988). *Giving USA: 1987 Annual report*. New York: AAFRC.

Berger, P. L., and J. Neuhaus (1977). *To empower people: The role of mediating structures in public policy*. Washington, DC: American Enterprise Institute.

Blau, P. L. (1964). *Exchange and power in social life*. San Francisco: Chandler Publishing Company.

Boulding, K. (1973). *The economy of love and fear: A preface to grants economics*. Belmont, CA: Wadsworth Publishing Company.

Crimmins, J. C., and M. Keil (1983). *Enterprise in the nonprofit sector*. Washington, DC: Partners for Livable Places; New York: Rockefeller Brothers Fund.

Fink, J. (1989). Community agency boards of directors: Viability and vestigiality, substance and symbol. In R. D. Herman and J. Van Til, eds., *Nonprofit boards of directors: Analyses and applications*, pp. 89–117. New Brunswick, NJ: Transaction Books.

Gassler, R. S. (1986). *The economics of nonprofit enterprise*. Lanham, MD: University Press of America.

Hansmann, H. (1980). The role of nonprofit enterprise. *Yale Law Journal* 89, 835–901.
———. (1987). Economic theories of nonprofit organization. In W. W. Powell, ed., *The nonprofit sector: A research handbook* (pp. 27–42). New Haven: Yale University Press.

Herman, R. D., and R. D. Heimovics (1986). Critical events in the management of nonprofit organizations: initial evidence. Paper presented at the 1986 annual meeting of the Association of Voluntary Action Scholars, Harrisburg, PA.

Homans, G. (1958). Social behavior as exchange. *American Journal of Sociology* 63, 597–606.

James, E. (1983). How nonprofits grow: A model. *Journal of Policy Analysis and Management* 2, 350–65.

Kiritz, N. (1979). *Program planning and proposal writing*. Los Angeles: The Grantsmanship Center.

Kotler, P. (1975). *Marketing for nonprofit organizations*. Englewood Cliffs, NJ: Prentice-Hall.

Kramer, R. (1987). Voluntary agencies and the social services. In W. W. Powell, ed., *The nonprofit sector: A research handbook* (pp. 240–57). New Haven: Yale University Press.

Lauffer, A. (1984). *Strategic marketing for not-for-profit organizations*. New York: Free Press.

Lovelock, C. H., and C. B. Weinberg (1984). *Marketing for public and nonprofit managers*. New York: John Wiley.

Mauss, M. *The Gift* (1954). Glencoe, IL: Free Press.

Milofsky, C. (1980). *Structure and process in self-help organizations: Working paper # 17.* New Haven: Yale University, Institute for Social Policy Studies.

———. (1987). Neighborhood-based organizations: A market analogy. In W. W. Powell, ed., *The nonprofit sector: A research handbook* (pp.277–95). New Haven: Yale University Press.

O'Connell, B. (1983). *America's voluntary spirit.* New York: The Foundation Center.

Salamon, L. M. (1987). Partners in public service: The scope and theory of government-nonprofit relations. In W. W. Powell, ed., *The nonprofit sector: A research handbook* (pp. 99–117). New Haven: Yale University Press.

———. (1989). The voluntary sector and the future of the welfare state. In *1988 Spring research forum working papers.* Washington, DC: Independent Sector.

Seltzer, M. (1987). *Securing your organization's future.* New York: The Foundation Center.

Skloot, E. (1988). *The nonprofit entrepreneur.* New York: The Foundation Center.

United Way of America (1976). *UWASIS II.* Alexandria, VA: United Way of America.

Weisbrod, B. (1977). *The voluntary nonprofit sector.* Lexington, MA: D. C. Heath.

White, P. E., S. Levine, and G. Vlasak (1980). Exchange as a conceptual framework for understanding interorganizational relationships: Application to nonprofit organizations. In A. R. Negandhi, ed., *Interorganizational theory* (pp. 182–95). Kent, OH: Kent State University Press.

Wolch, J. R. (1985). The urban voluntary sector: An exploration of basic issues. In Tobin, G. A., ed., *Social planning and human service delivery in the voluntary sector* (pp. 29–45). Westport, CT: Greenwood Press.

Wolpert, J., and T. Reiner (1985). The nonprofit sector in stable and growing metropolitan areas. *Urban Affairs Quarterly* 20, 487–510.

Young, D. R. (1987). Executive leadership in nonprofit organizations. In W. W. Powell, ed., *The nonprofit sector: A research handbook* (pp. 167–79). New Haven: Yale University Press.

9

Operations Planning and Control

PRAFULLA JOGLEKAR

Although work in human service organizations (HSOs) can be very rewarding, it can—like any other work—have its share of frustrations. Internal inefficiencies that interfere with doing one's job well can be particularly frustrating. For example, employees may complain about having to take too much time to complete client reports, not having such simple technological support as automatic telephone dialers or word processing equipment, not knowing what procedures to follow when certain recurrent problems arise, being short on help during peak hours, running out of supplies when they are most needed, and even having to walk too far to talk to the most frequently visited colleagues.

It seems that work specialization is a foreign concept to many HSOs. I have heard many executive directors confess that they have no time for long-range or strategic planning since they do their own paperwork, typing, and cleaning.

Similarly, active and planned employee training is not very common among the HSOs. How many times have you encountered a new colleague trying to rediscover the wheel in developing his or her own procedures for dealing with standard (typical) situations?

Some of the most common frustrations of HSO workers are expressed as

"If only my client knew exactly what his/her problem is,"

"If only my client would come to the point quickly,"

"If only my client were cooperative,"

"If only my client followed my advice."

Clearly, both the efficiency and the effectiveness of an employee-client interaction in an HSO depend upon the cooperation (i.e., the productive contribution) of the client. Yet, have HSOs thought of looking at their clients as productive resources to be trained, motivated, helped, and actively used (almost as if they were the employees) to contribute their full potential to the organization's efficiency and effectiveness?

Perhaps the most frustrating situation is an HSO's involvement in procedures and paperwork that could have been avoided altogether. I know of a newly appointed executive director of a mental health facility who, having discovered that the agency was using three pencils per employee per day, required that all supplies be kept under a lock and key, requested in writing, and issued by his secretary only after a review of the concerned employee's prior requests. This was clearly penny-wise and pound-foolish. The new procedure cost considerably more (in the paperwork and in the secretary's time) than the pencils ever did. None of the other supplies showed any reduction in consumption due to the new procedure. More importantly, the procedure created a serious morale problem since the employees felt that they were no longer trusted!

As I see it, these types of problems are more common with service industries in general, and HSOs in particular. The reason is that, traditionally, managers in these organizations have had little exposure to the concepts and techniques of operations planning and control (OPC), commonly known as "production management" in the manufacturing sector.

Courses in production management have always been mandatory in business administration curricula. The production function in an organization is responsible for the effective and efficient conversion of an organization's inputs into desired quantity and quality of outputs. In the manufacturing sector, this function has been recognized as the backbone of industrial revolution. However, over the last two decades, a number of scholars and innovative service managers have come to recognize that even in service industries, the central function is to convert an organization's inputs into desired outputs. In the service sector, inputs include the customer, the information and cooperation provided by the customer, and so forth, in addition to the standard inputs of capital, equipment, materials, supplies, employee skills and time, and management competencies. Desired outputs include services, client satisfaction, and funder satisfaction in addition to the standard outputs of goods, compliance with government regulations, profits or surplus, and so forth. It is recognized that the value of the outputs produced by an organization (whether measured in revenue dollars or in client satisfaction units) must be greater than the cost of the inputs it uses.

Insofar as the operations planning and control function focuses on maximizing the difference between the value of an organization's outputs and the cost of its inputs, its study is recognized to be vital for potential managers of service industries as well. Consequently, business schools across the nation have replaced their traditional production management courses with courses in production and operations management that cover the OPC function in both the manufacturing and the service industries. Indeed, today several business schools are offering more specialized courses in service operations management.

In what follows, I shall highlight some of the rich concepts and techniques from the literature on service operations management and discuss how these may apply in your HSO as well. Finally, I shall also discuss the inevitability of the application of these concepts and techniques for HSOs at large.

INCREASING EFFICIENCY IN SERVICE OPERATIONS

Theodore Levitt (1972, 1976) was perhaps the first one to point out that service industries can and should use the principles of production management so commonly used in the manufacturing industries. He noted that when faced with problems of efficiency and effectiveness, a manufacturing organization looks for solutions inside the very tasks to be done, whereas historically, services often looked for the solutions in the performer of the task. This approach kept the services from redesigning the tasks themselves, from creating new tools, processes and organizations, and from eliminating the conditions creating the problems. To appreciate the validity of this concept, all you need to do is to reflect on your own career in an HSO. When things went wrong, how many times were the problems blamed on your lack of motivation or skills, rather than on the way the tasks were designed?

Levitt gave several eye opening examples of efficient service operations such as those introduced by fast food restaurants, automatic car washes, airport X-ray surveillance equipment, automatic bank transaction machines, and fast, low-priced automobile repair shops for standardized repairs. For instance, he noted that in some automobile repair shops tasks are so carefully designed and standardized that workers with little education and a few days of training can easily perform them to the desired level of quality. Levitt also stressed the importance for several service industries of using the consumer as a productive resource. Self-service has become common in a number of service operations including supermarkets, bank transactions, and telephone dialing. Based on my earlier comments, I hope that you already recognize the importance of client cooperation in your operations.

Following up on Levitt, Chase (1976, 1982, 1984) distinguished between high-contact and low-contact service operations, and pointed out that a number of principles of mass production (including standardization of products, work specialization, automation of standardized operations, demand pooling, and economies of scale) could be used effectively to boost productivity in low-contact operations. According to Chase, consumer contact refers to the physical presence of the consumer in the system during the production of a service. The degree of consumer contact can be measured by the amount of time the consumer is in the system relative to the total service time.

Health centers, hotels, and public transportation are services characterized by high contact, whereas bank loan operations, and the sorting and delivery of mail are operations characterized by low contact. Chase observed that low-contact operations could be located in remote locations, standardized, and even automated to an extent. On the other hand, high-contact operations had to be located near the consumer, required workers with technical as well as behavioral skills who were paid for their time rather than output, and needed excess capacity to accommodate peak loads. He pointed out that Levitt's concept of using consumer self-service was almost unavoidable for efficient and effective performance in high-contact operations. You may want to identify the low-contact operations (minimally, the administrative operations) in your agency, and think about how they can be standardized, and/or automated. Also think of the ways to encourage client cooperation in the high-contact operations in your HSO. The suggestions from other authors below may help in this effort.

Lovelock and Young (1979) elaborated further on strategies that managers can employ to exploit the self-service concepts, such as developing client trust, understanding client habits, pretesting procedures and equipment, and teaching clients how to use service innovations. Gartner and Reissman (1977), Mills, Chase and Margulies (1983), and Schmenner (1986) represent other works that have suggested important ways of using the client as a productive resource.

Shostack (1984) pointed out that the engineering approach of designing a blueprint can work in the systematic design and control of a service delivery system as well. She pointed out that even in high-contact services, techniques such as "scripting dialogues" for various employee-client interaction situations, training the staff thoroughly, establishing procedures, keeping records, and monitoring performance can help improve the service delivery systems. Albrecht and Zemke (1985), Mabert (1982), and York (1985) also emphasize the need for planning the service delivery system.

DISTINCTIVE CHARACTERISTICS OF SERVICE ORGANIZATIONS

While much literature has focused on the similarities between service and manufacturing operations, a number of scholars have helped identify the many distinguishing features of service industries and their implications for the strategy and operations in service industries. Fuchs (1969) observed that the output of services is intangible and that service production is difficult to separate from the presence of the customer. Hyatt (1972) discussed the problems and the successes in setting productivity standards and increasing output in white-collar jobs (e.g., typing, phoning, mail opening, processing applications, etc.) in private as well as public sectors. He showed the feasibility and usefulness of such a "productivity push."

Still, the intangibility of service output continues to defy the complete application of manufacturing management principles to service industries. Nevertheless, substantial progress in the measurement of productivity in the service industries seems evident from the works of Adam, Hershauer, and Ruch (1981),

Buehler and Shetty (1981), Czepiel, Solomon, and Surprenant (1985), Fuchs (1969), Heaton (1977), Parks (1984), Reubens (1981), Rohrbaugh (1981), Rowe (1981), Longest (1977), Mark (1981), and Maister (1983). Hostage (1975), Human Services Research Institute (1983) and Adam, Hershauer, and Ruch emphasize the need for the measurement of quality in addition to productivity in service organizations. They also demonstrate some practical ways for such a measurement of quality and productivity. You may want to study this literature and see how you could measure and control the productivity and the quality of service in your organization.

The presence of the customer during the production of many services led Sasser (1976) to observe that in services, employees may be seen as minifactories in themselves. Their activities transcend mere production into the selling of the service. The presence of the customer during the production process also implies that unlike goods, services cannot be inventoried and service organizations must possess the equipment and labor capacities to meet peak demands. Fitzsimmons and Sullivan (1982) pointed out the time perishability of these excess capacities in service organizations and suggested several useful strategies, including smoothing the demand through reservations, appointments, price incentives, and so forth; adjusting short-term capacity through part-time help during peak periods and proper scheduling of work shifts; and increasing the self-service content of a service. Can you think of ways by which you could shift some of your peak-hour demand to off-peak hours? If your peak hours are predictable, you may want to schedule employee shifts so that more employees are available during those hours. Finally, as already mentioned, there may be a need for education, training, and motivating clients to be cooperative, if not self-servicing.

Although service industries do share a number of distinguishing characteristics, the fact that they are also very different from one another led Sasser, Olsen, and Wyckoff (1978) to present a collection of case studies of service industries. These cases may enable managers to discern the similarities of their situations with those faced by managers of other service organizations and thus identify common management principles. At the same time, these cases help managers develop an appreciation for the uniqueness of each service operation including their own. You should certainly pay attention to the unique characteristics of your services and design your own strategies and operations accordingly. However, do avoid assuming that almost everything about you is unique; most of the time it is not.

TYPOLOGIES OF SERVICE ORGANIZATIONS

The study of the distinguishing features of various services has also led to several conceptually rich classification schemes for the service industries. We have already mentioned Chase's (1976) distinction between high-contact and low-contact services. Hasenfeld and English (1974) distinguished between the people-changing (e.g., the hospital, the prison, the university, and the church) and the people-processing (e.g., the employment center, the diagnostic clinic, and the court system) human services. To this typology, Fitzsimmons and Sullivan (1982) added a dichotomy of services for the consumer (e.g., airline, TV, insurance, and restaurants) versus services to the consumer (what Hasenfeld and English called the "human services"). Fitzsimmons and Sullivan argued that the appropriate "service package" consisting of the supporting facilities, the facilitating goods, the explicit services, and the implicit services differs from one type of service to another in their classification scheme. You may want to think about your own services and identify the facilities and goods you need (as against the ones you have) to support the provision of your services. Also recognize some of the "implicit services," for example, courtesy, confidence-building, confidentiality of information obtained, and so forth, that you are (or should be) providing in addition to the explicit services such as child care, counseling, work-therapy, and so forth. How would you go about making the total "service package" most valuable for the client (and/or the funder) per dollar of expenditure?

Capitalizing on Thompson's (1967) notion that information is the fundamental raw material of service organizations, Mills and Margulies (1980), and Mills (1986) developed a taxonomy of service organizations based on the nature of the client-employee encounter and the production and distribution skills required on the part of the employee. Mills's maintenance-interactive service organizations (e.g., retail organizations, fast-food restaurants, and banking institutions) are characterized by stable environments, little uncertainty about customers' needs, and short but repeated encounters between customers and employees. Mills points out that services in the maintenance-interactive organizations can be standardized and offer great room for planning and realizing economies of scale.

On the other hand, task-interactive service organizations (e.g., legal, accounting, brokerage, and engineering firms) operate in complex environments with a moderate to high degree of perceived uncertainty. Mills suggests that in these organizations there is much dependence on clients and customers by the service provider for the completion of the task. In these organizations, the provider must possess the technical skills and abilities to address the problems in his environment.

In contrast, the personal-interactive services (e.g., welfare, health care, religious, and psychological consulting organizations) are characterized by an environment that is dynamic and complex and in which clients are generally unaware of or imprecise about what their problems are and how to go about remedying them. The abilities and skills necessary to address the problems of a client are not as technical as in the earlier types. Instead, the providers need training and knowledge derived from wide exposure to many situations. What works in rendering the service to one client may not be effective for others. There is a need for a long-term relationship between the client and the employee, and the need for creativity and frequent novelty on the part of the provider.

Mills exploited his taxonomy to explain, both descriptively and prescriptively, the differences in service design parameters, organizational structures, and performance control procedures among the various types of service organizations. Mills's flexiform design concept addresses the needs of the personal-interactive systems very well.

The flexiform structure consists of a set of concentric power circles. The model can be perceived as a three-dimensional sphere that decreases in power but simultaneously increases in authority as one moves towards the center of the sphere. The outer circle is the most powerful segment and constitutes the fundamental operational unit in which the service provider and the client are integral parts.

The second dimension of the model consists of the unit heads, who have relatively more authority than the operational people, but who are not as powerful since they are not involved in the pivotal encounters with the clients. The third dimension consists of the main administrative body including the chief executive officer, whose client encounters are primarily peripheral, that is, supportive to the pivotal encounters of the operational people. Recognition of this disparity between power and authority in personal interactive services can certainly help explain the dynamics of HSOs, although some of them may be task-interactive systems.

THE ROLE OF INFORMATION TECHNOLOGY

Noting that two simultaneous revolutions are shaking the American business community—the extraordinary boom in computer and communication technology and the service sector's rapidly growing share of gross national product—Faulhaber, Noam, and Tasley (1986) assessed the past and future impact of information technology on service productivity in industries such as health care, insurance, and financial services. Together, the readings in Faulhaber, Noam, and Tasley observed a blurring of the concepts of industry and services, with services increasingly intensive in information capital, and industry more and more reliant on information services such as programming, data bases, internal communications, and automated purchasing and distribution. They pointed out that service providers, traditionally decentralized and often small-sized, were being linked through communications technology and could be organized on a national scale. Taylor (1981), Mills and Moberg (1982), and Collier (1983) have elaborated particularly on the applications of modern technology in the service sector.

Later in this chapter, I describe my own experience in helping an HSO decide on the appropriate technology for its operations. Here, my point is that today HSOs must actively identify technologies that may help them become more effective and efficient, and carefully choose among the alternative technologies.

QUANTITATIVE TECHNIQUES IN OPERATIONS PLANNING AND CONTROL

In the foregoing discussion, I have highlighted a body of literature that focuses primarily on the qualitative concepts of operations and planning in service industries. An equally important body of literature has demonstrated that a number of quantitative techniques, widely used in production management, are also applicable to determining optimal solutions to the problems of service delivery. To do full justice to that body of literature requires considerable time and space. Here I shall only provide a few examples and highlight appropriate references for further study of the quantitative techniques.

Fitzsimmons and Sullivan (1982) have presented the applications of many quantitative techniques including linear programming, queuing theory models, service scheduling models, and decision tree analysis to management problems in service organizations. As one illustration, let us consider their discussion of a shift-scheduling problem for a police patrol unit. The demand for patrol officers varies by the hour of the day. For example, around midnight one needs almost four times as many patrol officers as at 4 A.M. Yet patrol officers work on eight-hour shifts and report to duty at one of the six reporting times: 8 A.M., noon, 4 P.M., midnight, or 4 A.M. The problem is how many officers to schedule for each reporting time so as to minimize the total number of officers hired and still meet the minimum patrol requirement of each hour of the day. Fitzsimmons and Sullivan (pp. 86–88) show that this problem can be mathematically formulated as a linear program and an optimal solution can be found. In general, work scheduling is a common problem. Mathematical techniques can help you reduce the total number of workers required by 10 to 20 percent compared to the more frequent trial and error approach.

Most of the examples given by Fitzsimmons and Sullivan are from for-profit or public sector services. Joglekar (1983) illustrated some of the applications in nonprofit organizations. Bartholdi et al. (1983), Cerveny (1980), and Grant (1980) describe specific applications of quantitative analyses in HSOs that are easy to understand even for the nonquantitative reader. A number of scholarly papers in such journals as *Interfaces, Management Science*, and *Decision Sciences* provide more in-depth and exciting examples of such applications, and deserve to be on your reading list if you have the necessary quantitative background.

Unfortunately, there are some existing barriers to the use of OPC concepts in HSOs, and these are discussed in the section that follows. On the other hand, there also appear to be some emerging conditions that may make the use of OPC concepts practically unavoidable for HSOs in the future.

BARRIERS TO THE USE OF OPC CONCEPTS

The skeptic may point out that in the available literature, most of the examples of the application of OPC concepts to services come from the for-profit sector, or at best, from very large nonprofit organizations. I believe that an important reason for this is that managers of HSOs have persistently ignored, if not actively resisted, the use of OPC concepts. These managers often argue that HSOs are unique in that their mission is to focus on equity, service, and humane treatment of their clients and employees; consequently, they must not focus on efficiency. Others proudly say that theirs is already the most efficient of all the sectors insofar as they use volunteers, that is, minimum-cost labor. Some argue that they are faced with situations where each client is different; as such it is difficult to standardize the service. Some of the other unique characteristics of HSOs include the distinction between the buyer (i.e., the funding agency) and the consumer, the lack of inventories, the preponderance of nonmeasurable, non-quantifiable performance attributes, the short-term budgetary cycles, and the lack of ability to exploit economies of scale.

While these and other unique characteristics of HSOs deserve to be recognized, they must not become alibis for the lack of a professional management. In fact, the literature we have reviewed here suggests that one must exploit the knowledge of these unique characteristics in designing careful applications of OPC concepts to HSOs. After all, effectiveness and efficiency are not mutually exclusive. If a mission is worth carrying out, it is worth twice as much to carry it out efficiently. HSO managers owe a special responsibility to their volunteers in making sure that volunteer time is used most productively. Furthermore, from the literature I have cited, it is clear that OPC concepts do focus as much on the effectiveness of an operation as they do on its efficiency. Thus, resistant HSO managers should reconsider their attitudes towards the concepts of operations planning and control.

EXTERNAL CONDITIONS THAT MAY FORCE THE USE OF OPC CONCEPTS

In any case, I believe that in the coming years HSO managers will be forced to change their traditional attitudes. OPC applications in HSOs will be increasingly popular, if not practically unavoidable.

During the sixties and seventies, since resources available to HSOs were growing, they could afford to ignore efficiency considerations. Now, with shrinking resources, they must focus on efficiency. A number of funders have begun to insist on efficiency. Insofar as the efficient HSO is more likely to obtain the funding for its mission, application of OPC concepts will prove to be of strategic value to many HSOs.

In view of shrinking grants, today a number of HSOs are engaged in entrepreneurial activities (Crimmins and Keil, 1983; Young, 1987) including contract services that must meet specified efficiency standards and deadlines to obtain a renewal of the contract. In 1983, I had the privilege of helping Programs for Exceptional People (PEP), an agency for the mentally retarded in Philadelphia, to meet a contract they had to stuff pre-addressed envelopes with Christmas advertising inserts, seal them, bundle them by zip code, and bag the bundles by state. I showed that rational work methods could help the handicapped workers as well as their social worker—now a production manager—be more productive (Joglekar, 1985).

The 25 advertising inserts PEP had to stuff in envelopes included cards and fliers in six different sizes. The social worker wanted to be equitable to his workers. He created a production line of seven workers (all mentally retarded) along a table, where these inserts were arranged in no particular order. Each of the first six workers were to pick up four inserts and pass them on to the next worker on his or her right, along with the collection of inserts received from the worker on the left. The seventh worker was to grab the total pile of inserts from the sixth worker, pick up the 25th insert, stuff them all in an envelope, and drop the unsealed envelope in a receiving bin. An eighth worker (not mentally retarded) inspected these envelopes (randomly) for the proper inserts (no missing insert and no duplicate) and sealed the good and the uninspected envelopes. A ninth worker (not mentally retarded) sorted and bundled them by zip code and bagged them by state.

With my OPC background, the first thing I recommended was that the mailing labels (and not the envelopes) ought to be sorted by zip code and state. Also, the envelopes were to be sealed as soon as they were stuffed—so that no fliers would be lost between the stuffing process and inspection. The quality controller had to (randomly) open some of the sealed envelopes and reseal them if accurate. The inaccurate ones were handled as before. Perhaps my most important rec- ommendation was to forget the false notion of equity that the various size pieces ought to be arranged in random order, and that each worker must pick ''his fair share'' of four pieces. From a work-equity or line-balancing (as it is called in OPC) point of view, I suggested that the inserts be ordered by their size (for it is easiest to pick up and collate pieces of the same size), and that the first worker on the line (who does not have to carry and pass on items collected from the worker to his left) should pick up seven items, but the next worker should pick up only six, transmitting the collection from the left-hand worker, along with his own, to the right-hand worker. Similarly, the third worker should pick up only five while transmitting the collection by the workers from his left, along with his own collection, to the worker on his right. There were other subtle improvements that allowed the workers to see and chat with each other, listen to rhythmic music, and so forth. Together, the changes I proposed improved productivity significantly enough for PEP to complete its contract a week ahead of schedule when PEP's estimate prior to my intervention was that they would be three to four weeks behind the contract deadline.

My recounting of the PEP situation is not exhaustively detailed, but I hope it illustrates the value of OPC.

Another external force requiring the use of OPC concepts in HSOs in the coming years is that today a number of HSOs are observed to be merging and/ or sharing resources in search of economies of scale. Moreover, there is increased realization that although most HSOs are what Mills calls person-interactive organizations, at least the peripheral (i.e., administrative) activities of these organizations can benefit from work-flow study, design, and standardization. Even the core activities can benefit from Shostack's concepts of staged dialogues and careful staff training.

Finally, technological developments in recent years are also ready for exploitation by the HSOs. Not only do advances such as automatic telephone dialers and word processors facilitate all kinds of office work, the advent of microcomputers promises to handle a variety of once nonstandardizable, white-collar tasks if they are standardized (Collier, 1983).

A full exploitation of the available technology requires an orientation to study the existing operations, work flows, database organizations, and so forth. In 1982 I helped a nonprofit telephone referral service evaluate its technological choices through the application of a queuing theory model (Joglekar and Tavana, 1983). The referral system consisted of five interconnected telephone lines that a client could call to seek legal advice and, if necessary, referral to a lawyer specializing in the client's problem area. The telephone company had reported that, on average, the referral service handled 195 calls per day but had 524 busy signals per day. The busy signals represent the number of times prospective clients tried to call when all five lines were occupied, but they do not represent the number of clients who never got through. The referral service wanted to increase the number of clients served as long as it was cost-justified. Towards that goal the referral service could (a) add one or more telephone lines, (b) hire additional paralegals to answer the phones, (c) provide clerical assistance to the paralegals, and/or (d) provide computer terminals to the paralegals.

We identified the subtasks involved in answering a call (e.g., interview the client, locate the name and address of the attorney to be referred, and complete the paperwork), and through a time study, estimated the time taken by each subtask under the existing conditions. We estimated the impact of each of the options on the time required by each subtask. Finally, using a mathematic model from queuing theory, we assessed the impact of each option on the increase in the number of clients served (the model also enabled us to estimate the number of potential clients who were being denied the service). Comparing these increases with the costs of each of the options enabled us to recommend that the referral service add two more lines and hire an additional paralegal on a part-time basis to serve during typical peak hours. A surprise element of our recommendation was that in 1982 providing computer terminals to the paralegals was not cost-justified. Perhaps the situation has changed by now. Here, my point is that prudent technology choices in HSOs call for adequate background in OPC concepts and techniques.

All of the above developments and trends represent external forces that will ultimately require that all HSOs use the OPC concepts. Even if you do not have the time to study OPC concepts and techniques your self, you may be able to increase their use in your organization by bringing in OPC consultants. However, as noted earlier, HSOs that want to be leaders in the implementation of the coming changes may first need an internal change in management attitude.

REFERENCES

Adam, E., J. Hershauer, and W. Ruch (1981). *Productivity and quality: Measurement as a basis for improvement*. Englewood Cliffs, NJ: Prentice-Hall.

Albrecht, K., and R. Zemke (1985). *Service America: Doing business in the new economy*. Homewood, IL: Dow Jones-Irwin.

Bartholdi, J. J., L. K. Platzman, R. L. Collins, and W. H. Warden (1983, June). A minimal technology routing system for Meals on Wheels. *Interfaces* 13(3), 1–8.

Buehler, V. M., and Y. K. Shetty, eds. (1981). *Productivity improvement: Case studies of proven practice*. New York: AMACOM.

Cerveny, R. P. (1980, December). An application of warehouse location techniques to bloodmobile operations. *Interfaces* 10(6), 88–94.

Chase, R. B. (1976). Where does the customer fit in a service operation? *Harvard Business Review* 56(6), 137–42.

Chase, R. B., G. B. Northcraft, and G. Wolf (1984). Designing high-contact service systems: Application to branches of saving and loan. *Decision Sciences* 15(4), 542–56.

Chase, R. B., and D. Tansik (1982). The customer contact model for organization design. *Management Science* 29, 1037–50.

Collier, D. A. (1983, December). The service sector revolution: The automation of services. *Long Range Planning* 16(6), 12–22.

Crimmins, J. C., and M. Keil (1983). *Enterprise in the nonprofit sector*. New York: Rockefeller Brothers Fund.

Czepiel, J., M. Solomon, and C. Surprenant, eds. (1985). *The service encounter*. Lexington, MA: Lexington Books.

Faulhaber, G., E. Noam, and R. Tasley, eds. (1986). *The impact of information technology on the service sector*. Cambridge, MA: Ballinger.

Fitzsimmons, J. A., and R. S. Sullivan (1982). *Service operations management*. New York: McGraw-Hill.

Fuchs, V. R. (1968). *The service economy*. National Bureau of Economic Research. New York: Columbia University Press.

Fuchs, V. R., ed. (1969). *Production and productivity in the service industries*. Washington, DC: National Bureau of Economic Research.

Gartner, A., and F. Reissman (1977). *Self-help in human services*. San Francisco: Jossey-Bass.

Grant, F. H. (1980, October). Reducing voter waiting time. *Interfaces* 10(5), 19–25.

Hasenfeld, Y., and R. English (1974). *Human service organizations*. Ann Arbor, MI: University of Michigan.

Heaton, H. (1977). *Productivity in service organizations: Organizing for people*. New York: McGraw-Hill.

Hostage, G. M. (1975, July–Aug.). Quality control in service business. *Harvard Business Review* 53(4), 89–106.

Human Services Research Institute (1983). *Assessing and enhancing the quality of ser-*

vices: A guide for the human services field. Boston: Human Services Research Institute.

Hyatt, J. C. (1972, April 25). Productivity push: Firms seek to upgrade white-collar output. *The Wall Street Journal.*

Joglekar, P. (1983). New decision-making tools: Applying management science in nonprofits. *Nonprofit Management Association conference report,* 32–34.

Joglekar, P. (1985, April). Improving work methods at a social service agency. Paper presented at the ORSA/TIMS Conference, Boston.

Joglekar, P., and M. Tavana (1983). Application of queuing theory to a nonprofit referral system. *Proceedings of NEAIDS,* 150–52.

Levitt, T. (1972). Production-line approach to service. *Harvard Business Review* 50(5), 41–52.

Levitt, T. (1976). The industrialization of a service. *Harvard Business Review* 54(5), 63–74.

Longest, B. (1977). Productivity in the provision of hospital services: A challenge to the management community. *Academy of Management Review* 2, 475–83.

Lovelock, C. H., and R. F. Young (1979, May–June). Look to consumers to increase productivity. *Harvard Business Review* 57(3), 168–78.

McCallum, R., and W. Harrison (1985). Interdependence in the service encounter. In John Czepiel, Michael Solomon, and Carol Surprenant, eds., *The service encounter,* (pp. 35–48). Lexington, MA: Lexington Books.

Mabert, V. A. (1982). Service operations management: Research and application. *Journal of Operations Management* 2(4).

Maister, D. (1983). *Professional service firm management.* Boston: Harvard Business School.

Mark, J. (1981, March). Measuring productivity in government. *Public Productivity Review* 5, 21–44.

Mills, P. (1986). *Managing service industries.* Cambridge, MA: Ballinger.

Mills, P., R. Chase, and N. Margulies (1983). Motivating the client/employee system as a service production strategy. *Academy of Management Review* 8, 301–10.

Mills, P., and N. Margulies (1980). Toward a core typology of service organizations. *Academy of Management Review* 5, 255–65.

Mills, P., and D. Moberg (1982). Perspectives on the technology of service operations. *Academy of Management Review* 7, 467–78.

Parks, R. (1984, March–April). Linking objective and subjective measures of performance. *Public Administration Review* 8, 118–27.

Reubens, E. (1981). The services and productivity. *Challenge* 24, 59–63.

Rohrbaugh, J. (1981, June). Operationalizing the competing values approach: Measuring performance in employment service. *Public Productivity Review* 5, 141–59.

Rowe, D. L. (1981). How Westinghouse measures white collar productivity. *Management Review* 70(11), 42–47.

Sasser, E. (1976). Match supply and demand in service industries. *Harvard Business Review* 56(2), 133–48.

Sasser, E. E., R. P. Olsen, and D. D. Wyckoff (1978). *Management of service operations: Text, cases and readings.* Boston, MA: Allyn and Bacon.

Schmenner, R. W. (1986, Spring). How can service business survive and prosper. *Sloan Management Review* 27(3), 21–32.

Shostack, G. L. (1984). Designing services that deliver. *Harvard Business Review* 62(1), 133–39.

Taylor, J. B. (1981). *Using microcomputers in social agencies*. Beverly Hills: Sage.

Thompson, J. D. (1967). *Organizations in action*. New York: McGraw-Hill.

York, R. O. (1985). *Human service planning: Concepts, tools, and methods*. Chapel Hill, NC: University of North Carolina Press.

Young, D. R. (1987). Entrepreneurial activities of the nonprofit sector. *Independent Sector Spring Research Forum Working Papers*. Washington, DC: Independent Sector.

10
Management
Information Systems

LESTER BARENBAUM
AND PATTY A. COLEMAN

INFORMATION AS A RESOURCE

The advent of microprocessor chips and personal computers has placed advanced information processing technology well within the reach of most social service agencies. Information systems consultants now receive many requests from agencies to help them purchase and learn to use computers. Administrators sense that there are ways to improve productivity and ease the accomplishment of routine tasks, and typically have these needs in mind when they seek consultation.

This desire to computerize places the cart before the horse; it focuses on mechanization of a system before clearly defining the system itself. Computers do have tremendous potential for enhancing agency effectiveness, but what does not exist cannot be automated. Computerization assumes that there are effective systems already in place for collecting and utilizing agency data, and that the pressing need is for conversion of those manual systems into faster and more productive ones by means of computers.

Information is a vital organization resource, much as are personnel and money. Organizations must know what information they have, how it is being and will be used, and what will be needed in the future. While organizations have been accustomed to managing fiscal resources and more recently have accepted the import of managing human resources, information remains the neglected stepchild of human service management. A common problem observed in our consultation work is a failure to take information systems management as seriously as fiscal or personnel management. The positioning of the management information system within the organization therefore needs to be addressed before looking at components of the system itself.

One example is illustrative: a multifaceted health services agency had evolved a very segmented departmental structure, for example, educational indirect services were very segregated from patient services activities, and development staff worked far apart from public relations staff. At the top of the organizational hierarchy, an executive director, associate director, and several staff members coordinated the activities of all the departments. But within that structure, management of the computer system was the job of a junior level staff person in the finance department, and management of information resources was nonexistent. As a result, we found that the agency generated a lot of reports at high costs, but these reports contained very little useful information and left large gaps. Information that patient services managers desperately needed was found readily available in the education department, but the staff had never known it was there. Every department had its own mailing list, and names were not shared among them. The computers became the possession of the finance staff, other staff members avoided using them, and software systems reflected the narrow perspective of fiscal control rather than overall organizational objectives. No one was in control of information, and top management was not in control of information technology. Enormous waste was occurring, and the staff was becoming increasingly resistant to using the computer.

No efforts consisting solely of systems design at the department level would have cured these ills. Such design would merely have created stronger little fiefdoms that replicated each other's efforts and reflected narrow departmental biases and agendas rather than comprehensive vision or organizational purpose and direction. These systems could not hope to generate information useful for planning. Only an integrated system can approach that level of contribution, and integration requires top management involvement and control.

While prescriptions ignore the vast diversity in agency structures, we have never worked with an organization where we have not recommended consolidation of information systems and computer management in a top management position. In a smaller agency, this may well be a small component of a top manager's job description. In larger settings, it has required a full-time appointment. Information systems management can be handily combined with responsibilities for strategic planning. But the systems must be managed, and failure to do so while designing new systems often results in chaos and mismanagement of precious resources.

With top management in control of information resources, the system can be established in a way that not only addresses reporting requirements, but also enhances daily operations and supports future growth and continuing viability of the organization.

In general, human service managers have information needs of three types: reporting, evaluating, and planning. Reporting constitutes answering the questions What are we doing? How do we do it? What is it costing us? Answers include facts such as numbers of clients seen, demography of the client population, fees received, service units delivered, cost of each service unit, levels of employee compensation, and funding received.

Evaluating seeks to address the question What effect are we having? Providers want to know their impact on the needs of the target population, the extent to which services are delivered efficiently, effectively, and humanely. Planning questions include What should we anticipate for the near and distant future? Do we project changes in client needs? What is going on in the immediate vicinity or the country as a whole that may change the nature of our services over time?

It is vital that these three areas be addressed by the agency managers and that effective, useful, and well-controlled manual systems be in place before any attempt is made to introduce computers.

THE DECISION TO AUTOMATE

A critical step in the agency's progression towards computerization is to ask the question Should we? The introduction of computers has often been a vehicle for change in the organizations with which we have worked. The benefits agencies receive are often tied to better information systems rather than computerization itself.

The three types of information must be examined closely with automation in mind. It is necessary to understand how a computer functions, what it can and cannot do, what financial and human resources will be required, what information will be generated, and how the agency will use that information. Other important considerations are the amount of time involved in designing a system, concerns related to the training of staff, and the potential impact of the sometimes painful conversion from manual to computerized management of information.

Most of these issues are familiar to agency managers, but much of the language is not. Jargon is used to describe even basic concepts and entities. The computer itself is referred to as hardware and the instructions used by the computer are termed software. The following section is intended to provide an overview of computer function and use.

BASIC COMPUTER CONCEPTS

Every computer system is comprised of the following components:

Input and output devices
Central processing unit (CPU)
Operating software
Main memory
Storage devices
Application software

An input device such as a keyboard sends information to the CPU. Output devices receive information from the CPU and display it through screen displays and printers. An analogy to manual work may be drawn by comparing the keyboard to a pen (input) and the printer or screen to paper (output).

The CPU is analogous to the human brain. It contains the electronic circuitry that controls the computer in terms of its speed, how it performs arithmetic and logical functions, and how it interfaces with various input and output devices. Operating software is the set of programs (software) written to control the CPU. For example, MS–DOS is software that controls the CPU of IBM-compatible computers. DOS is the acronym for Disk Operating System.

Main memory or RAM (random access memory) is composed of computer chips which, in our analogy, are equivalent to a person's desk. The main memory is where the computer does its work. Memory is measured in bytes, with each byte representing one character, that is, one number or letter of the alphabet. Early microcomputers came with 16k, or 16,000 bytes, of memory. That is, they had a desk large enough to hold 16,000 characters. Because prices for memory have fallen, computers are commonly available with 640k of memory. This increase in standard memory has allowed programmers to develop more sophisticated software applications that can only operate on a computer with sizable memory.

Main memory is volatile: when you turn off your computer whatever data were in memory are lost forever. In order to preserve the data, the computer uses storage devices. Devices such as hard disks and floppy disks store data even when the computer is turned off. In our analogy, disks can be compared to file cabinets. For instance, information we want to keep may be moved from our desk to the file cabinet before we change tasks. It is where we keep our information when we are not using it. At the present time, computers normally come with a hard disk that holds 20 megabytes (1 megabyte [1 mg] = 1 million bytes) of information. This seems like a great deal of storage, but just as with file cabinets a lot of storage can be very useful.

AN ILLUSTRATION

Application software packages represent a series of instructions sent to the CPU to be executed. Typical application software packages, such as a word processing package, may contain several hundred thousand instructions.

To see how these components work together, consider a situation in which we sort and print a list of 5,000 names that were stored on a hard disk. With the operating software acting as a translator, the CPU receives commands from an applications software package designed to sort data. The CPU controls the copying (not the moving) of data from the hard disk into the main memory, at which time the sorting begins. Data are continually copied to and from the hard disk as the sorting takes place. If the main memory area is small, only a few names can be sorted at a time and the process moves slowly. If the memory is large, many names can sorted at once; because less movement between the hard disk and memory will be required, the process will move more quickly. All work is done in the main memory and the hard disk is where the sorted data are stored. Once the sorting is completed the names can be printed out.

To follow through our manual analogy, a copy of the names is moved from the file cabinet to the desk and sorted. The larger the desk, the more names that can be spread out for sorting. Once each batch is sorted the names are replaced in the file cabinet. Ultimately the sorted names are copied to paper. This example illustrates a task that can be quickly accomplished by a computer but which, depending on the number of names, might be virtually impossible to do manually.

The questions regarding how much to automate and with what level of technological sophistication are issues that must be addressed repeatedly during the computerization process. One increasingly popular innovation is the Local Area Network (LAN). LANs physically connect computers and other peripherals through coaxial cable or telephone wire. LAN software then allows each member of the network to have decentralized access to centralized data. Thus, a client database could be stored on one computer and other computers could access data, update it, and create reports from that centralized database. LANs also allow several computers to share an expensive printer such as a Laserjet. Other advantages include the abilities to send electronic mail and share software packages across the network.

LANs do require greater technical skill of users and usually one person with superior computer ability becomes the LAN administrator. Thus the advantages must be balanced against increased technical demands on information management. It is frequently advisable to start small, while at the same time insuring that additional capabilities and sophistication can be introduced at reasonable intervals. Most often computerization begins with application software that is easy to use and helps agencies understand how computer technology will affect their organization.

An issue that confronts every computer user is whether a generic package is available to meet one's needs or whether an application must be customized to the user's specification. The trade-off is typically a complicated set of issues. For example, an agency may be forced to modify its fund-raising information system to conform to the constraints of an existing applications software package. The benefits may be that the package is inexpensive and requires little or no dependence on a consultant. On the other hand, by using a consultant the agency could design a custom fund-raising application that would generate exactly the information they specify. The cost of the system would be greater and some dependence on the consultant would be required. The following sections will discuss generic as well as customized software applications and address the issues an agency must explore.

APPLICATION SOFTWARE: GENERIC PACKAGES

Two areas in which agencies frequently begin the computerization process are word processing and automated spreadsheets. There are several widely available programs that are useful to almost anyone who wishes to type text or manipulate a large amount of quantitative data. They typically come with training manuals and most bookstores carry additional support material.

Other types of generic programs include application packages to handle, for example, accounting or mailing list preparation and a wide range of utility software programs to make it easier to manage the computer. An example of a utility program would be an off-the-shelf backup program that helps one make backup copies of data stored on a hard disk.

Modern word processing packages allow managers to dramatically change how an office operates. The essence of word processing is that parts of a typed document can be changed while maintaining the integrity of the unchanged text. To revise a document on a typewriter, you must retype it. When using a word processor a sentence can be removed from page 3 of an eight-page document and the word processor takes care of reformatting the text after the unwanted sentence is removed.

This ability then allows managers to work through several drafts of a document without an undue burden on typing resources. Managers can delegate the task of drafting correspondence and then simply edit the letters before they are sent out. This upgrades the skill level of the clerical staff as well as making managerial time more productive.

Electronic spreadsheeting allows one to manage numbers in the same way word processing allows one to manage documents. A calculator helps us perform numeric functions with a few numbers. A spreadsheet performs numeric functions on rows and columns of numbers with great ease. One can ask and answer "what if" questions such as How would my budget be affected if salaries increased by 6 percent, 8 percent, or 10 percent next year and other expenses increased by 5 percent?

AUTOMATED ACCOUNTING SYSTEMS

Automated accounting system applications have become widely available in the last five years. They are different from word processing and spreadsheet applications, however, in that they require a well-thought-out systems design in order to be of maximum value to the agency. Specifically, designing the system's reports and structuring the chart of accounts to allow access to relevant accounting information is critical.

Properly employed accounting software can enhance business productivity by transforming the accounting function from one of retroactive reporting to one of proactive financial planning. Automated accounting systems place more emphasis on the accounting knowledge of the user. This is because much of the accounting process is done in the background (through the accounting software); thus there is less visible input and output and users must have a better grounding in accounting theory than that required for a manual system.

The introduction of microcomputer accounting software over the last five years has had a dramatic impact on pricing. For example, Peachtree repackaged its eight-module accounting software and repriced it from $4,750 to $200 in June 1986 with virtually no loss in functionality. Most packages are integrated in that the general ledger, accounts receivable, accounts payable, and inventory functions work either together as a unit or separately.

Automated accounting systems often do not save time. Debits and credits still must be either written or keyed in. The ability to generate timely management reports is one major advantage of automated systems; however, all major accounting packages allow one to move data to spreadsheet packages such as Lotus. Once the data are in Lotus it is a relatively straightforward process to create reports that compare monthly budgets to actual results and to prepare financial forecasts based upon recent experience.

When one automates an accounting system, the key ingredient for success is to develop a reporting framework that both meets current reporting and planning needs and has the capability to change as the organization changes. This is accomplished by creating a chart of accounts that organizes the accounting information. Each account within the chart of accounts represents a bucket of accounting data. If the account is too aggregated, then information can get lost. For example, if all salaries go into the salary account, it may be difficult to get information concerning salaries across programs within an organization. If salary expense is broken down into too much detail, then one may see the detail and never get a good picture of overall financial health. Thus, in creating a chart of accounts one must think about the appropriate level of detail one needs for both internal reporting and planning purposes.

APPLICATION SOFTWARE: CUSTOM-DESIGNED SYSTEMS

Often, as mentioned above, the applications available do not meet the agency's needs. One type of applications software that normally requires customizing is a database management system (DBMS), that is, a system that manages large quantities of data such as are utilized in fund-raising activities and client tracking systems.

A database management system, whether manual or automated, allows one to transfer large amounts of data (facts) into information. The difference is that with a computerized database the transformation of data is accomplished through both structuring the data and utilizing the speed of the computer. Any question that can be answered through a computer-based system can also be answered in a manual system.

The first phase in developing a DBMS is the feasibility analysis. The feasibility analysis is comprised of three major segments.

- Identification of need or opportunity
- General statement of output requirements
- Specification of required and available resources

AN ILLUSTRATION

As an illustration of database concepts, consider one agency's conversion from a manual fund-raising system to an automated one. The manual system contained data on approximately 1,000 individuals and institutions. Several fund-raising appeals and newsletters were sent each year. Contribution data were recorded on 5 x 7 index cards that also contained demographic data for each potential donor. It was felt a computerized DBMS would provide

- improved tracking of active and inactive donors,
- the ability to target mailings to selected groups, and
- faster processing of labels and letters.

Overall, it was believed that the major benefit would be to provide better management control over the mailing list. The information system would move from one focused on reporting how much money was being raised to one that could evaluate the success of various fund-raising activities and provide information to help plan future activities. This discussion of needs led directly to the specification of desired outputs. Major output requirements were as follows:

- Donation and demographic data on each supporter as well as groups of supporters should be easy to generate.
- Mailings to selected groups should be possible. Of particular interest is mailing to inactive donors.
- The DBMS should be capable of printing labels and letters.

A computerized database is structured through the use of fields, records, and files. A field represents a data item being collected. For example, donor zip code was one field in our database. The information for a donor is called a record. All donor records together form our donor file. Our donor file contains approximately 1,000 records, each comprised of 30 fields of data. The layout of the donor file is shown in Exhibit 10.1 and definitions of the variables are shown in Exhibit 10.2.

Our Donation File contains fields relating to donations that donors make. Each record in the donation file represents a donation. Exhibits 10.3 and 10.4 illustrate the layout and variable definitions in the donation file.

A key attribute of most computer databases is the ability to relate data between files. A database that has this ability is called a relational database. Databases that do not have this ability are called flat file databases. In our relational database we enter donations into the donation file and the system makes entries in the donor file for us. For example when a donation is entered into the donation file, that information is updated in the individual's donor record.

Reports can be generated using data from both files at the same time. The

Exhibit 10.1
Donor Information Input Screen

Donor ID [5]   Donor Type [2]   Activity Status [1]

Title [10   ] First Name [10   ] Last Name [15   ]
         Position   35
         Organization Name   35
         Address   35
         Street   35
         City   20   ] State [2] Zip [5] [4]

Referral   Interest
Source   Group   Date of First Contact [   ]
[5]   [5]

                              No.   Amount   No.   Amount
Contributions This Year   [ ]   [   ]   [ ]   [   ]
Lifetime Contributions   [ ]   [   ]   [ ]   [   ]
                              Last Year   Year Before Last

Note: The length of the fields is shown within the brackets where necessary. For example, the donor ID number is five characters in length.

Exhibit 10.2
Donor File Definitions

DONOR ID

This ID number will be controlled by the system. The system will not allow for duplicate ID numbers to be used.

DONOR TYPE

This field denotes the type of contributor the donor is. One example of a typical set of codes is shown below:

Student	ST	Other	GE
Individual	IN	Corporate	CO
Family	FA	Foundation	FO

ACTIVITY STATUS

Valid codes here are "A" for active and "I" for inactive. The data entry screen assumes a default of "A".

176

ADDRESS

A 6-line address is possible as shown.

REFERRAL SOURCE

Each donor can have a referral source. Typical codes are: Former Client, United Way, Board Member.

INTEREST GROUP

Each donor can be assigned to an interest group. Typical codes are:

Education   EDUC   Conservation   CONSV
Politics   POL   Health Care   HCARE

DATE OF FIRST CONTACT

Manually entered into the system.

CONTRIBUTION FIELDS

These fields require no manual entry. As contributions are entered into the donations file they will be automatically posted to the proper donor based upon the donor id number and fiscal year entered.

Exhibit 10.3
Donation Information Input Screen

Donor ID [5   ]

Program   [4   ]

Activity Date [   ] Fiscal Yr [2]

Donation Type [3   ] Donation Amount [7   ] Account Code [9   ]

In-kind Code   [3   ] Acknowledgment Code [1]

Entry Date   [6   ]

Note: *The length of the fields is shown within the brackets where necessary. For*
example, the donor ID number is five characters in length.

Donor Activity History shown in Exhibit 10.5 was created by drawing data from both files using the donor ID# as the link (key) that relates data for a donor from the donor file with donation data from the donation file.

Let's assume that the agency wants to send a mailing to donors who live in Bucks County, Pennsylvania and who have not made a contribution this year but have made a contribution over the past three years. In the manual fundraising system one could look through the approximately 1,000 donor records to find those donors. If the managers knew ahead of time that they would need this data, they could have had the donor records filed in county order to greatly reduce the search time. But if in the next mailing they wanted to find donors across all counties interested in education, then having donor records categorized by counties rather than by the interest of the donors would not be of great help.

The power of a computerized system is that donor records can be sorted very quickly without any preclassification to speed searches. Generating mailing labels for the 200 donors in the database who live in Bucks County and are interested in education would take less than 30 minutes. Thus one advantage of a computerized database system is the ability to search through data at high speed.

The query function, which asks questions of the database, is one of the most powerful features of a computerized system. Shown below is a series of questions

Exhibit 10.4
Donation File Definitions

DONOR ID

An entry will not be allowed unless this donor is on the donor master file. The donor's name will be displayed to help verify data entry.

ACTIVITY DATE

Date of contribution activity. This date is used to update the donor master file. It must be filled in for monetary transactions.

DONATION TYPE

Cash "CSH" and check "CHK" are the only two valid codes. All monetary activities must have one of these codes entered.

ACCOUNT CODE

Reference for accounting purposes.

FISCAL YR

Reference for accounting purposes. Default set to current year.

DONATION AMOUNT

The dollar amount of a donation is entered here. This amount is automatically posted to the donor file.

IN-KIND CODE

Use this field to mark the type of in-kind donation made. No dollar value is attached to this. No posting takes place.

ACKNOWLEDGMENT CODE

Denotes the type of letter one will receive. This code will tell the word processor which letter is to be sent. Mailing labels for acknowledgment letters will be prepared by the word processor.

ENTRY DATE

Requires no manual entry. Will use the system date. For audit purposes.

Exhibit 10.5
Donor Activity History

09/01/87 THRU 08/31/88

DONOR   Edwards, Cherylyn   DONOR ID# 12345

DONATIONS - THIS YEAR $ 75.00   LIFETIME $ 275.00

ACTIVITY DATE	DONATION TYPE	AMOUNT $	INKIND CODE
09/15/87	CSH	50.00	
03/22/88			TOYS
08/05/88	CHK	75.00	
TOTAL		$125.00	

---

posed in both simple English and computer syntax. As you can see, the difference between the two is not great.

Who made donations last year but not this year?

LIST DLNAME WHERE $LYEAR > 0 and $TYEAR = 0

where: DLNAME   =   Donor Last Name

$LYEAR   =   Dollars of donations last year

$TYEAR   =   Dollars of donations this year

Which individuals referred to us by board members have not made any donations ?

LIST DLNAME WHERE REF = ''BRD'' AND $LTIME = 0

where: REF   =   Referral source of donor

$LTIME   =   Lifetime donations for a donor

Which individuals living in Bucks County are interested in education and have made lifetime donations over $250?

LIST DLNAME WHERE COUNTY = ''BU'' and $LTIME > 250 AND INTGRP = ''EDUC''

where: COUNTY   =   County
      INTGRP   =   Interest group

For each of these questions we have asked the computer to list the donor's last name. We could have just as easily told the computer to print mailing labels sorted by zip code for individuals fitting each of the above criteria.

Furthermore, the ability to answer such questions in under five minutes and to prepare mailing labels or names and addresses to be "mail merged" for printing as part of a cover letter in under 30 minutes allows one to change the way the fund-raising system is managed. It allows managers to think about micromanagement. Targeted mailings instead of mass mailings now become possible. More precise evaluation of fund-raising activities becomes possible. Through proper construction the computerized database can not only speed up the time-consuming tasks but also change how you conduct your business.

IMPACT OF MIS ON THE ORGANIZATION

The introduction of sophisticated information systems and supportive technology can have quite dramatic effects on organizational culture, structure, staff morale, relations among managers, and operational priorities. These are changes that must be managed if they are to be of maximum benefit rather than being a traumatic boondoggle. In many ways, such management is no different than control over other processes of organizational change. For example, the smooth introduction of any innovation requires a strong commitment from top management; the leadership must clearly communicate the objectives of the change and support staff during the transition.

Some organizations found that the introduction of large computer systems (mainframes) had the effects of increasing the division of labor, centralizing authority, and exacerbating hierarchical stratification. Although there is currently little data on whether the smaller microcomputers have the same effects, there is some suggestion that they may decentralize authority, because they can be dispersed and operated throughout the agency and at all levels of staff.

One obvious consequence of system development is the need for staff time to manage the systems. This is true from the beginning; systems design is best accomplished when that top manager who will be responsible for the system is in position and assigned to oversee the process. While a manager must guide the system, however, agencies risk devastating consequences if they let all of the system expertise reside in only one person. Control should be centralized, but expertise needs to be diffused across departments and levels of the organizational hierarchy. This permeation may shift the hierarchy as distributed expertise and shared information result in distributed power.

Consultants from outside the organization may play a vital role in successful systems design and implementation. There are several reasons why retaining a consultant can ultimately serve an organization well. Staff members cannot be assumed to have an objective perspective regarding their existing methods of information collection, whereas consultants can question each instrument's utility and simplicity without restraint. There is no need for most human service agencies to have a technical expert on staff, but such expertise must be available in order to design useful systems and put appropriate technology in place. Experienced consultants can anticipate and therefore prevent many problems endemic to implementation.

Perhaps the most difficult commitment required is the organizational investment of both staff hours and patience; this commitment may be considerable before obvious benefits are reaped. For this reason it is helpful to plan small victories very early on; introducing word processing is usually a very quick fix that delights staff and management alike. If proficiency in word processing is accomplished, staff members may have more patience for the time-consuming process of database implementation. And managers who are given an introduction to the use of spreadsheets for accomplishing some of their routine and complex calculations may also experience some relief.

Staff resistance to new systems can also be reduced by communicating the purposes of the changes clearly and involving employees directly in the systems design process. Organizations have consistently found that support for a new system is greatly increased by including staff members from the start.

The actual users of the technology often are also the best advisers regarding ergonomic concerns. Computers require changes in work stations to accommodate the equipment, minimize the noise created by printers, and facilitate the comfortable use of keyboards and video display screens.

Efficiency and productivity in an organization are dependent upon the existence of an effective and effectively used information system. In thinking about a management information system, including both the actual system and its operations, a number of basic principles must be kept in mind. First, an information system must mirror the goals, objectives, and work style of an agency, and not the reverse. Second, an information system should not be seen as simply a collection of data, but instead as a vehicle that collects data and organizes, synthesizes, and converts that data into knowledge capital. Third, well-planned manual information systems must be designed and in place before automation is introduced. Fourth, an information system is not the answer, but is part of an answering process in effective management.

11
Evaluating Program Outcomes

LYNN E. MILLER

A drug abuse clinic finds that 72 percent of its clients report total abstinence after six months of treatment.

The director of an employment program observes that over half of the people who complete the program find employment within three months. In a comparison group of people who did not enroll in the program, only 22 percent found employment in the same time period.

A family counseling center finds that, on average, family members report a substantial improvement in their abilities to communicate with one another after completing a program of counseling sessions for families with troubled teens.

A therapist treating a group of people with public speaking phobias has clients present a speech to a group of strangers both before and after treatment. On average, ratings of speech anxiety are much lower following therapy.

Have the agencies in these four examples been successful in meeting their program goals? Possibly. Unfortunately, however, it is difficult to determine whether the observed changes are actually attributable to the agencies' interventions. This chapter will discuss some of the common pitfalls that produce inconclusive program evaluations. It will also discuss ways to design evaluation projects so they can more convincingly demonstrate the value of human service programs.

COMMON THREATS TO THE VALIDITY OF PROGRAM EVALUATIONS

Our goal in evaluating a human services program or intervention is to determine whether the program has in fact made a difference. In carrying out evaluation projects, however, a number of factors can cause the actual effects of programs to be either overstated or understated. The project is considered to be invalid to the extent that the observed changes in the clientele can be attributed to factors that may have biased the results rather than to the treatment program. In what is now considered a classic book on research design, Donald Campbell and Julian Stanley (1966) identified the following as being among the most common threats to the validity of evaluation research:

a. Maturation. Some changes that occur in program clientele may simply reflect the normal changes that take place when individuals mature. For example, families with troubled teens may find that some communication problems resolve themselves as time passes. This may be especially likely for families who seek out professional help. That is, those families who recognize problems and feel it is important to improve the situation may be the ones who would—with time—be able to work things out. Thus some of the changes that appear to be the result of counseling may simply be changes that would have occurred without counseling.

b. Historical events. In addition to "maturational" processes that occur normally with the passage of time, some specific events—outside of the treatment program—can also affect program clientele. For example, drug use by clients who enter a drug rehabilitation program may be affected not just by the treatment they receive, but also by whatever events motivated them to seek treatment (e.g., loss of a job or pressures from family members). Thus, it again can be difficult to determine whether changes are due to receiving professional help or to other factors.

c. Differential selection of individuals for comparison groups. Individuals who undergo some program of treatment are often compared in evaluation projects to those who did not enter the program. However, individuals entering a treatment program often do so because they are particularly motivated or have particularly severe needs. Those unemployed individuals who enroll in an employment training program, for example, may differ from those who do not. They may have better skills to start with—making them more optimistic about the usefulness of such a program—or they may be more motivated to find employment. Thus, a difference in the posttraining employment rates for the self-selected groups of program enrollees and nonenrollees may be attributable either to the training program or to initial differences between the two groups.

d. Effects of initial extremity. People are often motivated to enter a treatment program when their problems reach "crisis proportions." When a problem reaches such an extreme level that it causes the individual to seek help, it may be the case that "there is no where to go but up." Since full-blown crises are often short-lived, improvements that appear to be the result of a treatment intervention may simply reflect the normal diminution of problems that occur over time.

e. Changes in measuring techniques. Some apparent changes that occur are really just the result of changes in the way the variables of interest are measured. For example, a counselor's views about what are acceptable family communication patterns can change throughout the course of a program of counseling as he or she has the opportunity to view the effects of the many different ways that family members interact. The result may be that families who have not changed their interaction patterns receive a more or less favorable evaluation than they did initially.

f. Effects of testing. In research that involves "before and after" comparisons, the testing that occurs before an individual participates in the intervention program may influence how he or she performs on a later test. For example, once speech phobics have been rated while speaking to a group of strangers, they will know more about what to expect when postintervention ratings are made. Thus, they may be less anxious about making the second speech.

   Testing not only affects overt behavior, but it can influence responses on a paper-and-pencil test as well. Clients who are given tests to assess their psychological adjustment have time to think about the test and their responses if they are assessed before participating in some treatment program. That alone can cause their postintervention responses to change.

ETHICAL CONCERNS

How can these problems be avoided? It is often difficult to design evaluation projects that will not be biased by the factors discussed above. Ethical concerns create a major obstacle to carrying out research in a manner that ensures that conclusions are valid. For example, to determine whether cigarette smoking really causes lung cancer in humans, we could randomly assign individuals to two groups, force the members in one group to smoke and those in the other not to smoke, and then compare their health over a long period of time. However, because most people would agree that it is ethically improper to constrain behavior to such a great extent, comparisons that have been made of who chooses to smoke or not smoke are subject to the argument that factors other than smoking (e.g., personality traits or nutrition) may differ between the two groups and may be responsible for the difference in cancer rates. Although researchers can avoid some threats to research validity by using statistical techniques and sophisticated research designs that account for initial differences between smokers and non-smokers, the research on humans cannot be as conclusive as the results of more controlled animal experimentation.

In human service settings, it is similarly unethical to deny people what is believed to be the best treatment available simply so a control (comparison) group can be created. At the same time, however, it is unethical to continue to treat people with techniques that have not been demonstrated to be efficacious. Consequently, agencies often seek ways to both carry out a valid evaluation project and provide quality treatment. The sections that follow contain some suggestions, largely based on the work of Campbell and Stanley (1966), for designing research that both allows for appropriate research control and avoids denying appropriate treatment to individuals.

RESEARCH DESIGNS TO AVOID

Some forms of research are subject to severe threats to internal validity. One research design that is very commonly used but that at the same time provides little conclusive evidence regarding treatment efficacy is the one-shot case study. In one-shot case studies individuals participate in a treatment program and then are assessed in some way. For example, a person who has completed a series of counseling sessions may be asked to complete a questionnaire measuring certain aspects of his or her psychological adjustment. Similarly, a person who has undergone therapy for a public speaking phobia may be rated while presenting a speech to a group of strangers. A score indicating healthy psychological adjustment or low speech anxiety is then taken as evidence of the efficacy of the counseling or therapy.

Assuming that the assessment devices are valid measures of mental adjustment or public speaking anxiety, there is certainly nothing wrong with using a good score as evidence that counseling can be terminated. Moreover, positive scores can provide suggestive evidence regarding the effectiveness of the intervention programs. That is, if the assessments indicate that the individual has not overcome his or her problems, we may assume that the treatment is not as helpful as would be desirable.

Scores in one-shot case studies should not be taken, however, as evidence that the program caused or failed to cause any changes to take place. Maturation, historical events, and the effects of initial extremity are among the possible rival explanations for why an individual's behavior may have changed. More fundamentally, though, the one-shot case study does not provide us with any evidence regarding whether individuals have changed. Without any data for comparison, we cannot rule out the possibility that clients who scored well on the assessment tool after undergoing treatment would have scored just as well if they had been assessed before treatment. Similarly, if clients score poorly after treatment, we cannot say they did not improve; it is possible that they might have been much worse off before treatment.

Only slightly more informative is the pretest-posttest design, in which individuals are assessed both before and after treatment. Such research does provide some information regarding whether individuals have changed in some way; consequently, evaluation reports often present information gathered by this method. However, it is still impossible to determine whether the treatment—as opposed to other factors—caused any of the observed changes. The changes may be simply due to a normal maturation process or the tendency for the passage of time to bring some relief to the crises that drive people into therapy. Perhaps events outside of the treatment program—the support and counsel of friends or other types of help people might tend to seek while participating in a treatment program—are responsible for the changes. Perhaps pretesting itself helps people think about or work through some of their problems. Or perhaps changes in the measuring process merely give the impression that program participants have changed in some way. Especially when the assessment involves some subjective judgment on the part of the observer, it is possible that the respondents are held to different standards during the posttest phase than they are during the pretest stage.

TRUE EXPERIMENTS

While not always feasible in human service settings, research designs that represent true experiments avoid the problems that can threaten the validity of evaluation projects. In a true experiment, individuals are randomly assigned to different groups and the groups are treated identically except for the intervention program under study. The simplest true experiments are those that use just two groups, a treatment group that participates in the intervention program and a control group that does not. More elaborate variations are those that compare several different forms of treatment on groups comprised of randomly selected people.

The rationale for conducting a true experiment is that if two groups differ only in that one group receives a particular treatment and the other does not, then any differences observed between the two groups should be attributable to the treatment. Consequently, true experiments are considered to have much greater validity than the one-shot case study and the pretest-posttest design, which have no control groups.

Individuals are randomly assigned to the various groups in an experiment to help ensure that the groups will be roughly equivalent. As noted earlier, comparing individuals who sign up for a program with those who do not confounds the research by making it impossible to determine whether initial differences in the two groups—as opposed to the intervention under study—are the cause of observed differences between the groups.

Does random assignment really ensure that the groups will be equivalent? The groups, of course, cannot be perfectly equivalent because the backgrounds, attitudes, personalities, and abilities of individuals are unique. What we hope for is that the average characteristics of the groups—the average assertiveness, the average sociableness, the average intelligence, and so on—will be about the same. Even so, randomly assigned groups can, by chance, be quite different from one another. The statistical tests that are used to compare group outcomes do take that possibility into consideration, however. The analyses determine the odds of getting—by chance—differences in group outcomes as large as the ones observed; if that probability is small (less than .05), then the difference in outcomes is probably not just the result of randomization having produced non-equivalent groups.

To carry out a true experiment properly, the treatment and control groups should be treated identically except for the intervention under study. One problem that can arise is that the clients' expectations, that is, their beliefs that the therapy or treatment will be efficacious, are often enough to change attitudes or behavior. Many evaluation projects therefore include a placebo control group of individuals who are led to believe they are undergoing therapy, but who are actually given a form of treatment that is not likely to be effective. For example, a study of the effectiveness of a dieting program may include a placebo control group of individuals who are told to "think thin" while listening to music. If the dieting program actually under study results in greater weight loss than the placebo treatment, then we have greater confidence that the program did not cause weight loss simply by convincing the participants that attending a program would result in weight loss.

Many human service agencies are understandably reluctant to provide individuals either with no treatment or with what is believed to be a nonefficacious treatment in order to have control groups. One way to both conduct a valid experiment and provide treatment to all subjects is to do those two things sequentially. That is, after the evaluation project is completed, treatment is provided to the individuals who were randomly assigned to the control group. Some organizations have waiting lists and normally provide treatment to some individuals later than others. For such organizations, research in which individuals in the control group do not receive the actual treatment until after others do is quite acceptable. For organizations that cannot withhold treatment from some individuals for a period of time, the research suggestions in the section on quasi-experimental designs may be useful.

The two most commonly used true experimental designs are the pretest-posttest control group design and the posttest-only control group design. Both designs compare outcome measures for a randomly assigned treatment group and a randomly assigned control group. In the former design, however, pretest measures are obtained to help assure the evaluator that the treatment and control groups did not differ—at least on the outcome measures of interest—before the treatment program began. However, pretests are not considered to be necessary in true experiments. Randomization will provide the best assurance that the groups will not be substantially different prior to treatment (Campbell and Stanley, 1966). Consequently, a posttest-only control group design should be adequate for most research situations.

QUASI EXPERIMENTS

Quasi experiments have many of the characteristics of true experiments but still have some potential threats to their validity. Such studies are conducted in situations that do not permit all of the controls necessary for a true experiment. The evaluator should be aware of the potential limitations of the various quasi-experimental designs and should choose one that would not be likely to result in interpretive problems for his or her particular project.

One such design is the nonrandomized control group design, in which re-spondents are assigned to treatment and control groups on a nonrandom basis. In this type of quasi experiment it is crucial that pretests be given to determine whether the two groups are fairly equivalent prior to the administration of the treatment being evaluated. Sometimes evaluators attempt to match the two groups on characteristics that might make a difference in how individuals would respond to treatment (e.g., each individual in the treatment group is matched with a person in the control group for age, gender, certain personality characteristics, and scores on pretest measures).

The nonrandomized control group design is sometimes used when individuals are self-selected into the treatment program. In such situations, however, even if the treatment and control groups are pretty well matched on relevant char-acteristics, there still exists some reason why the members of the treatment group sought help and the members of the control group did not. That factor, rather than the treatment program, could be the true reason for any posttest differences observed between the treatment and control groups. Consequently, it is best to avoid this quasi-experimental design when self-selection is used to differentiate the experimental and control groups.

The nonrandomized control group design works best when assignment to different groups, although not random, has little to do with the group members' own choices. For example, individuals living in a neighborhood in which a particular recreation or employment program is initiated could be compared with a matched group of individuals living in a neighborhood without such a program. Similarly, a therapist might introduce a new technique to one intact group re-ceiving therapy, but not to another therapy group determined to be similar in composition.

Another potentially useful quasi-experimental design is the time-series ex-periment. This design involves the study of only one group, but rather than collecting just one set of pretest and posttest measures, multiple measures are taken at various time intervals both before and after the treatment is given. The goal is to be able to provide evidence to show that any changes that take place can be traced to the point in time that the intervention was introduced. For example, to study whether a wellness program provided to a corporation is effective in reducing absenteeism, it would not be appropriate to compare the average absenteeism for a one-year period before the program is introduced with the average absenteeism for a one-year period after the program is introduced. Any improvements in absenteeism rates could be attributed to factors other than the program, such as general societal trends toward greater health consciousness or changes in the ages of personnel. However, it may be possible to attribute the changes to the program if the monthly absenteeism figures are shown for one year before and after the wellness program is introduced. By showing the monthly rates over time, rather than just the single average rates, it becomes possible to pinpoint when in the course of time absenteeism rates began to change. If it can be demonstrated that there was no trend toward improvement during the 12 months before the introduction of the program, but that improvements began shortly afterwards, the organization providing the program will have much more convincing evidence of their program's effectiveness.

Time-series quasi experiments are not without potential threats to their validity. When conducting such a study, evaluators must be alert for events that coincide with the introduction of the treatment program and that might, therefore, compete as explanations for observed changes. If the researcher does suspect that extraneous events might coincide with the treatment intervention, the research design should be altered, perhaps by adding a control group. In a control-group time-series quasi experiment, the control group is observed at the same times as the treatment group. If the observed changes in the members of the treatment group are attributable to the treatment rather than to other events, then similar changes should not be observed in the control group. A nonrandomly assigned control group can often be used in this type of research without seriously threatening the validity of the project.

OUTCOME MEASURES

Selecting outcome measures is a process that should involve many people in the organization and perhaps some individuals outside the organization (e.g., previous clients and intended consumers of the study findings). Different people will have different perceptions of the various potential outcomes of the intervention. Sometimes the desired outcomes may only *appear* to be quite obvious. For example, a program to improve the reading skills of young children should have improved reading skills as its primary objective. However, the agency may find that in actual practice a great deal of its work is aimed at increasing the esteem of the children or counseling the children on family problems. By soliciting suggestions from a variety of sources, the evaluator is more likely to arrive at a set of outcome measures that can allow him or her to assess the true impacts of the program.

Of course, when designing an evaluation study, the evaluator should review other studies that might be relevant. It is particularly useful to consult published literature when selecting methods for measuring outcomes. Reference librarians at university libraries can be a very helpful resource to individuals trying to locate such material. Evaluators should utilize well-researched, standard measurement tools when possible to help ensure that the tools are actually valid measures of the outcomes of interest. For example, the evaluator would want to avoid asking respondents for self-reports of their behavior if previous research has indicated that self-reports of the particular behavior of interest are not to be trusted.

DATA ANALYSIS

For the types of research designs discussed here, the goal of data analysis generally will be to compare posttest outcome measures for program participants with those same individuals' pretest measures and/or with posttest measures for members of a control group. Even if the treatment program has no effect, at least slight differences are likely to be observed in the sets of outcome measures being compared. Consequently, tests of statistical significance should be conducted to determine whether any observed differences between pretest and posttest measures or between the treatment and control groups are more substantial than what would just be expected by chance. In certain instances, statistical procedures will be applied to control for the effects of some variables that were measured but could not be controlled experimentally.

Obviously, statistical analysis can be difficult. Before conducting the evaluation study, the evaluator should determine what statistical procedures will be used. This decision can affect decisions regarding the type of data to be collected (e.g., many statistical procedures that can be applied to ratings made by respondents cannot be applied to rank orderings). Evaluators who are not well-versed in statistical analysis should seek help. Universities can be a source of inexpensive consultation; for many disciplines, university departments are likely to have at least some faculty members who are extensively trained in research design and analysis.

INFORMED CONSENT

Hargreaves and Attkisson (1978) have noted that "informed consent is appropriate whenever research or evaluation alters a client's activities in the program from those that are a routine and necessary part of service delivery—if the client is thereby put at risk with respect to any physical, psychological, or social harm" (p. 329). Typically, clients are told if they are to be randomly assigned, what additional activities will be asked of them as a result of participation in the evaluation project (e.g., the completion of follow-up questionnaires), and what potential risks and benefits may result from their participation in the evaluation project. Participants should be told that they can withdraw from the project at any time without losing the opportunity to receive regular program services (see Hargreaves and Attkisson, 1978, for further information).

OTHER FORMS OF EVALUATION

This chapter has focused on what often is referred to as "impact evaluation." This type of evaluation is conducted to determine whether a program has desirable effects, and the results are used to make decisions regarding whether a program should be continued, modified, or discontinued. There are, however, other types of evaluations that agencies utilize (see Patton, 1982, and Rossi, Freeman, and Wright, 1979, for discussions of different types of evaluations). Perhaps the most commonly used is program monitoring, in which the agency monitors and reports on service delivery. Program monitoring includes activities such as counting the number of clients served and periodically checking to determine whether referral forms are being completed properly. Licensing and accrediting bodies often emphasize this type of evaluation procedure. Also, it is often useful to conduct program monitoring evaluations and impact evaluations simultaneously. For example, if the program is found to have no impact, information collected while monitoring the program can be used to determine whether the program was properly implemented (see Rossi, Freeman, and Wright, 1979, for further information on program monitoring).

Cost-effectiveness studies, in which the costs of service delivery are compared with the benefits, are also commonly conducted to evaluate agencies or their programs. Cost-effectiveness analyses may use information derived from program monitoring or from impact evaluations. One variation is the cost-benefit analysis, which compares program costs and benefits expressed in monetary terms. For human service agencies, cost-benefit analyses frequently require the translation of nonmonetary outcomes into dollar figures. This is difficult to do and requires a very thorough analysis of the different ways that monetary benefits can be directly or indirectly attributed to the program. Often, many assumptions have to be made in assigning monetary values to outcomes. Thus agencies are advised to proceed very cautiously in carrying out cost-benefit analyses.

Agencies frequently conduct formative evaluations when programs are relatively new. These evaluations are often informal and used to obtain information needed to "tinker" with particular aspects of an intervention program. For example, staff and clientele might be asked for their opinions regarding how well certain program features seem to work, and the program might then be modified accordingly.

REFERENCES

Campbell, D. T., and J. C. Stanley (1966). *Experimental and quasi-experimental designs for research*. Chicago: Rand McNally.

Hargreaves, W. A. and C. C. Attkisson (1978). Evaluating program outcomes. In C. C. Attkisson, W. A. Hargreaves, M. J. Horowitz, and J. E. Sorensen, eds., *Evaluation of human service programs*. New York: Academic Press.

Patton, M. Q. (1982). *Practical evaluation*. Beverly Hills: Sage.

Rossi, P. H., H. E. Freeman, and S. R. Wright (1979). *Evaluation: A systematic approach*. Beverly Hills: Sage.

ANNOTATED BIBLIOGRAPHY

Campbell, D. T., and J. C. Stanley (1969). *Experimental and quasi-experimental designs for research*. Chicago: Rand McNally. Although written for evaluators of educational programs, this book can be (and frequently has been) applied to the evaluation of human service programs. Considered "must" reading by many program administrators, this book identifies the various threats to the validity of evaluation projects, describes different basic research designs, and indicates the ways in which the validity of each design is (and is not) threatened.

Evaluation Review The issues of this journal, formerly *Evaluation Quarterly*, contain examples of evaluation projects and discussions of issues in the field of evaluation research.

Rossi, P. H., H. E. Freeman, and S. R. Wright (1979). *Evaluation: A systematic approach*. Beverly Hills: Sage. This book explains how to conduct evaluations for a variety of purposes (e.g., program planning, implementation, and impact assessment). It contains descriptions of numerous evaluations that have been conducted.

PART IV
HUMAN RESOURCE SYSTEMS

12
Effective Communication

STEVEN I. MEISEL

COMMUNICATION AS A KEY TO EFFECTIVE ORGANIZATIONAL BEHAVIOR

All organizations start out with good intentions. The formal charter or statement of purpose is idealistic and optimistic about the positive changes that will come about as the organizational goals are achieved. All too often, however, the organization falls short of its goals and finds itself bogged down in the struggle to cope with day-to-day operating problems.

Many of the minor breakdowns in organizational functioning are the result of failures in internal organizational communication. Without adequate communication within the organization the goals become unclear. The parts of the organization lose coherence and the overall purpose of the organization gives way to agency politics and fighting for "turf" between the various departments or offices. Communication breakdowns lead to an increase in information gathered through the grapevine, destructive rumors, and a sense of alienation and isolation on the part of the members of the organization. No one wants to feel cut off from the flow of important information. Certainly there are reasonable secrets to be kept and plans that need be examined by only a few people to determine usefulness. However, few manifestations of organizational functioning are so potentially damaging as the belief that information is being withheld or that workers are receiving deliberate misinformation.

The internal communications process has been described as being as essential to organizational development as language is to thought (Maddalena, 1981). This chapter will present some concepts for understanding the state of your organizational system of internal communications. This is known as a communication audit. In addition, ideas will be presented for examining communication between the organization and its environment of clients, regulatory agencies, and funding sources. The objective is to provide some specific methods to increase understanding of organizational communication with the intent to increase effectiveness of the organization as a whole.

THE COMMUNICATION AUDIT

The goal of the communication audit is to generate information about the communication system currently in use. Information gained through the audit procedure should result in a picture of the formal and the informal communication networks as well as the use or misuse of the system. Most people in the organization will have an opinion as to the nature of the communication design and flow. The greatest advantage of the communication audit project is that it results in objective data from all levels of the organization. The development of facts rather than opinion will give the agency director or executive a broadly based fund of information to provide a diagnosis of the existing system and to support change where needed. Specifically, the communication audit is a planned procedure that examines the flow of information through the organization. It provides answers to several important areas of questioning: How well is the entire communication system working? Does the system of internal communications have the elements required to achieve its objectives? How effective are the specific communication activities currently in use? Which activities require increased managerial attention and support?

The great value of the communication audit comes through the comparison of communication objectives and actual performance. The internal communication system generally has four important goals. They are to inform the staff of ongoing objectives, policies, and plans; to control the work of the staff members to assure that individual effort is congruent with organizational goals; to assist in problem solving at all levels of the organization; and to develop team building by sharing information and providing opportunities for input from members of the organization. In addition, it is important to know if the communication activities of the organization are operating efficiently; that is, are they reaching the right people at the right time with the right message?

These questions represent the critical components of an effective communication system. In most cases, there is more than enough communication activity, but the goal of the activity may be unclear or disguised. Meetings may be called discussions when they are really designed to simply inform. Messages may solicit feedback on decisions after the decision has been implemented. Everyone who works in an organization knows the frustration of learning too late about matters of importance to the work.

By comparing objectives to activities and activities to a performance standard, the not-for-profit executive can get systematic information on what is working and what is in need of change. The analysis and recommendations of the audit committee will provide support for effective communication strategies and useful ideas for the revamping of those activities judged ineffective or harmful. In addition, the audit process often opens up new areas and approaches to internal communication that enliven the process and increase organizational morale.

The communication audit represents a positive and proactive approach to dealing with organizational communication problems. It increases awareness of the importance of good communication and builds commitment among co-workers to better communication and, ultimately, a more effective organization. The communication audit design presented in this chapter is called a "communication system appraisal." The entire audit process from data collection to the analysis and recommendation state is generally completed in two months. The advantages to this design are that it is accessible and readily understood at all organizational levels.

WHO SHOULD DO THE COMMUNICATION SYSTEM APPRAISAL?

Whether the communication audit is being done for the entire organization or for one department, it is obvious that the wholehearted commitment of top management is necessary. Normal defensiveness and career worries indicate that people will have a hard time reporting communication breakdowns. In order to create broad-based acceptance of the system appraisal project, the International Communication Association has recommended the establishment of an audit liaison committee comprised of a representative group (from three to nine members) drawn from various departments and levels of the organization (Goldhaber, 1986). This committee will (1) help implement audit logistics (conduct interviews, design and distribute questionnaires, etc.); (2) collect the information and prepare interim audit reports; (3) communicate preaudit, audit, and postaudit information to the organization (via newsletters, memos, meetings, etc.); and (4) write the final audit report including conclusions and recommendations.

The audit process will not be a full-time job for committee members, but will require some release time from day-to-day tasks. This is one other reason for developing the audit process from the top of the organization downwards. The audit liaison committee cannot be expected to be expert at all phases of the appraisal process. Appropriate resources should be used for questionnaire development and analysis of content. Some organizations will want to use outside consulting to help train the audit committee.

It is also strongly suggested that a timetable for implementing the various parts of the communication system appraisal be developed. This should be a formal schedule indicating each part of the audit process, with the amount of time needed for completion. While the timetable can be amended when necessary, lack of a timetable will stretch the process out long enough for enthusiasm to falter and commitment to give way to frustration.

PREPARING THE ORGANIZATION FOR A COMMUNICATION AUDIT

The communication system appraisal or other form of communication audit represents a major step for any organization. People are understandably wary of any process that records their work and provides for comparison against a standard. In addition, most people are not used to charting everyday transactions that seem informal. Finally, although most people complain about internal communication from time to time, relatively little attention is paid to specific means for increasing effectiveness.

Given these concerns, it is a good idea to do some work to ready the organization or department for the audit process. This can be accomplished in two ways: (1) sharing the reasons for the decisions to undertake the audit and (2) increasing awareness of communication as a specific work activity.

It is important to involve a broad and diverse group of people in the discussion of how to proceed with the audit project. The work to be done, the goals of the audit process, and the selection criteria for the audit liaison committee should be part of an open decision-making process. The audit will involve increased work for committee members as well as greater effort on the part of those who will have to share the daily work of the committee members while they are involved in the audit process.

Time and effort spent in answering questions, soliciting feedback, and building commitment for the communication audit will pay off in increased cooperation and more useful data generated by the audit process. A simple truth of organizational behavior is that individuals respond in a more positive way when they feel involved in a decision. Increased awareness of communication as a planned work activity comes from seeing the amount of time and effort expended on communication activity. Communication theorists have suggested that between fifty and ninety percent of all organizational activity is devoted to the transfer of information within the organization (Gibson, 1986). But for many people, only a sense of "telephone phobia" at the end of a work day remains to serve as an indicator of the great amount of time spent communicating.

A positive outcome of the audit process is a heightened awareness of communication objectives. Every organization needs to consider its communication activities, but this is especially important in the nonprofit sector. The nonprofit organization is driven by its values, and success is often a function of how well those values are shared by the staff. The internal communication system is the vehicle used to share the policies and objectives through which values are put into operation.

THE COMMUNICATION SYSTEM APPRAISAL

The communication system appraisal is divided into two sections (see Exhibit 12.1). Section A is concerned with the overall internal communication system and begins with the task of examining the process by which organizational goals and policies are communicated to members of the organization. Section B examines specific communication activities such as new employee orientations and in-service training programs. The objective of Section B is to record the many specific communication activities of the organization along with the performance standards for each activity.

The communication system appraisal begins with "Fact Finding," in which the audit committee examines communication policy (Section A, Stage 1). In this stage, the auditors list organizational communication objectives and policies and the specific activities associated with meeting these objectives. This information comes from written policy and from interviews with team leaders, department supervisors, and the agency director. Very often communication activities have not been previously documented.

The audit process then involves asking and discussing questions, giving the individual time to think about the policy-activity linkage, and finally, getting the information. A master list should be maintained on which all answers can be easily recorded. When the information is complete, a listing is made charting responsibility for the outcome of the activity. Exhibit 12.2 provides examples of results of this initial fact-finding stage.

The final task in fact finding is to identify areas of organizational responsibility for each policy and activity area. For example, is training the work of the personnel department or of the team leader? Job descriptions are places to begin looking, but informal communication activities may have shifted these responsibilities into unofficial areas. It is important to record the real (not the ideal or official) functioning of the organization.

The second step (Stage II) of the communication audit is the analysis of the overall communication system. This stage looks at communication activities on the basis of objectives and levels of communication in the organization. All communication systems have four basic objectives: to inform, to control, problem solving, and team-building.

The level of communication refers to the functional units of the organization within which the communication takes place. The levels are: interpersonal, small group (departmental), and the complete organizational unit. Exhibit 12.3 provides examples of the types of information recorded in this stage.

Stage II provides a good measure of the existing communication system. The best way to approach this analysis is to gather as much data and opinion as possible. Members of the organization at different levels should be asked and given the opportunity to express their opinions in detail. A systematic data-gathering effort (e.g., questionnaires, planned interviews) should be used to get the broadest possible sense of the members' views.

Exhibit 12.1

Work Plan for a Communication System Appraisal

Section A. Overall Communication System

Stage 1. Fact Finding

1. Determine organizational communication objectives and policies.

2. Inventory the communication activities and classify in relation to specific communication policies.

3. Identify the nature of communication system responsibilities and the organizational department with communication as a key responsibility.

Stage II. Analysis

1. Study the communication activities in terms of objectives and organizational levels.

2. Utilize appropriate measurement techniques to judge the strengths and weaknesses of the overall communication system.

3. Note the strengths and weaknesses of overall system in relation to organization situational factors including structure, processes, and leadership.

Stage III. Evaluation

1. Summarize the data obtained and arrive at conclusions concerning the adequacy of existing activities to implement policies.

2. Recommend necessary changes and/or supportive communication programs and furnish details as to implementation

Section B. Specific Communication Activities

Stage I. Fact Finding

1. Determine the nature and objectives of the activity.

2. Identify the objectives for the activity with reference to applicable communication performance criteria.

3. Arrive at performance standards which will determine satisfactory performance for each procedural instruction.

Stage II. Analysis

1. Employ appropriate measurement techniques to estimate actual performance and deviation from standards.

2. Study deviations representing important weaknesses in the communication activity. Identify situational factors influencing communication behavior.

Stage III. Evaluation

1. Summarize the data obtained and arrive at conclusions concerning the adequacy of the specific communication activity to meet the objectives set for that activity.

2. Recommend corrective measures with suggestions for implementation. Report on the presence of organization situational factors preventing accomplishment of objectives.

Exhibit 12.2

Examples of Communication Policies and Corresponding Activities

Policy	Activities	Responsibility
Help employees understand the agency's objectives, plans, and policies.	Personnel Handbook Director's Memos Administrative Team Meetings Staff Meetings	Administrative Team Executive Director Asst. Director Director and Supervisor
Provide employees with the essential information to do their jobs.	New Staff Orientation Job Description Organizational Chart Team Meetings	Asst. Director Administrative Team Executive Director Dept. Supervisors
Provide effective channels for internal communication; encourage free exchange of views and recommendations; and facilitate individual professional development.	Team Meetings Staff Meetings Performance Reviews Exit Interviews In-service Training	Dept. Supervisors Director and Supervisors Admin. Team/Supervisors Asst. Director Asst. Director

Exhibit 12.3

Examples of Classification of Communication Activities by Objectives and Level

	Organizational Level of Communication		
Objective	Interpersonal	Small Group	Organizational
To Inform	Hiring Interview Orientation Performance Review Oral and Written Reports	Team Meetings In-Service Training Admin. Team Meetings	Director's Memos Job Descriptions Personnel Handbook Rumors/Grapevine
To Control	Performance Reviews	Project Status Annual Dept. Review	Policy and Procedures Directives Director's Memos Job Descriptions
Problem-Solving	Request for Recommendations Exit Interviews	Team Meetings Admin. Team Meetings	Staff Meetings Policy and Operations Handbook
Team-Building	Annual Review Outstanding Employee Award	Monthly Breakfast Interdepartmental Lunches Softball Games	Staff Meetings Awards Luncheon Volunteer Appreciation Dinner

The issues of organizational structure and leadership can be addressed with objective appraisal of the mechanisms which help or hinder communication. Satellite offices or other kinds of geographic dispersal make communication more difficult. If the executive director spends a great deal of time dealing with the board of directors or funding sources and has little time left for the line work of the organization, this could be a structural weakness. Some of these structural problems can be thought of as necessary evils, but all should be recorded.

The final step (Stage III) of Section A is the development of recommendations and conclusions regarding the overall communication system. Some areas will be seen to be effective; other areas (as determined by the performance standards) will probably require change. Recommendations for new communication activities should be made along with dates for implementation and suggestions as to which people will be affected by the change. Above all, the changes must be realistic and capable of being implemented. A suggestion that would require an upheaval of the entire organization is probably not going to be accepted—or even feasible.

SECTION B: SPECIFIC COMMUNICATION ACTIVITIES

In Section A, the communication objectives for the overall organization are audited. The next step in a communication system appraisal is to examine the internal communication activities specific to each department or function. Exhibit 12.4 illustrates the objectives and performance criteria and standards relating to the activity of "performance assessment." In Stage I, each unit of the organization will develop a similar list of communication objectives and standards for performance for each of its functional areas. If the audit is being done for just one department, then a final list will include all the activities for each of that department's functions. For example, the same unit that deals with volunteers might also handle community information and liaison to United Way.

Each communication activity needs to be thought about in terms of content (what information should be conveyed?); media used (is the communication in the form of memos, newsletters, etc?); timing (how often or by what date should the communication take place?); participation (who is involved in this communication activity?); and feedback (how will responses to the communication be obtained?). Some of the communication activities will be the result of agency policy, but others will have grown up through informal means and must also be recorded.

If bulletin boards are changed only once a year rather than the stated goal of once a month, then this represents a deviation from the standard and should be recorded. In Stage II, such deviations should be noted and presented in a way that is relatively nonthreatening and nonjudgmental. There may be good reasons for the deviation from the standard or goal that can be identified and discussed in the conclusion stage. The communication audit should not be used or perceived as a work review and employee evaluation. The evaluation (Stage III) entails

Exhibit 12.4

Examples of Objectives, Performance Criteria, and Standards for a Specific Communication Activity: Performance Assessment

Objectives	Performance Criteria	Performance Standards
Develop clearly understood goals with periodic reviews of performance	Content Feedback	Formal meetings with supervisor twice a year.
Set initial goals and objectives Interim review Final evaluation	Timing	January/July March/August June/December
Performance plan Develop and prioritize Objectives-Goal Statement	Content Media Used Timing Participation	Signed plan within two weeks of initial meeting Use of Agency performance assessment document Signed by employee and supervisor
Work closely with supervisor to determine your objectives in an atmosphere of open, two-way participation	Participation	On-going

summarizing the findings and analysis relative to each specific communication activity. This process is used to generate conclusions about the success or failure in meeting objectives and performance standards.

Because communication activities are part of the overall functioning of the unit or agency, a breakdown in one area may actually be the consequence of a larger organizational problem. Variables such as organizational structure or unusual events may have had an impact on the planned communication activity and should be identified and discussed. In many cases, the problem stems from a source other than the responsible individuals. In other words, a good plan or activity can be easily disrupted by conflicting demands from other (especially, higher) parts of the organization.

SOME IDEAS FOR DATA COLLECTION

The communication system appraisal needs a great amount of reliable data in order to be useful to the organization. There are many ways to gather information for this audit process, including interviews, reviews of documents, communication logs, and survey forms.

Interviews are facilitated through the use of an interview guide that can be prepared and distributed prior to the interview. The guide should state the purpose of the interview and several of the topics or questions about communication activity that the audit committee will examine. Use of the interview guide allows members of the organization time to consider the nature and effectiveness of their communication activities before being questioned.

The review of agency documents can also yield important information on the written policies of the organization. Useful areas of research are newsletters, personnel manuals, and operations manuals, as well as the documents that set out the original charter or purpose of the organization. These documents often contain statements of intent regarding the need to keep members of the organization informed of policy, activities, and goals. Many nonprofit organizations maintain files of directors' memos, exit interviews, or performance assessment materials that can be combined to create a paper trail that can be followed by the audit committee.

Two data-gathering instruments of particular use to an audit committee are the communication diary instrument and the organizational communication survey. The International Communication Association (ICA) has developed a format to record daily communication activity. This form is reproduced here as Exhibit 12.5 and may be copied for general use. The communication diary instrument can be made available to all members of the organization or to a representative sample from several areas or levels of the agency. People should be asked to keep the diary as accurately as possible for one week.

Use of the diary heightens awareness of communication patterns and activity. It will help members of the organization to appreciate both the quantity and quality of ongoing communication activities and can serve as an introduction to the idea of a wide-ranging audit. The diary will provide information on channels, types, and perceived effectiveness. The audit committee should collect the diaries at the end of the week and use the data to develop a quantitative picture of the organizational communication activity. The communication diary is a good preparation activity for the communication system appraisal or can stand alone as a useful data-gathering tool for the organization.

Another ICA instrument that may be useful for understanding internal communication practices is the organizational communication survey (Exhibit 12.6). This uses a closed- and open-ended items to obtain feedback on individual satisfaction with current internal communication practices. The form gives the respondent an opportunity to indicate information desired and information received, and can be used as a one-shot exercise. It can serve as valuable feedback to a supervisor from those being supervised or from the organization to the director. The evaluation process can also be enriched through this opportunity for workers to evaluate their superiors in a constructive and specific way. Further, the communication survey is another consensus-building activity that can support the communication system appraisal project.

THE AUDIT PROCESS: IN SUMMARY

The audit committee will meet to plan the communication system appraisal and to design the data-gathering instruments. They will interview members of the organization, review documents, interpret data, and write the final report on the state of communication activities, goals, and policies. In doing so, the committee will develop important information regarding issues of administrative competence, organizational goal clarity, turnover rate, and general employee satisfaction. In short, the communication audit will shed needed light on the larger issues of organizational effectiveness. The audit provides quantitative information that may be used to support planned change or it may offer the same support for the continuation of successful policies and procedures. It is a managerial tool that gathers data and at the same time demonstrates administrative concern for the human processes of the nonprofit organization.

EXTERNAL COMMUNICATION: THE FEEDBACK LOOP

How does an organization know it is doing a good job? In fact, what does "doing a good job" really mean? Answers to these questions are often intuitive and lack quantitative data to support the impressions of the administrative team. A private sector business relies on sales figures or the measurement of profit. The nonprofit organization must use other sources to measure effectiveness. Every organization exists to meet the needs of some group of people. The nonprofit enterprise, no less than a business or government agency, will find its very survival threatened if it is perceived as being inattentive to the needs of its

Exhibit 12.5

ICA Communication Diary Instrument

Your name _____ Date _____

Daily Communication Interactions

	1st	2nd	3rd	4th	5th	6th	7th (etc.)
INITIATOR							
Self	—	—	—	—	—	—	—
Other party	—	—	—	—	—	—	—
CHANNEL							
Face-to-face	—	—	—	—	—	—	—
Telephone	—	—	—	—	—	—	—
Written	—	—	—	—	—	—	—
KIND							
Job-related	—	—	—	—	—	—	—
Incidental	—	—	—	—	—	—	—
Rumor	—	—	—	—	—	—	—

LENGTH

Less than 3 minutes   —

3 to 15 minutes   —

15 minutes to 1 hour   —

Over 1 hour   —

QUALITIES

Useful   —

Important   —

Satisfactory   —

Timely   —

Accurate   —

Excessive   —

Effective   —

Exhibit 12.6

Example of an Organizational Communication Audit Survey

PLEASE CHECK THE APPROPRIATE BOX
AND USE THE SPACES PROVIDED OR
THE BACK FOR ADDITIONAL COMMENTS

	very dissatisfied 1	2	3	4	very satisfied 5
1.) Are you dissatisfied or satisfied with communication and the availability of information?	☐	☐	☐	☐	☐

	very seldom 1	2	3	4	very often 5
2.) How often do you read:					
Bulletin boards?	☐	☐	☐	☐	☐
Memos?	☐	☐	☐	☐	☐
Newsletters?	☐	☐	☐	☐	☐

	very little 1	2	3	4	very much 5
3.) How much information about your work and organization do you get now from:					
Supervisors and Directors	☐	☐	☐	☐	☐
Other employees?	☐	☐	☐	☐	☐
Bulletin boards?	☐	☐	☐	☐	☐
Newsletters	☐	☐	☐	☐	☐
Staff meetings?	☐	☐	☐	☐	☐
Rumors?	☐	☐	☐	☐	☐

4.) How much information about your work and organization would you like to get from:

	very little 1	2	3	4	very much 5
Supervisors and Directors?	☐	☐	☐	☐	☐
Other employees?	☐	☐	☐	☐	☐
Bulletin boards?	☐	☐	☐	☐	☐
Newsletters	☐	☐	☐	☐	☐
Staff meetings?	☐	☐	☐	☐	☐
Rumors?	☐	☐	☐	☐	☐

5.) What is the amount of information you receive now about the following job items?

	very little 1	2	3	4	very much 5
Your own work	☐	☐	☐	☐	☐
Changes in policies	☐	☐	☐	☐	☐
Training and courses	☐	☐	☐	☐	☐
Employee benefits	☐	☐	☐	☐	☐
Organizational changes	☐	☐	☐	☐	☐

6.) Are there negative aspects in communication within your organization? What are they?

_____

_____

7.) Are there outstanding aspects in communication within the organization? What are they?

_____

_____

213

Exhibit 12.6 (Continued)

	disagree strongly 1	2	3	4	agree strongly 5
8.) I would like to see improvement in communication:					
From Supervisors & Directors to personnel	☐	☐	☐	☐	☐
From Personnel to Supervisors & Directors	☐	☐	☐	☐	☐
With my own Supervisor	☐	☐	☐	☐	☐
Among fellow employees	☐	☐	☐	☐	☐

	very dissatisfied 1	2	3	4	very satisfied 5
9.) Are you dissatisfied or satisfied with the following aspects of your job?					
Supervision of work	☐	☐	☐	☐	☐
Chances for promotion	☐	☐	☐	☐	☐
Wages and salaries	☐	☐	☐	☐	☐
Employee benefits	☐	☐	☐	☐	☐
Opportunities to participate in influencing matters that concern my work	☐	☐	☐	☐	☐

	very dissatisfied 1	2	3	4	very satisfied 5
10.) Are you satisfied with the current performance appraisal system?	☐	☐	☐	☐	☐

primary beneficiaries or benefactors or both. It is easy for an organization to lose track of its goals or to attempt to meet new goals without adequately testing its assumptions of need or relevance. This need to be in touch with the work-related environment is met by external communication strategies, and the relative effectiveness of these strategies will have great impact on the effectiveness of the organization.

Some ideas for developing adequate feedback systems will be presented here, and references contained in the annotated bibliography offer further guidance in design and implementation.

FEEDBACK VERSUS THE FEEDBACK LOOP

It is likely that most, if not all, nonprofit managers would agree with the notion that feedback from clients, funders, and boards is important to overall organizational effectiveness. This fact is recognized and widely understood if not always acted upon. However, the concept of the planned feedback loop—that is, a continuous formal interchange of information between the organization and the environment—may be a new idea. In our personal lives, it is not enough to ask friends how they are feeling and then receive a standard response. A good relationship depends on a continuing conversation with appropriate responses to changing feelings. It entails modification of behavior to reduce the problem areas and support the parts of the relationship that are working well.

The organization has a relationship with its environment and needs the same continuing dialogue to keep that relationship healthy. This is the purpose of the feedback loop.

DESIGN AND IMPLEMENTATION

There are many possible designs for a feedback loop, but generally these fall into two broad categories. The first is based on personal contact through meetings and phone conversations. An example of this type of system is the advisory board. In this design, the organization finds a group of typical consumers of its services who will meet regularly to comment on quality, program relevance, and general organizational effectiveness in their environment. An example of this design would be a training program with an advisory board comprised of employers of program graduates, other employers who have not hired the trainees, and recent graduates. The discussion focuses on what skills are needed in the marketplace for the present and the near future. The graduates can give feedback on the usefulness of their training. In this way, the agency offering the training program can modify its curriculum to better meet the needs of its students and at the same time show a willingness to listen to recommendations and to learn from the end users of the service.

Effectiveness of the advisory board model depends on two things. First, there must be a formal, ongoing series of meetings with a good mutual understanding of the goals of the feedback process. Second, the director of the organization must be committed to effective use of the advisory board. Information that is not acted on is useless, and board members who suspect that their role is largely ceremonial will soon resign. The dialogue must be honest and reasonable with good faith on both sides. This can only be demonstrated by actions on the part of the organization.

The second broad category of feedback loop is the survey model. This design is somewhat less demanding than the advisory board process but requires no less a commitment to straightforward action and response.

The survey model makes use of questionnaires and other market survey techniques. Surveys can be conducted by phone, administered in an interview setting, or done through the mail. The most typical survey is the needs assessment in which prospective clients and other members of the community are asked to make recommendations as to the goals and best use of the agency's resources. In any of these cases, the concept of the feedback loop must be followed. The loop is completed when data generated by the survey are used to modify organizational operation. The next set of questionnaires will then inform potential respondents of the changes and attempt to gain further feedback to judge the effectiveness of the new programs or policies. Effective use of the survey model is dependent on this mutual exchange of information between the organization and individuals and on the planned, regular implementation of the survey.

There are several limitations to the survey method (Micheli et al., 1984) and administrators contemplating use of this model should be aware of potential problems of design, timing, cost, and interpretation.

Effective questionnaire design requires skill and practice. Anyone who has ever tried to respond to the type of question that asks Would you rather see Congressman Bob returned to office *or* have the communists take over? certainly is aware of the importance of the kinds of questions used. Several good sources for information on questionnaire design have been included in the bibliography of this chapter. Another possibility is the use of a market research firm to help design the initial effort. Nonprofit organizations are increasingly making good use of these private-sector specialists. Another good source of market research assistance is the local university. Marketing research instructors are often eager to find projects for students. These projects often yield very professional results at minimum cost.

A questionnaire can be sent out at varying intervals. The challenge is to find the right balance between too few and too many mailings to get the most useful information. Many organizations can get maximum benefit from four mailings per year. This allows ample time for interpretation and implementation of suggested changes. However, the numbers may vary according to the sample and issue being surveyed. There are some general guidelines in timing a survey that are useful to keep in mind. People respond less often during the Christmas season and during the July and August vacation period. If the interview technique is used, morning appointments are usually more productive.

Another consideration is cost. Mailing with return envelopes is expensive, and the organizational time spent in analysis of the survey has to be considered. If a marketing firm or other consultant is used for design, training, or analysis, then the operational cost of the survey will be increased. Cost of the survey should not deter the use of this model. The benefits may be substantial in increased effectiveness of external communication and, therefore, worth the cost.

The final limitation is in the area of interpretation. Making the best use of the data is important to the organization and crucial for holding the trust and interest of respondents. The best guideline is contained in the understanding that the survey is another kind of management tool. It brings in information that may or may not be useful but certainly needs to be considered. Even faulty perceptions or biased answers give clues as to how the organization is getting its message across to its working environment.

EXTERNAL COMMUNICATION: A FINAL NOTE

Whatever format the feedback loop may take, it can have a powerful influence on the organization. This influence must be managed so that the organization is not constantly changing goals according to the trend of the latest information. Change and response must be a steady but measured process. Communication is best served when the organization is aware of the changing needs and desires of the clients, funding bodies, and community groups in the agency's environment. The commitment to maintaining an ongoing dialogue with important groups outside the organization through the use of a feedback loop is a good indicator of an effective external communication system.

REFERENCES

Gibson, J. W. and R. M. Hodgetts (1986). *Organizational communication*. New York: Academic Press.

Goldhaber, G. M. (1986). *Organizational communication*. 4th ed. Dubuque, IA: William C. Brown.

Maddalena, L. A. (1981). *A communications manual for nonprofit organizations*. New York: AMACOM.

Micheli, L. M., F. V. Cespedes, D. Byker, and T. J. Raymond (1984). *Managerial communication*. Glenview, IL: Scott, Foresman.

ANNOTATED BIBLIOGRAPHY

For information on the design of effective questionnaires and other survey instruments see the following works:

Dillman, D. A. (1978). *Mail and telephone surveys: The Total Design Method*. New York: John Wiley. This is a very direct, how-to manual on the design and use of a variety of survey methodologies. The advantages and disadvantages of mail, phone, and face-to-face surveys are thoroughly covered. In addition, this book provides general principles for writing effective survey questions, structuring the questionnaire, and drawing out the desired information.

Varner, I. I. (1987). *Contemporary business report writing*. New York: Dryden. This is an excellent guide to effective business writing and examines a number of different types of reports and other presentations of data. Chapter 10 provides very good information on sampling procedure and the design of questionnaires. Chapter 11 provides an excellent overview (for the nonstatistician) on the use of statistical techniques to analyze and interpret the data collected by the surveys.

For information on other available communication assessment tools see

Cummings, H. W., L. W. Long, and M. L. Lewis (1987). *Managing communication in organizations: An introduction*. 2nd ed. Scottsdale, AZ: Gorsuch Scarisbrick. This introductory text can serve as a useful tool for the nonprofit organization manager with no prior experience in the area of organizational communication. Topics include strategic communication planning, information management, and a number of useful ideas on communication assessment. The book includes samples of a number of assessment tools and a bibliography of additional measures.

To learn more about the relationship between organizational structure and communication see

Farace, R. B., P. R. Monge, and H. Russell (1977). *Communicating and organizing*. Reading, MA: Addison-Wesley. In this work, the internal and external organizational environments are explored, with particular emphasis on communication processes and behavior. The structure of the organization dictates the flow of information throughout the hierarchy. Changes in organizational structure create consequences for the communication efficiency and effectiveness.

Galbraith, J. (1973). *Designing complex organizations*. Reading, MA: Addison-Wesley. This book examines information processing as the central issue in organizational functioning. It is of particular interest to organizations in which decision making is shared across departmental boundaries. Four critical areas of organizational process are examined as they relate to problems in the flow of information through the organization.

13

The Management of Volunteers

LYNN E. MILLER

The problems of recruiting, motivating, and retaining workers who are not paid for their work pose special challenges for volunteer administrators. Actually, much has been written on techniques for managing volunteer programs, and the reader is referred to the bibliography for a variety of helpful materials. This chapter attempts to summarize much of the available advice, but in addition it applies current management and psychological theory to help determine under what circumstances and with what individuals certain techniques will be effective. Although this chapter is primarily intended for individuals who are involved in administering a volunteer program or supervising volunteers, it may be of interest to managers of paid employees as well. Especially given the limited funds of many nonprofit organizations, understanding techniques that do not rely on financial incentives to enhance employee performance and satisfaction should prove helpful.

To understand effective volunteer management, it is useful to examine the factors influencing behavior in general. Social psychologists have identified three types of factors that directly affect our actions: attitudes, social norms, and past habits (Bagozzi, 1981; Bentler and Speckart, 1979). Other factors, such as personalities, needs, and various aspects of the specific situation, appear to affect behavior indirectly by influencing either attitudes, social norms or habits, or the weights placed on them (Fishbein and Ajzen, 1975). For example, some individuals are very reflective and internally motivated; their own attitudes towards activities (such as volunteering) greatly affect their actions. Other individuals seem to be very concerned with "fitting in," and are more influenced by social norms—that is, the behaviors and expectations of others (Miller and Grush, 1986). In many cases, though, a major determinant of behavior is simply habit, and the volunteer administrator must find ways of changing the habit of not volunteering to one of active and productive volunteering. This chapter discusses ways to get, keep, and motivate volunteers by taking into consideration the roles of attitudes, social norms, and habits.

RECRUITING VOLUNTEERS

Attitude Influence as a Recruiting Tool

Recruiters' attempts to attract new volunteers often involve trying to change the prospective volunteers' attitudes. Attitudes are commonly viewed as being composed of the beliefs we have towards an activity or issue and the favorableness of those beliefs. Thus, to change beliefs, a recruiter may point out the various consequences of volunteering, including consequences for the volunteer, the agency, the clients, and society. To change perceptions of the favorableness of the effects of volunteering, the recruiter may discuss the value or importance of the consequences.

Unfortunately, decades of research have indicated that changing peoples' attitudes does not typically lead to changes in behavior (Festinger, 1964; Grush and Schersching, 1978)—a finding that is probably not surprising to many frustrated volunteer recruiters. Some work, however, has found ways to increase the probabilities of behavior change. For example, attempts to change behavior have been found to be most successful when the individuals can gain personally from their behavior change (Grush and Schersching, 1978). The implications for recruiters are obvious. Potential volunteers should be convinced that volunteering can be personally beneficial to them, for example, by providing job skills, references, academic credit, company leave time, social rewards, a sense of fulfillment, or other rewards that the individual may seek (factors influencing what a volunteer finds rewarding will be discussed later in this chapter).

Giving clear behavioral guidelines has also been found to be important for changing past habits (Leventhal, Singer, and Jones, 1965; Leventhal, Watts, and Pagano, 1967). Potential volunteers should be given clear directions on how to become a volunteer, and the process should be as simple as possible. Giving vague guidelines, such as "call me at the agency," is less likely to be effective than distributing cards with one's name, phone number, and best times to be reached, or distributing maps that show how to get to a scheduled training session.

Realistic Job Previews

Although recruiters should clearly explain the advantages of volunteering, they should probably avoid creating overly positive views of the volunteer activities. Studies of paid employees have found at least somewhat lower turnover rates for individuals who were provided with realistic job previews (RJPs) during recruiting (Meglino et al., 1988; McEvoy and Cascio, 1985). Since turnover is more likely with volunteers than with paid employees, RJPs would seem to be especially advantageous for recruiting volunteers.

In RJP recruiting, all pertinent information—both positive and negative—is presented. Although it is not known why this technique is more effective than the traditional approach of "selling" the individual on the job and the organization, several possible reasons have been offered (Wanous, 1980). First, by creating expectations that are congruent with reality, later disappointment is unlikely to develop and cause dissatisfaction. In addition, RJPs may help people make more informed decisions. Thus, those who later decide to volunteer should be both better "matches" for the organization and more committed to their decisions. RJPs may also help people develop mechanisms for coping with what they expect to be the more difficult or unpleasant aspects of their tasks. Finally, RJPs may create a perception of the organizational members as being caring, honest, and noncoercive.

Although a recruiter may be reluctant to talk about the negative aspects of volunteering, several studies with paid employees have found that RJPs do not affect the number of people who accept job offers. In addition, they have been found to lead to greater job satisfaction (Wanous, 1980). In fact, it is likely that many potential volunteers already assume that volunteering is unpleasant, at least in some facets. An honest description of the volunteer tasks may keep the negative aspects of the work in perspective, so that exaggerated assumptions about the unpleasantness of the work will be less likely to discourage people from volunteering. On the other hand, some research suggests that RJPs can still be effective in reducing turnover if they are presented after individuals commit themselves to the organization (Ilgen and Seely, 1974; Meglino et al., 1988). In other words, a recruiter who is apprehensive about presenting negative information to prospective volunteers should at least provide a realistic preview of the activities before individuals who have agreed to volunteer actually begin work.

RJPs may be presented to potential volunteers by means of training sessions, booklets describing the activity, chats with current volunteers, oral and/or audiovisual presentations on the volunteer work, or even by having the volunteer try the activity for an hour or two. Procedures that require the volunteer to make a small commitment, for example, by agreeing to come to an informational meeting or to try volunteering for an evening, may be especially effective for recruiting. The "foot-in-the-door" technique, in which individuals are asked to make a small commitment before they are asked to make a large commitment, has been found to be an effective procedure for changing peoples' behavior in many situations (Beaman et al., 1983; DeJong, 1979).

Utilizing Social Influences

Effective recruitment involves more than influencing individuals' attitudes towards volunteering. Social factors are very important determinants of whether people will volunteer. For example, a recent Gallup poll found that most people started volunteering because someone asked them to or because they participated in an organization that got them involved in volunteering, and that very few people volunteered after seeing or hearing an advertisement (Independent Sector, 1986).

There are a number of ways that the recruiter can utilize social pressures to attract volunteers. Obviously, the Gallup results imply that making appeals in person or to groups should draw more responses than public service announcements or bulletin board notices. For strong personal appeals, volunteers can be—and very often are—asked to encourage their friends to volunteer. In fact, some agencies not only have volunteers recruit their friends, but have them work with their friends as teams; this approach would appear to capitalize well on social normative pressures. Similarly, the recruiter could present appeals to groups or organizations such as church groups, fraternities and sororities, scouting troops, and community groups. To capitalize on group norms in those situations, the members of the audience could be asked to "sign up" at the meeting along with their friends rather than just to contact the agency later if they are interested. Where feasible, one could ask the group to initially volunteer as a whole for a group project. Group members could then be asked after the group project if they would be interested in further group or individual work.

Introducing people to the volunteer activity through group projects would appear to be especially useful for recruitment. The potential volunteers get a realistic job preview and, if the group project went well, are likely to feel that their peers support the cause. In addition, the group project can provide the recruiter with an opportunity to identify individuals who might be interested in or well-suited for the volunteer work. Moreover, because the potential volunteers have already made a small commitment by participating in the group project, the recruiter may have a "foot in the door." In fact, the recruiter may have become friends with a number of the group members and thus be more influential with them.

Another recommendation for utilizing the power of social norms when recruiting is to indicate that many other people are volunteering, rather than to suggest that the agency is desperate for volunteers. If potential volunteers believe that the agency is unable to attract or retain volunteers, they may fear that the cause is an unworthy one, that the agency staff members are incompetent, that those who do volunteer would be burdened with too much work, or that the agency is not able to accomplish much. One can still indicate a need for volunteers, for example, by talking about the growing demand for the agency's services in the community.

Finally, the importance of positive publicity for recruiting volunteers should be apparent. Although agencies may not always see direct effects of publicity on contributions or requests for service, current and potential volunteers are more likely to want to work for agencies that are viewed positively by others in the community.

RETAINING VOLUNTEERS

Turnover among paid employees is often desirable. In many cases, it is the poorer performing employees who leave. In addition, one can often bring in less experienced replacements at lower wages or offer promotions to deserving employees. Moreover, the person who fills the vacancy may have new ideas that create positive changes for the organization (Dreher, 1982; McEvoy and Cascio, 1985; Staw, 1980). While turnover among volunteers may have similar advantages in many situations, very harmful consequences can also result. For example, serious disruptions in learning can occur when volunteer tutors must be replaced in literacy programs. Similarly, the resignation of a "Big Brother" or "Big Sister" may, contrary to program goals, contribute to a child's feeling abandoned and unwanted. Moreover, turnover not only hinders service delivery, but can drain financial resources. Imagine, for instance, the burden of recruitment and training to the small rape crisis center, already understaffed and strapped for funds, that must constantly find and train new hotline counselors.

Unfortunately, much of the turnover among volunteers cannot be prevented. The 1981 Gallup survey on volunteering (Americans Volunteer, 1982) found that of those who had quit volunteering within the preceding three years, 12 percent said that they quit because they moved and 10 percent said that they quit because they went to a paying job or to school. Another 33 percent said that they were too busy to continue volunteering, and 18 percent quit for personal reasons. (Some respondents gave more than one reason.)

In actuality, very few respondents in the Gallup survey said that they quit because they were dissatisfied with volunteering. Nine percent said that they no longer found it interesting; 4 percent said that they went into more important volunteer work; 2 percent said that it was too expensive; and 1 percent felt that there was nothing useful for them to do. On the other hand, a recent survey of volunteers that I conducted found that those who planned to quit volunteering in the near future because they were too busy were less satisfied with various aspects of volunteering than were those who did not say that they were too busy. Presumably, a more rewarding experience might convince people to continue despite other demands on their time.

In summary, volunteer turnover is frequently due to extraneous factors over which the administrator has little control. However, while volunteers generally do not report highly dissatisfying experiences as factors causing them to quit, a lack of strong incentive to continue may contribute to the turnover rate in many agencies. Consequently, to reduce turnover administrators must find ways to ensure that their volunteers' needs will be highly satisfied by their volunteer activities.

Meeting Needs

A number of theorists have attempted to identify the different types of needs that people seek to satisfy in their lives. One particularly well-tested model is

Alderfer's (1972) ERG theory, a modification of the well-known Maslow need hierarchy theory. According to Alderfer, needs can be categorized into three groups: existence, relatedness, and growth needs (hence "ERG"). Existence needs are those that must be satisfied to ensure a comfortable existence for the individual. Relatedness needs are the needs people have to feel accepted, respected, and loved by others. Growth needs are those needs we have to obtain creative, fulfilling, and meaningful growth in our lives.

Different volunteer activities can satisfy these needs in a variety of ways. However, it is neither possible nor necessary for a given volunteer activity to provide all of the possible rewards that might satisfy these needs. Rather, as will be discussed, different things are satisfying to different people at different times, and administrators should design volunteer programs and place volunteers with that view in mind.

The most obvious rewards of volunteering are those that satisfy growth needs, especially the rewards that result from feeling that one's work is significant and meaningful. By giving volunteers feedback about the impact that their individual or group work has had on clients, the agency, or society, such rewards may be made even more salient. In addition, volunteer administrators may make such rewards more likely by providing the training and support that is necessary to ensure success and a sense of accomplishment. On the other hand, there is reason to believe that not all volunteers are motivated by a desire for worthwhile accomplishment. One study (Miller, 1985) found that volunteers whose paid employment did not offer opportunities for meaningfulness and fulfillment were involved in and committed to volunteering to the extent that they expected the volunteer work to be meaningful and interesting. Volunteers whose paid employment did satisfy such needs, however, were apparently not motivated to do worthwhile volunteer work. Instead, they were found to be involved in and committed to volunteering to the extent that they perceived the staff as supportive, felt that volunteering offered useful experience, found their volunteer activities to be enjoyable, and believed that volunteering would leave them with sufficient time for other activities. In other words, volunteer administrators may find it necessary to assess the needs of volunteers and carefully match the volunteers to tasks that will be rewarding to them.

Although the volunteer activity may be perceived as meaningful and significant, it can—at the same time—be perceived as being dull and routine. Yet, doing work that is interesting and varied is considered to be important for satisfying growth needs. Ways to make volunteering more interesting include having paid staff take on a greater proportion of the necessary paperwork and other tedious chores, encouraging some joking and socializing among volunteers while they work, and having volunteers engage in a variety of activities that utilize their skills.

Developing and utilizing one's skills as a volunteer can lead to greater personal growth as well as to greater enjoyment of the activity. Volunteer administrators should therefore try to create opportunities to enable those volunteers seeking self-development to learn new skills. Again, good training and staff support will be helpful and necessary. Moreover, varied activities, such as giving talks to groups, training new volunteers, using computers or other equipment, or working with others who are more experienced, can result in personal growth. Providing opportunities for volunteers to be "promoted" to more challenging and prestigious activities may help volunteers see their own development more clearly. In addition, arranging for volunteers to obtain college credit and letters of reference for their work allows individuals to use their volunteer activities to obtain personal growth in other aspects of their lives.

For some volunteers, a sense of freedom and control will be important to their growth. Freeing volunteers from close supervision, allowing them to use their own procedures for doing tasks when appropriate, and having volunteers participate in decision making relevant to their work are ways to enhance volunteers' perceptions of their self-worth and personal contributions. Of course, a supervisor may be reluctant to allow such initiative under certain circumstances, and at times the volunteer may prefer greater help and supervision. For example, the path-goal theory of leadership (see chapter 3) would suggest that volunteers will be more likely to appreciate autonomy and relaxed supervision when tasks are very clear and structured than when tasks are ambiguous and unstructured. The theory also predicts that there are personality differences in the types of supervision that people prefer. For example, "authoritarians"—people who tend to believe that status and power differences are important to effective organizational functioning—are predicted to respond better than nonauthoritarians to directive leadership. On the other hand, "internals"—people who feel that they, rather than external forces, are in control of their fates—are expected to be more appreciative of participative leadership styles than are others (House and Baetz, 1979).

The close relationships that volunteers often develop with clients, staff, and other volunteers can serve to satisfy relatedness needs. Relationships with staff members have been found to be especially important to volunteers (Briggs, 1982), and unsatisfactory volunteer-staff relations are a major cause of turnover for some agencies (Miller, 1985; Pierucci and Noel, 1980). Marx (1981) has argued that a major impediment to positive volunteer-staff relations is the stress that results from a lack of role clarification; he recommends that responsibilities of staff and volunteers be negotiated and defined. In addition, a number of other writers have recommended training staff to work with volunteers, involving staff members in the design of the volunteer program, and improving communication between staff and volunteers in order to improve volunteer-staff relations (see Hodgkins, 1979; Lauffer, 1977; Stenzel and Feeney, 1976; and various articles on board-staff relations in the Spring 1981 issue of *Voluntary Action Leadership*).

In general, showing volunteers the respect, concern, patience, and appreciation that they deserve will help make volunteering a more satisfying experience. Once-a-year recognition ceremonies are not sufficient for this (in fact, although some volunteers are very appreciative of such ceremonies, many volunteer administrators report that they are poorly attended). Rather, informal expressions of thanks, prompt attention to personality conflicts and other problems, adequate support and encouragement on difficult or stressful tasks, and utilization of volunteers' suggestions are among the ways in which positive relationships can be developed on a personal and daily basis.

Existence needs are less obviously satisfied through volunteering than are growth and relatedness needs, although there are some important things that administrators can do to help satisfy these needs. A comfortable and safe working environment is, of course, necessary, and some volunteers will need to have transportation and meals paid for or provided. Consideration should be given to volunteers' time constraints; many people have limited time to contribute and many require flexible scheduling. Mechanisms for preventing or dealing with fatigue problems, especially for volunteers who work overnight or at tiring tasks, may also need to be developed. In addition, instruction in stress management, time management, or self-defense may be necessary for individuals involved in some volunteer activities.

Assessing Needs

Administrators should either formally or informally assess the needs of their volunteers in order to determine how the activities may be made more rewarding and to match volunteers with tasks that they will find satisfying (see Francies, 1983). In doing so, administrators should be careful to assess more than just individuals' backgrounds and experiences, since a lack of experience does not necessarily indicate a lack of ability or interest. In fact, individuals may be volunteering primarily in order to satisfy some needs that have not been met by their other work or leisure experiences.

Since people's needs and abilities change over time, periodic reassessments of volunteers' needs should be made. For example, according to path-goal theory, autonomy and decision-making responsibilities will not be rewarding to a person who lacks experience and confidence. Once volunteers gain experience, however, greater autonomy is generally appropriate. In addition, people undergo many other changes in their lives that can affect the types of satisfaction they seek from volunteering. Older volunteers, for example, have been found to be more likely to volunteer for altruistic reasons and less likely to volunteer for self-serving reasons (e.g., career development) than younger people (Frisch and Gerrard, 1981). In addition, the degree of participation in volunteer activities has been found to be related to factors such as age, marital satisfaction, and number of children (Schram and Dunsing, 1981). In other words, changes in volunteers' responsibilities may be warranted as their lives change.

Influences of Norms and Habits on Turnover

Providing volunteers with strong incentives to continue helps to maintain positive attitudes towards volunteering. However, habits and social norms also play important roles in the retention of volunteers. Administrators are generally more successful at retaining volunteers than recruiting them, perhaps because inertia may be a barrier to changing old habits. However, many individuals quit during the first few months of volunteering, before volunteering has really become a habit. When a new volunteer indicates an intention to quit, the administrator might therefore ask the person to continue for a while longer, especially if the volunteer shows potential for fitting in well.

To help create social norms for continuing as a volunteer, administrators can team new volunteers with role models—volunteers who have been active for a long time. They can also indicate at meetings, in newsletters, or informally that many people have continued to volunteer for long periods of time and that their long-term commitments have helped make the program successful.

MOTIVATING VOLUNTEERS

Contingent Rewards

Worker satisfaction has been found to be related to lower turnover and absenteeism and, moreover, is a worthwhile outcome in itself. However, substantial research has shown that happier workers are not necessarily harder workers. Rather, greater effort and better performance result when rewards are made contingent upon good performance (Greene and Craft, 1979; Lawler, 1983). These findings are the basis for path-goal theory (see chapter 3), which states that a leader's actions are motivating to the extent that they (1) make satisfaction of subordinates' needs contingent upon effective performance and (2) complement the environment by providing the coaching, guidance, support, and rewards necessary for effective performance.

In the case of volunteering, some of the rewards are intrinsic—that is, they result from the process of doing the work—and thus are already contingent upon effort. For example, many volunteer activities are fun and interesting, so that volunteers who seek those rewards should be motivated to put in a lot of time and effort. On the other hand, some of the rewards of volunteering are extrinsic— that is, they are potential outcomes of the work—and either are or can be made contingent upon successful performance. "Promotions" to more prestigious or interesting volunteer work, opportunities for special training, a sense of accomplishment, good job references, and appreciation from clients or staff are among the rewards that can be tied to performance. Supervisors or administrators of volunteer programs can help motivate volunteers by finding ways to build intrinsic rewards (e.g., fun and variety) into the volunteer task and to make extrinsic rewards contingent upon successful performance. In some cases, feedback indicating that a volunteer's work has had a significant impact may be enough to produce a sense of accomplishment and fulfillment. More creative approaches, though, may be needed to provide other extrinsic rewards.

Moreover, there are a number of ways in which the volunteer administrator or supervisor can help volunteers see how their effort will lead to effective performance. One way is to clarify the volunteers' responsibilities, for example, by realistic job previews and written job descriptions. (There is actually some debate as to whether volunteers should be given written job descriptions. While many writers endorse written descriptions, Schindler-Rainman and Lippitt (1975) advise that job descriptions should be either nonexistent or written by the volunteer after several weeks of experience.) Periodic, one-on-one evaluations of volunteers are a useful device for providing feedback and setting new goals to be achieved. Proper task design that minimizes wasted effort is also important for enabling volunteers to see how their effort leads to effective performance (see chapter 9). For example, forms that the volunteer must complete should be as brief and simple as possible. In addition, volunteers should be provided with the materials that are necessary for effective performance.

Obviously, adequate training and assistance should be provided to help assure successful performance. As mentioned previously, however, highly directive behavior may be seen as inappropriate and overly controlling, especially if the task is clear and the subordinate is experienced and knowledgeable. Also, the odds of successful performance may be improved if clients and volunteers are carefully matched for compatibility, where appropriate.

Influences of Norms and Habits on Motivation

The motivational techniques discussed in this section have been concerned with helping volunteers see how their time and effort will eventually lead to rewards. This approach, in other words, focuses on creating positive attitudes towards working hard as a volunteer. Once again, though, the importance of habits and social norms should not be ignored. For example, some people may have "Protestant work ethics" and habitually work hard at what they do. Thus, just because some volunteers seem to be highly motivated does not mean that the agency's motivational techniques are sufficient.

Some of my own survey research on volunteers has indicated that social norms may be important motivational forces for volunteers. In one study, volunteers' beliefs about how much time their families, friends, and clients wanted them to spend on volunteering each week were substantially related to how much time they actually spent. However, their views about how much time the agency staff members, other volunteers, and religious leaders wanted them to spend did not predict who would volunteer more hours. On the other hand, it would be wrong to conclude that the agency has no influence over the time that volunteers will spend. In the agencies that were studied, clear agency norms established a minimum amount of time that volunteers were expected to spend each week, and most volunteers met this standard.

The effects of work group norms on productivity are also well documented, and under some circumstances may be very strong influences on behavior (Feldman, 1984). For example, when the group members work closely together and the group is highly cohesive, performance standards tend to be "enforced."

People do not always conform to social norms in order to gain acceptance or avoid rejection, however. Rather, they often merely use social norms as a source of information on how to act in ambiguous situations (Deutsch and Gerard, 1955). Norms should therefore have an especially strong influence on new volunteers who are likely to be concerned with clarifying their roles. Consequently, it is important for new volunteers to work with staff members or other volunteers who can establish norms for high quality performance. On the other hand, some people are more apt to be influenced by social norms than others. As noted earlier, some research has found that attitudes predict behavior best for people who are highly self-reflective and who are relatively unconcerned with meeting others' expectations. Social norms, on the other hand, seem to predict behavior well for people who are either not very self-reflective or who have a desire to please others. Past work and volunteer experiences, hobbies, and reasons for volunteering may provide clues regarding individuals' levels of internal motivation. Recruiters may find it useful to assess such information prior to placing volunteers to work with others.

EVALUATING YOUR VOLUNTEER PROGRAM

The following is a list of questions based on this chapter to aid in evaluating agency procedures for recruiting, motivating, and retaining volunteers.

1. How does your agency meet volunteers' existence needs? That is, how does the agency deal with the following issues as they affect volunteers?
   A. Safety
   B. Fatigue
   C. Comfort
   D. Stress
   E. Meals
   F. Transportation
   G. Insurance
2. How are relatedness needs met?
   A. How does the agency provide opportunities for volunteers to develop close relations with clients? other volunteers? staff members?
   B. What mechanisms exist for detecting and overcoming problems in volunteers' relations with clients? other volunteers? staff members?
3. How are growth needs met?
   A. In what ways, and to what degree, are the volunteer activities enjoyable?
   B. In what ways, and to what degree, are the volunteer activities varied?
   C. In what ways, and to what degree, are the volunteer activities seen as worthwhile?
   D. In what ways, and to what degree, do volunteers develop their skills through volunteering?
   E. In what ways, and to what degree, do volunteers gain self-esteem through volunteering?

4. What can be done to make volunteering more likely to satisfy the following types of needs?
   A. Existence needs
   B. Relatedness needs
   C. Growth needs
5. What are the potential drawbacks of volunteering for your agency?
6. When recruiting, do you give potential volunteers a realistic preview that describes the volunteer activities, the personal benefits of volunteering, and the drawbacks of volunteering?
7. When recruiting, do you spell out clearly how a person goes about becoming a volunteer for your agency?
8. Do you offer potential volunteers the opportunity to make a small commitment to your agency (for example, by just volunteering for a few hours, observing other volunteers, or working on a "one-shot" volunteer project) before making a large commitment to volunteer for your agency?
9. Do you ask current volunteers to recruit their friends?
10. Do you present appeals to groups when recruiting, giving the group members the opportunity to sign up with their friends?
11. Do you present a positive image of your agency as one that is able to attract committed volunteers?
12. Is it possible for you to assign volunteers to different areas of responsibility? (In some agencies, all volunteers engage in the same activities.)
    A. If yes, do you attempt to assess the needs and interests of the volunteers and assign responsibilities accordingly?
    B. Do you periodically reassess the needs and interests of the volunteers and make appropriate changes in their assignments?
13. Do you have new volunteers work with experienced, committed, and hard-working volunteers and/or staff members?
14. What are the expectations that are communicated to volunteers (either formally or informally, through staff members or other volunteers) regarding the following?
    A. The amount of effort that volunteers should exert
    B. The quality of the work that is expected
    C. The number of hours that volunteers should put in
    D. The length of time that people usually remain volunteers
15. Can volunteers adjust their schedules to meet other demands on their time (for example, time demands from family, friends, school, or work)?
16. To what extent do volunteers believe that their effort will lead to successful performance?
    A. Are the volunteers trained as well as possible?
    B. Are volunteers' responsibilities clearly specified?
    C. Are necessary materials and support available?
    D. Are volunteers provided with appropriate feedback regarding their performance?
17. To what extent is the process of engaging in the volunteer work rewarding?
18. Have desirable outcomes of volunteering been made contingent, to the extent possible, upon how much effort the individuals exert?

REFERENCES

Alderfer, C. P. (1972). *Existence, relatedness, and growth.* New York: Free Press.
Americans volunteer 1981: A Gallup survey on volunteering. (1982, Winter). *Voluntary Action Leadership*, 21–32.

Bagozzi, R. P. (1981). Attitudes, intentions and behavior: A test of some key hypotheses. *Journal of Personality and Social Psychology* 41, 607–27.

Beaman, A. L., C. M. Cole, M. Preston, B. Klentz, and N. M. Steblay (1983). Fifteen years of foot-in-the-door research: A meta-analysis. *Personality and Social Psychology Bulletin* 9, 181–96.

Bentler, P. M., and G. Speckart (1979). Models of attitude-behavior relations. *Psychological Review* 86, 452–64.

Briggs, D. L. (1982). On satisfying the volunteer and the paid employee: Any difference? *Volunteer Administration* 14 (4), 1–14.

DeJong, W. (1979). An examination of self-perception mediation of the foot-in-the-door effect. *Journal of Personality and Social Psychology* 37, 2221–39.

Deutsch, M., and H. B. Gerard (1955). A study of normative and informational social influence upon individual judgment. *Journal of Abnormal and Social Psychology* 51, 629–36.

Dreher, G. F. (1982). The role of performance in the turnover process. *Academy of Management Journal* 25, 137–47.

Feldman, D. C. (1984). The development and enforcement of group norms. *Academy of Management Review* 9, 47–53.

Festinger, L. (1964). Behavioral support for opinion change. *Public Opinion Quarterly* 28, 404–17.

Fishbein, M., and I. Ajzen (1975). *Belief, attitude, intention, and behavior: An introduction to theory and research.* Reading, MA: Addison-Wesley.

Francies, G. R. (1983, Summer). The Volunteer Needs Profile: A tool for reducing turnover. *Journal of Volunteer Administration*, 17–33.

Frisch, M. B., and M. Gerrard (1981). Natural helping systems: A survey of Red Cross volunteers. *American Journal of Community Psychology* 9, 567–79.

Greene, C. N., and R. E. Craft (1979). The satisfaction-performance controversy—revisited. In R. M. Steers and L. W. Porter, eds., *Motivation and work behavior.* 2nd ed. New York: McGraw-Hill.

Grush, J. E., and C. Schersching (1978, May). Does attitude change lead to behavior change? Paper presented at the meeting of the Midwestern Psychological Association, Chicago.

Hodgkins, D. (1979, Spring). What is supervision? *Voluntary Action Leadership*, 24.

House, R. J., and M. L. Baetz (1979). Leadership: Some empirical generalizations and new research directions. In B. M. Staw, ed., *Research in organizational behavior* vol. 1. Greenwich, CT: JAI Press.

Ilgen, D. R., and W. Seely (1974). Realistic expectations as an aid in reducing voluntary resignations. *Journal of Applied Psychology* 59, 452–55.

Ilsley, P. J., and J. A. Niemi (1981). *Recruiting and training volunteers.* New York: McGraw-Hill.

Independent Sector. (1986). Americans volunteer 1985. Washington, DC: Independent Sector.

Lauffer, A., and S. Gorodezky (1977). *Volunteers.* Beverly Hills: Sage.

Lawler, E. E. (1983). Satisfaction and behavior. In R. M. Steers and L. W. Porter, eds., *Motivation and work behavior.* 3rd ed. New York: McGraw-Hill.

Leventhal, H., R. P. Singer, and S. Jones (1965). Effects of fear and specificity of recommendations upon attitudes and behavior. *Journal of Personality and Social Psychology* 2, 20–29.

Leventhal, H., S. Watts, and F. Pagano (1967). Effects of fear and instructions on how to cope with danger. *Journal of Personality and Social Psychology* 6, 313–21.

Marx, M. J. (1981, Fall). Role review. *Voluntary Action Leadership*, 22–26.

McEvoy, G. M., and W. F. Cascio (1985). Strategies for reducing employee turnover: A meta-analysis. *Journal of Applied Psychology* 70, 342–53.

Meglino, B. M., & A. S. DeNisi, S. A. Youngblood, and K. J. Williams. (1988). Effects of realistic job previews: A comparison using an enhancement and a reduction preview. *Journal of Applied Psychology* 73, 259–66.

Miller, L. E. (1985). Understanding the motivation of volunteers: An examination of personality differences and characteristics of volunteers' paid employment. *Journal of Voluntary Action Research* 14, 112–22.

Miller, L. E., and J. E. Grush (1986). Individual differences in attitudinal versus normative determination of behavior. *Journal of Experimental Social Psychology* 22, 190–202.

Pierucci, J., and R. C. Noel (1980). Duration of participation of correctional volunteers as a function of personal and situational variables. *Journal of Community Psychology* 8, 245–50.

Schindler-Rainman, E., and R. Lippitt (1975). *The volunteer community*. La Jolla, CA: University Associates.

Schram, V. R., and M. M. Dunsing (1981). Influences on married women's volunteer work participation. *Journal of Consumer Research* 7, 372–79.

Staw, R. M. (1980). The consequences of turnover. *Journal of Occupational Behaviour* 1, 253–73.

Stenzel, A. K., and H. M. Feeney (1976). *Volunteer training and development: A manual*. New York: Seabury Press.

Wanous, J. P. (1980). *Organizational entry: Recruitment, selection, and socialization of newcomers*. Reading, MA: Addison-Wesley.

ANNOTATED BIBLIOGRAPHY

Ellis, S. J. (1986). *From the top down: The executive role in volunteer program success*. Philadelphia: Energize Books. This book provides useful information on many aspects of running a volunteer program. Included are discussions of how to set policies pertaining to volunteers, establish good volunteer-staff relations, and determine budgets and select staff for the volunteer program. Many administrators will find the sections on legal concerns and accounting for volunteer time in financial records to be particularly helpful.

Lauffer, A., and S. Gorodezky (1977). *Volunteers*. Beverly Hills: Sage. This book discusses the pros and cons of utilizing volunteers and the tasks involved in operating a volunteer program. A worksheet is provided for analyzing the tasks involved in the volunteer activities. Detailed suggestions for recruiting, selecting, training, and supervising volunteers are presented.

Presson, B., comp. (1980, Spring). Training volunteers—An introduction. *Voluntary Action Leadership*, 23–28. This special "chapter" in *Voluntary Action Leadership* is a set of articles that specify how to conduct a successful volunteer training program. A step-by-step planning guide is included, and ways to be a successful trainer are discussed.

Schindler-Rainman, E., and R. Lippitt (1975). *The volunteer community*. La Jolla, CA:

University Associates. This book thoughtfully analyzes topics such as volunteer-staff tensions, volunteer motivation, and the role of the volunteer administrator. Chapters 4 through 8 discuss motivation, recruitment, training, and program administration, and are especially useful for individuals running volunteer programs. Other chapters, however, provide interesting insights into societal trends and the roles of volunteers.

Stenzel, A. K., and H. M. Feeney (1976). *Volunteer training and development: A manual*. New York: Seabury Press. This book provides detailed suggestions for developing a volunteer program. A variety of forms and charts are provided to help in such areas as assessing volunteers' skills, abilities, and interests; describing the volunteers' jobs; planning a training event; and evaluating volunteers.

Index

About the Contributors

LESTER BARENBAUM is professor in the Finance Department at La Salle University in Philadelphia, Pennsylvania. His research interests are in the area of financial analysis of the non-public firm. Recent publications have appeared in the *Journal of Accounting Auditing and Finance*, *Valuation* and *Business and Tax Planning Quarterly*. He is a senior business analyst at Financial Research, Inc. Dr. Barenbaum received his M.A. and Ph.D. in economics from Rutgers University.

PAUL R. BRAZINA is assistant professor of accounting at La Salle University. Prior to joing La Salle, he worked for both Coopers & Lybrand and Price Waterhouse & Company in Philadelphia. Paul is a CPA and CMA in Pennsylvania, has served as a private consultant for financial accounting systems and accounting services, and is a member of the Advisory Council of Community Accountants in Philadelphia. Professor Brazina received his B.S. and M.B.A. from Pennsylvania State University.

RADHA CHAGANTI is associate professor in the Department of Business Policy and Environment at Rider College in Lawrenceville, New Jersey. Her research interests are in the areas of strategic planning in profit and not-for-profit organizations, strategic management and entrepreneurship. She has published in the *Journal of Small Business Management*, *Entrepreneurship*, *Advances in Strategic Management*, and the *Handbook of Business Strategy*. Dr. Chaganti received her M.A. from Osmania University (India), her M.B.A. from Indian Institute of Management, and her Ph.D. from State University of New York at Buffalo.

PATTY A. COLEMAN is assistant professor in the Department of Sociology, Social Work and Criminal Justice and Director of the Women's Studies Program at La Salle University. She has fourteen years of experience in social service agencies as a licensed social work clinician, agency administrator, and management consultant. Her current research interests include women and technology, family and child welfare policy, management of chronic illness, health services, and grassroots social movements. Professor Coleman received her B.A. from Kirkland College, and her M.S.S. from Bryn Mawr College where she is currently a Ph.D candidate in Social Work and Social Research.

JUSTIN FINK has taught organizational theory and management at La Salle University, and is proprietor of Community Nonprofit Services, a Philadelphia-based firm specializing in providing development and management assistance to small and mid-sized organizations in human services and the arts. He has been active in the study of voluntary organization behavior and is Associate Editor of *Nonprofit* and *Voluntary Sector Quarterly*. Mr. Fink has contributed to the volume *Nonprofit Boards of Directors: Analyses and Applications*, and to a forthcoming study on contemporary issues in philanthropy sponsored by the American Association of Fundraising Counsel. He received his B.A. from the University of Pennsylvania and holds a M.S.S. from Bryn Mawr College, Graduate School of Social Work and Social Research where he is currently completing his doctoral dissertation.

EVERETT FRANK is Director of the Nonprofit Management Development Center at La Salle University. He was Staff Vice President of Corporate Planning at Scott Paper Company before coming to La Salle in 1981. He was one of the founders of the Philadelphia Branch of the North American Society of corporate planning. He has run management training programs for and consulted with over 300 nonprofit organizations in the Philadelphia area. Mr. Frank received his M.B.A. from Harvard University.

PRAFULLA JOGLEKAR is professor of information systems and management sciences at La Salle University. As the founding director of the Applied Research Center, he obtained funding for management training and research to serve human service agencies in the Philadelphia area. His research focuses on the application of operations reserach to government policy determination and the management of service organizations. Dr. Joglekar's articles have appeared in *Decision Sciences*, *Evaluation and the Health Professions*, *Journal of Health Economics*, *Management Science*, and *Public Choice*. He serves on the editorial board of *Evaluation and the Health Professions* and on the board of directors of the Nonprofit Management Association (NMA), and is the content editor of NMA's

Working Papers Series. Professor Joglekar received his B.S. in math from Nagpur University, India, his M.B.A. from the Indian Institute of Management, Ahmedabad, India, and his M.S. and Ph.D. in operations research from the University of Pennsylvania.

BRUCE V. MacLEOD is associate professor in the Management Department at La Salle University. His current research interests include the organization and management of nonprofit boards of directors and strategic management in profit and nonprofit organizations. A recent publication on nonprofit boards of human service organizations appeared in the *Journal of Voluntary Action Research*. Dr. MacLeod received his master's degree in organizational behavior from Yale University and his Ph.D in organizational behavior from Case Western Reserve University.

STEVEN I. MEISEL is assistant professor and chairman of the Management Department at La Salle Unversity. He has consulted and conducted management education programs for a wide variety of private and public nonprofit organizations. His current research interest is the study of internal organizational communication policies. He serves on the board of directors of the Eastern Academy of Management. Dr. Meisel received his master's degree and Ph.D. in group and organizational psychology from Temple University.

LYNN E. MILLER is associate professor of management at La Salle University. Her research interests include nonprofit boards of directors, work motivation, and the quality of work life. She has published in the *Journal of Voluntary Action Research*, the *Academy of Management Journal*, the *Academy of Management Review*, the *Journal of Experimental Social Psychology*, the *Journal of Personality and Social Psychology*, *Sociology and Social Research*, and *Human Relations*. She received her B.A. in psychology from Slippery Rock State College, and her M.A. and Ph.D. in social psychology from Northern Illinois University.

THOMAS MONAHAN is associate professor of accountancy at Villanova University. He is a CPA in New Jersey and has had articles published in a number of professional publications including the *Journal of Accounting Auditing and Fiances*, *CFA Digest*, *Issues in Accounting Education*, *Government Accountants Journal*, *Health Care Financial Management*, *Internal Auditor*, and *Valuation*. He has conducted executive development programs for a variety of companies including Ford Motor Company, Sun Company, Holiday Corporation, Arthur Young, and Union Carbide. Dr. Monahan received his B.S. from Hofstra University, and M.B.A. from Rutgers University and a Ph.D. in business administration from Temple University.

JOSEPH SELTZER is professor of management and Lindback Professor of Business Administration at La Salle University. His current research interests

include leadership and burnout, turnover among volunteers, nonprofit manage-
ment and innovative approaches to education. His articles have appeared in a
number of publications including the *Academy of Management Journal*, the
Organizational Behavior Teaching Review, and *Health and Human Resources
Administration*. He serves on the editoral board of the *Organizational Behavior
Teaching Review* and has held a number of offices in the Eastern Academy of
Management. He has worked with a number of nonprofit managers through La
Salle's Nonprofit Management Development Center as a consultant, seminar
leader and group facilitator. Dr. Seltzer received his B.S. from Carnegie Mellon
University and his Ph.D. in organizational behavior from the University of
Pittsburgh.

RICHARD M. WEISS is associated professor of business administration at the
University of Delaware. He is the author of *Dealing with Alcoholism in the
Workplace* and *Managerial Ideology and the Social Control of Deviance in
Organizations* (Praeger, 1986). Other work has appeared in the *Academy of
Management Review*, *Administrative Science Quarterly*, *American Psychologist*,
Contemporary Sociology, *Human Relations*, *National Productivity Review*, the
Journal of Voluntary Action Research, *Personnel Psychology*, *Research in the
Sociology of Organizations*, and *Sociology and Social Research*. He received an
M.S. and Ph.D from the School of Industrial and Labor Relations at Cornell
University.

JOHN D. ZOOK is assistant professor in the accounting department at La Salle
University. His research interests include taxation and accounting, and he currently serves in private practice as a consultant to corporations, nonprofit entities,
and individuals. His publications have appeared in *Taxation for Accountants*,
The CPA Journal, and *The Practicing CPA*. He is a licensed CPA in New Jersey
and Pennsylvania. He is also a member of the American, Pennsylvania and
Florida Institutes of Certified Public Accountants and the New Jersey Society
of Certified Public Accountants. Mr. Zook received his B.S. in mathematics
from St. Joseph's University and his MBA in finance from Drexel University.